Stretching the Sociological Imagination

Also by the Editors

Matt Dawson
LATE MODERNITY, INDIVIDUALIZATION AND SOCIALISM (Palgrave, 2013)

Bridget Fowler
PIERRE BOURDIEU AND CULTURAL THEORY (1997)
THE OBITUARY AS COLLECTIVE MEMORY (2007)

David Miller
CRITICAL TERRORISM STUDIES SINCE 11 SEPTEMBER 2001 (2013)

Andrew Smith
C.L.R. JAMES AND THE STUDY OF CULTURE (Palgrave, 2010)

Stretching the Sociological Imagination

Essays in Honour of John Eldridge

Edited by

Matt Dawson
Lecturer in Sociology, University of Glasgow, UK

Bridget Fowler
Emeritus Professor, University of Glasgow, UK

David Miller
Professor of Sociology, University of Bath, UK

Andrew Smith
Reader in Sociology, University of Glasgow, UK

Selection and editorial matter © Matt Dawson, Bridget Fowler, David Miller and Andrew Smith 2015
Individual chapters © Respective authors 2015
Foreword © John Holmwood 2015
Foreword © Greg Philo 2015

All rights reserved. No reproduction, copy or transmission of this publication may be made without written permission.

No portion of this publication may be reproduced, copied or transmitted save with written permission or in accordance with the provisions of the Copyright, Designs and Patents Act 1988, or under the terms of any licence permitting limited copying issued by the Copyright Licensing Agency, Saffron House, 6–10 Kirby Street, London EC1N 8TS.

Any person who does any unauthorized act in relation to this publication may be liable to criminal prosecution and civil claims for damages.

The authors have asserted their rights to be identified as the authors of this work in accordance with the Copyright, Designs and Patents Act 1988.

First published 2015 by
PALGRAVE MACMILLAN

Palgrave Macmillan in the UK is an imprint of Macmillan Publishers Limited, registered in England, company number 785998, of Houndmills, Basingstoke, Hampshire RG21 6XS.

Palgrave Macmillan in the US is a division of St Martin's Press LLC, 175 Fifth Avenue, New York, NY 10010.

Palgrave Macmillan is the global academic imprint of the above companies and has companies and representatives throughout the world.

Palgrave® and Macmillan® are registered trademarks in the United States, the United Kingdom, Europe and other countries.

ISBN 978–1–137–49363–7

This book is printed on paper suitable for recycling and made from fully managed and sustained forest sources. Logging, pulping and manufacturing processes are expected to conform to the environmental regulations of the country of origin.

A catalogue record for this book is available from the British Library.

Library of Congress Cataloging-in-Publication Data
Stretching the sociological imagination : essays in honour of John Eldridge /
  Matt Dawson, Bridget Fowler, David Miller, Andrew Smith.
    pages   cm
  Includes bibliographical references.
  ISBN 978–1–137–49363–7 (hardback)
  1. Sociology—Great Britain. 2. Sociology. I. Eldridge, J. E. T.
(John Eric Thomas) honouree. II. Dawson, Matt, 1983– editor,
contributor.
  HM477.G7S77 2015
  301.0941—dc23   2015021850

John Eldridge, © Christine Eldridge

Contents

List of Figures and Tables	ix
Foreword: For John Eldridge – Sociology in His Times and Ours John Holmwood	x
Foreword: John Eldridge and the Birth of the Glasgow Media Group Greg Philo	xiii
Acknowledgements	xvii
Notes on Contributors	xviii

1	Stretching Exercises: Stimulating the Sociological Imagination John Eldridge	1

Part I Sociology of Work and Industry

2	Exploring an Industrial Structure of Feeling: Creating Industrial *Gemeinschaft* in a Twentieth-Century Workplace Tim Strangleman	25
3	John Eldridge's Adventures with Cross-Classification in the Sociology of Work Tony Elger	43
4	'When All Hell Breaks Loose': Striking on the British Coalfields 1984–85 Huw Beynon	65
5	False Self-Employment Howard Davis	83

Part II Social Theory

6	On the (Alternative) Worlds That We Have Lost: *Sociology and The Third Way* Revisited Matt Dawson	101

7	The Media and Collective Memory: The Obituaries of Academics *Bridget Fowler*	120
8	The Humanitarian Crisis in Sociology *John MacInnes*	141

Part III Sociology of the Media

9	Sociology, Propaganda and Psychological Operations *David Miller*	163
10	Sociology of the Media: Towards an Ideal Journalistic Practice *Giuliana Tiripelli*	189
11	Sociology and Journalism: The Search for a Historical Imagination *Kevin Williams*	208
12	The Martian Invasion and the Sociological Imagination *Brian Winston*	226

Conclusion: Stretching the Sociological Imagination in the Neo-Liberal Academy 246
Matt Dawson, Bridget Fowler, David Miller and Andrew Smith

Appendix: Bibliography of the Writings of John Eric Thomas Eldridge (b. 1936) 263
Prepared by Alison Eldridge

Index 269

Figures and Tables

Figures

2.1	Construction of an office block, *c.* 1935	30
2.2	Park Royal Brewery, looking south, *c.* 1960	31
2.3	Worker purchasing the *Guinness Times*, 1947	34
2.4	Washing casks	35
2.5	Steaming metal and wooden casks	36
2.6	The Maltstore at Park Royal, *c.* 1950	37
3.1	Participation and worker responses	46
3.2	Occupational controls and workplace fiddles	51
3.3	Alternative politics of industrial relations	53
3.4	Patterns of compromise in workplace case studies, cross-classifying both 'concerns' and control capabilities of labour and capital	57
3.5	Authority and democracy in industry: First move (organisational structures x ideologies) and second move (exploring quadrants)	58
3.6	Third move (charting different strategies of legitimation and control) and fourth move (locating cases in matrix)	59
3.7	Fifth move (Thurley's matrix of organisational structures and forms of power) and sixth move (mapping cases into boxes)	60
9.1	Northern Ireland information organisations in January 1972	171
9.2	Organisational chart for Chicksands, 23 October 2008	180
9.3	Coalition air strike leaflets	183
9.4	Private Lynndie England with Iraqi prisoner on a leash	183

Tables

1.1	The research process for Mills	3

Foreword

For John Eldridge – Sociology in His Times and Ours

John Holmwood

I first came to know John and his work in 1980, when I took up my first academic job in the UK at the University of Edinburgh. I had just spent two years in Australia at the University of Tasmania and, returning to the UK, the post at Edinburgh was one of the last permanent jobs in sociology to be advertised for almost a decade. Higher education was subject to serious cutbacks, following the election of the first Conservative government under Mrs Thatcher in 1979. Shortly after, in 1982, her Secretary of State for Education and Science, Sir Keith Joseph, set up an enquiry into the Social Science Research Council (SSRC) – the forerunner of the Economic and Social Research Council (ESRC) – under Lord Rothschild, an enquiry whose remit also included special consideration of sociology and allegations of its supposed bias.

Mobilisation of the academic community, especially within sociology, and including John Eldridge, persuaded Lord Rothschild (against expectations – after all, he had just come from enunciating the 'customer-contractor' principle in his Report on The Organisation and Management of Government R&D) that the government's concerns and its plans for the SSRC were unfounded (albeit that Sir Keith was unpersuaded that the name 'science' was warranted, and the name of the Council was changed accordingly to ESRC). Lord Rothschild declared a moratorium of three years on any other changes and the academic community relaxed again. Unbeknown, higher education had embarked on a long process of neo-liberalisation, via the Jarratt Report (1985), which instituted managerial practices over collegial relations, the introduction of various audits (the Quality Assurance Agency or QAA and Research Assessment Exercise or RAE), the impact agenda and 'Pathways to Impact' and culminating in England, after the Browne Review of 2010, in the withdrawal of direct funding of undergraduate degrees in the social sciences, arts and humanities, the charging of student fees and opening up of the sector to for-profit providers operating without any of the wider obligations typically associated with universities and public universities in particular.

But I am running ahead of myself. Sociology in Scotland was barely 15 years old when the wider attacks upon it began. For reasons to do with the legislation then governing Scottish universities, any degree programme put forward at one institution had to be made available at all of them. This was a constraint on new disciplines such as sociology, and so most Scottish universities did not develop sociology programmes until the 1960s, after the relaxation of this legislation (and the projected expansion of student numbers after the Robbins Report of 1963).

John came to the University of Glasgow in 1972 and was part of the construction of the new discipline in that expansive moment. Like many others in British sociology, he was greatly influenced by C. Wright Mills's 'democratic' vision of the sociological imagination. Sociology had a distinctive viewpoint and body of expertise, but that expertise was tempered by its engagement with publics. It sought to uncover the wider social processes through which to locate 'private troubles' and, thereby, to make them available to public action to ameliorate them. Yet, more than anyone else, John was aware that this dialogic conception of 'sociological reporting' was at odds with the way in which mass media operated to secure the reproduction of existing social interests – those of a power elite – and to fuel the very anxieties that created scapegoats for private troubles. Indeed, it was precisely the uncovering of media 'bias' that gave rise to the accusation of 'bias' on the part of sociology, including in its sympathy toward trades unions (whether by the University of Warwick's SSRC-funded Industrial Relations Unit, or by the Glasgow Media Group's studies of media reporting of trades union disputes).

At around the same time – and with similar interest from British sociologists as provided to Mills – Howard Becker famously asked the question, 'whose side are we on?' For Becker, subordinate knowledges – even where presented neutrally by sociologist interlocutors – are perceived by those in authority as partisan. This reflected a 'hierarchy of credibility' in the value attributed to the views of different individuals and groups. Sociology's interest in addressing disadvantage and marginality among groups that were low in status meant that sociology would face a challenge to its own credibility. John was President of the British Sociological Association (BSA) between 1979 and 1981, just as these challenges were coming to the fore. In that role, he helped us face them and face them down. The mobilisation of academic debate and argument within the BSA and outside was impressive. The roll-call of sociologists providing written evidence to the Rothschild Report (available at Annex 5 to the report) is a tribute to the generation of which John was part and in which he played such a leading role.

Fast forward to the present. The silence of the academic community with regard to the most recent dismantling of public higher education is in striking contrast to the noisy and committed engagement of the past. There can be few who do not see in it the culmination of an ideological reorganisation begun in the 1980s. Yet our responses are mealy-mouthed just when we need to speak plainly. Echoes of the past are present when we endorse the importance of the impact agenda as showing a proper accountability of research to the public who funds it. We argue that the 'co-production' of research represents the dialogic commitment to *work with* the public, rather than do *research about* them. But do we really not see with whom we are enjoined to work? The absorption of research to the interests of power becomes increasingly evident – co-production *with* business, *with* policy-makers. We need research *about* business and *about* policy-making if democratic debate is to be facilitated. We are complicit in the instrumentalisation of dialogue, and the denial of its real promise, a promise exemplified in John's life and work.

It is usual when honouring a senior colleague to convey a sense of the baton being passed on, but when we reflect upon this succession in sociology, do we not get a sense of that baton being dropped? John provided for us an exemplary sense of sociology as a vocation, of sociology as a calling, albeit one conducted modestly. I shall close by modifying a passage from one of John's own inspirations, that we might understand how we have not fulfilled the promise of sociology that was given to us:

> For the last stage of this sociological development, it might well be truly said: 'sociologists without heart, specialists without spirit; this nullity imagines it has attained a level of world-leading originality, significance and rigour never before achieved'.
> [From Weber's *The Protestant Ethic and the Spirit of Capitalism*, and REF 2014 level and assessment criteria for 4* research]

Foreword

John Eldridge and the Birth of the Glasgow Media Group

Greg Philo

In October 1974, a motley group drawn from academia, TV and theatre assembled in a fine Art Nouveau building on Bute Gardens in Glasgow. Video recorders had just come on the market, and with them the prospect of storing TV programmes in large quantities for research analysis. They were incredibly expensive at £500 each; a one bedroom flat could be bought for £1700.

We looked at each other amid this fabulous technical wealth and wondered a little about what we would do with it. What would the methods be in such a new and fairly untried area? 'Aren't you supposed to know?' said Brian Winston from television. 'You are the sociologists!' – well, yes and no. We all had some sociology, but I was better known for theatre, Paul Walton was a prominent radical, Peter Beharrell had just finished his politics masters and Jean Hart was well known as an excellent jazz singer. 'Howard Davis knows about computers!' said Paul confidentially, which was pretty good at the time as none of the rest of us knew anything much about them.

But amongst us was John Eldridge, a bona fide top-notch sociology professor who added greatly to the volatile mixture of energy and varied experience which produced the Glasgow Media Group. We all in different ways knew about social science and its power to analyse and convince. But we had to feel our way through multiple techniques in a genuine process of trial and error, to explain the structures which underpinned meaning in television news. Could we, for example, explain its priorities by assessing expenditure on equipment and resources? Satellite use was expensive, so to employ them for news stories might indicate levels of importance. But then we found that the latest 'hot' news stories were being sent over on satellites originally commissioned for cricket coverage.

John, Paul and Brian had the original idea of comparing news coverage of strikes with other measures of their occurrence – such as official statistics on days lost. John's background in industrial sociology was very useful here. It proved invaluable again in his analysis of a pay claim by Arthur Scargill and the miners' union, showing how its very routine nature had been exaggerated and dramatised in the news.

But the agonies over method continued, and in the end we resolved them only by looking repeatedly at massive quantities of recorded TV programmes until patterns emerged and we could explain their regular features. Paul and Howard analysed news language, while Brian tackled visuals. Jean went off to interview journalists while Peter and I, joined by our great friend John Hewitt, developed case studies on news coverage of strikes at British Leyland and by the Glasgow dustcart drivers.

All this activity did not escape the attention of the Lords of Broadcasting. We were rather direct in our criticism, and at that time it was rare for academics to be impolite about television and especially the BBC. One senior figure termed our work 'Bad News for Scholarship'; another coined the gripping phrase 'a shadowy guerrilla force on the fringe of broadcasting'. But through these very turbulent moments, John was a stabilising influence, greeting each new argument with equanimity and good humour. We should also salute Glasgow University and its gloriously remote and unbothered attitude at the time. A complaint from the BBC chairman to the Principal made no difference at all. In the august and ancient environs of Hillhead, the attitude was more likely to be, 'the BBC, well, when was it set up? Only 1926?'. In comparison with the University, it was rather parvenu.

We survived, and somehow grew. The Media Group became a fixture of the University and we developed our research from content analysis to production studies and audience work. This development became what we are now best known for. We were able to pioneer research which linked all the key elements of communications and showed the interactions between them, which we termed the Circuit of Communications (production, content, reception and circulation). In this, we went a long way to resolving the key issue with which we had begun. This was essentially to understand the nature and extent of media power, and its influence if and where it existed. Our project became centrally concerned with how we might demonstrate possible links between the content of media and impacts on public belief and behaviour or the manner in which messages were resisted or reinterpreted. We were eventually able to do this by developing our new methods in audience research. In these, we went far beyond simply demonstrating a correlation between media accounts and public belief. With the new techniques in focus group work, we were able to show the exact moments in which beliefs were formed and the triggers for developments in attitudes and behavioural change. We could illustrate the conditions under which media messages were resisted and also when they were accepted as legitimate. This empirical work was developed across multiple examples in a wide range of different subject areas. For example, in our analysis of beliefs about the 1984/85 miners' strike, we found that everyone (including police and bystanders) who had been present at picketing rejected the predominant media images of the strike as very violent. Yet a majority of those who had not been present and who relied on the media as a source did believe that picketing was mostly violent; and beliefs were related directly to what had been seen in media, especially television (Philo 1990:148).

In our studies on mental health, we found that the fear generated by media images could actually overwhelm direct experience in the formation of belief. In this revealing comment, a young woman who lived next door to a hospital and worked as a volunteer described the impact of media on her own reactions when meeting the patients:

> The actual people I met weren't violent – that I think they are violent, that comes from television, from plays and things. that's the strange thing – the people were mainly geriatric – it wasn't the people you hear of on television. Not all of them were old, some of them were younger. None of them were violent – but I remember being scared of them, because it was a mental hospital – it's not a very good attitude to have but it is the way things come across on TV, and films – you know, mental axe murders and plays and things – the people I met weren't like that, but that is what I associate them with.
>
> (Philo 1996:104)

In our work on the Israeli/Palestinian conflict, we were able to show how structures of belief and the ordering of memories related directly to persistent themes in media accounts. For example, we showed in content analysis how TV frequently portrayed Palestinians as initiating violence and Israelis as 'responding'. We then demonstrated in focus groups how this led people to reorder their memories of sequences of events. The patterns of 'action' and 'response' are well described in this interchange from a focus group.

> Female speaker: You always think of the Palestinians as being really aggressive because of the stories you hear on the news. I always put the blame on them in my own head.

> Moderator: Is it presented as if the Palestinians somehow start it and then the Israelis follow on?
> Female speaker: Exactly, I always think the Israelis are fighting back against the bombings that have been done to them.
>
> (Philo and Berry 2004:222)

These methods became well known, and as we expanded our research programmes, we recruited a large body of researchers and postgraduates to pursue them. When they left, they took our methods and approaches, developing them further in many universities and schools of journalism. So the guerrilla force in which John Eldridge was such a central figure spread its messages, and let us hope it will continue to do so.

References

Philo, G. (1990) *Seeing and Believing*. London: Routledge.
Philo, G. (ed.) (1996) *Media and Mental Distress*. London: Longman.
Philo, G. and Berry, M. (2004) *Bad News from Israel*. London: Pluto.

Acknowledgements

The editors would like to thank all the contributors to this volume for their valuable contributions and patience during the editorial process. An especial thanks to Alison Eldridge for preparing the bibliography of John Eldridge's writings contained in this volume and to Lito Tsitsou for producing the index. His co-editors would particularly like to acknowledge and thank Matt Dawson, for his strenuous and thoughtful efforts to keep the whole project together.

This volume emerged from a Festschrift conference of the same title held at Glasgow University in September 2014. The editors would like to express their gratitude to all of those who contributed to the conference, including the School of Social and Political Sciences, University of Glasgow, for providing funding, Minna Liinpää and Maureen McBride for their help in organising the event and Maggie Nicol for her meticulous administrative assistance.

Thanks also to the team at Palgrave Macmillan, notably Philippa Grand and Judith Allan for their support for the project and advice in preparing the volume.

Finally, our thanks to John Eldridge himself. As the contributions to this volume make clear, John's work and collegial nature has inspired many of his colleagues and he has provided great support to us as editors in preparing this volume. We hope he enjoys it.

Contributors

Huw Beynon is Professor Emeritus at the Wales Institute of Social and Economic Research, Data and Method (WISERD) at Cardiff University, United Kingdom. He has written widely on issues relating to coal miners and the coal industry. In 1985, he edited a collection of articles dealing with the many issues involved in the miners' strike: *Digging Deeper*. Others of his books include *Masters and Servants: Class and Patronage in the Making of a Labour Organisation* (with Terry Austrin); *A Tale of Two Industries: The Decline of Coal and Steel in the North East of England* (with Ray Hudson and David Sadler); *Digging Up Trouble: Protest and the Environment on the Coal-fields* (with Andrew Cox and Ray Hudson); and *Coalfield Regeneration: Dealing with the Consequences of Industrial Decline* (with Katy Bennett and Ray Hudson).

Howard Davis is Professor of Social Theory and Institutions in the School of Social Sciences at Bangor University, United Kingdom, and Co-Director of the Wales Institute for Social & Economic Research, Data & Methods (WISERD). He worked previously at the universities of Kent, Glasgow (where he was a founder member of the Glasgow Media Group) and Edinburgh. His current research interests are in the sociology of culture, identities and belonging, and the impact of social change on individuals and communities. He is co-investigator on the ESRC large grant WISERD Civil Society (2014–19) which is examining civil society, participation and change in Wales and beyond.

Matt Dawson is Lecturer in Sociology at the University of Glasgow, United Kingdom, with research interests in social theory, political sociology, asexuality and the history of sociology. He is the author of *Late Modernity, Individualization and Socialism: An Associational Critique of Neoliberalism* (2013, Palgrave Macmillan) and *Social Theory for Alternative Societies* (2016, Palgrave Macmillan).

Alison Eldridge teaches sociology on Glasgow University's Access Course. She has recently completed her PhD which examines the relationship between sociology and photography. Drawing from the work of Pierre Bourdieu and Raymond Williams, the aesthetics, politics and ethics of conflict photography were explored in the context of a 'field' of photographic production including documentary, photojournalism and fine art photography.

John Eldridge is Emeritus Professor of Sociology at the University of Glasgow, United Kingdom. He was the founding Head of the Department of Sociology at Glasgow, having previously worked at the Universities of York and Bradford. He holds a BSc from the University of London, and an MA from Leicester University where he was taught by, amongst others, Norbert Elias and Ilya Neustadt.

His research has been path-breaking in at least three fields within the discipline, which are reflected in the organisation of the current volume. The first of these is the sociology of work and industry, in which regard he is the author of a series of highly influential studies including: *Industrial Disputes* (1968), *Just Managing: Authority and Democracy in Industry* (1985) and *Industrial Sociology and Economic Crisis* (1990). He was also the co-founder of the Centre for Research in Industrial Democracy and Participation at Glasgow.

He has, secondly, written widely on social theory including a series of insightful expositions of the writing of Max Weber (*Max Weber: The Interpretation of Social Reality*, 1972), Raymond Williams (*Raymond Williams: Making Connections*, with Lizzie Eldridge, 1994) and C. Wright Mills (*C. Wright Mills*, 1983).

Finally, he has been a highly innovative figure in the sociology of media. He was one of the co-founders of the Glasgow Media Group, which continues to develop pioneering research on the media and its effects 40 years on. His own contributions can be found in collaborative texts such as *Bad News* (1976), *More Bad News* (1980) and *Mass Media and Power in Modern Britain* (1997), and he is the author of important essays in edited volumes such as *Getting the Message: News, Truth and Power* (1993) and the *Glasgow University Media Group Reader, Volume 1* (1995).

All of his work has been marked by a characteristic concern to ensure that sociological research informs and shapes public debate, and by a commitment to the contribution that the sociological imagination can make to struggles for a more democratic and more equal society. A public sociologist *avant la lettre*, engaging with and writing for non-academic audiences has been a consistent part of John Eldridge's work throughout his career (see, for example, his contribution to the peace movement, *Taking Out Moscow*, 1992).

In addition to this, John was President of the British Sociological Association from 1979 to 1981 and was a crucial participant in the discussions with the UK government which led to the reorganisation of the Economic and Social Research Council in 1983. He was, in this respect, a central figure in the fight to resist moves to remove the term 'Social' entirely from the title of the organisation. He was also pivotal to the establishment of ALSISS (the Association of Learned Societies in the Social Sciences). In 2015, he was the recipient of the BSA's Distinguished Service Award, presented – appropriately enough, at Glasgow – by the current president, Professor Lynn Jamieson.

A selected bibliography of John Eldridge's academic and public writing is provided at the end of this volume.

Tony Elger is Emeritus Professor of Sociology at the University of Warwick near Coventry, United Kingdom, where he worked for most of his career. His teaching and research focused on the sociology of work and employment, comparative political economy, the problems and prospects facing workers and unions, and workplace case studies. Having retired to East Lothian in Scotland he retains a particular interest in these topics alongside walking, grandchildren and geology. He first encountered John's work when he was an undergraduate and post-graduate student and has been stimulated by it ever since.

Bridget Fowler is Emeritus Professor of Sociology at the University of Glasgow, United Kingdom. She is the author, amongst other works, of *The Alienated Reader* (Harvester Wheatsheaf, 1991), *Pierre Bourdieu and Cultural Theory* (1997) and *The Obituary as Collective Memory* (2007).

John Holmwood is Professor of Sociology in the School of Sociology and Social Policy at the University of Nottingham, United Kingdom. He has previously held appointments at the universities of Tasmania, Edinburgh, Sussex and Birmingham. He was a member of the Institute of Advanced Study, Princeton, in academic year, 2014–15. He was President of the British Sociological Association, 2012–14. He is co-founder of the Campaign for the Public University, and co-founder and joint managing editor of the free online magazine of social research, commentary and policy analysis, *Discover Society*.

John MacInnes is Associate Dean (Quantitative Methods) in the College of Humanities and Social Sciences and Professor of Sociology in the School of Social and Political Science at the University of Edinburgh, United Kingdom. From 2009 to 2014, he was strategic advisor to the ESRC on quantitative methods training. From 1978 to 1995, he worked at Glasgow University, first as a research assistant and later as a lecturer in sociology. His research interests include the links between sociology and demography and the nature and impact of population ageing.

David Miller is Professor of Sociology in the Department of Social & Policy Sciences at the University of Bath, United Kingdom. He was Global Uncertainties Leadership Fellow (2013–15) and is co-director of Public Interest Investigations, a non-profit company behind two websites: spinwatch.org and powerbase.info.

Greg Philo is Professor of Communication and Social Change at the University of Glasgow, United Kingdom, and Research Director of the Glasgow Media Group. He is the author of *Communicating Climate Change and Energy Security* (2013, with Catherine Happer), *Bad News for Refugees* (2013, with Emma Briant and Pauline Donald) and *More Bad News from Israel* (2011, with Mike Berry).

Andrew Smith is Reader in Sociology at the University of Glasgow, United Kingdom, and a member of the ESRC Research Centre on the Dynamics of Ethnicity. His research interests are with cultural sociology, imperialism and the sociology of racism. He is the author of *C.L.R. James and the Study of Culture* (2010, Palgrave Macmillan).

Tim Strangleman is Professor of Sociology at the University of Kent, Canterbury, United Kingdom. John Eldridge was the external examiner on Tim's PhD at Durham in 1998. He is interested in and has written on a wide range of areas around the sociology of work and economic life examining questions of work meaning and identity, deindustrialisation, memory, nostalgia and the experience of industrial change. He is the author of two books and currently working on a new book based on his Guinness research entitled *Imagining Work in the Twentieth Century: Guinness and the Transformation of Employment*.

Giuliana Tiripelli is a graduate assistant at Glasgow University, United Kingdom. Her interests lie in the fields of social change, the role of old and new media, and the present and future of journalism. Her work focuses on the analysis of formation and transformation of beliefs via the media. She is the author of *Media and Peace in the Middle East. The Role of Journalism in Israel-Palestine*, an ethnographic monograph about Peace Journalism and the Israeli-Palestinian conflict, to be published by Palgrave Macmillan in 2016 for the series Palgrave Studies in Compromise after Conflict.

Kevin Williams is Professor of Media and Communication in the Department of History and Classics at Swansea University, United Kingdom. His most recent publication is *International Journalism* (2011) and he is presently completing a book on the history of journalism.

Brian Winston holds the Lincoln Chair at the University of Lincoln, United Kingdom, and is a guest professor at Beijing Normal University. A television professional and prize-winning documentary scriptwriter, he was the Glasgow Media Group's first director and a member of the team which produced *Bad News* and *More Bad News*. Since that time he has held senior academic positions on both sides of the Atlantic and has written widely on media history and ethics, communication technology, documentary film and free expression.

1
Stretching Exercises: Stimulating the Sociological Imagination

John Eldridge

C. Wright Mills's *The Sociological Imagination* has achieved legendary status in the 50 or so years since its publication. I have always enjoyed it primarily for its intellectual and moral challenge but also for its mischievous sense of fun. According to Mills: 'To be aware of the idea of social structure and to use it with sensibility is to be capable of tracing such linkages among a great variety of milieux. To be able to do that is to possess the sociological imagination' (Mills 1959: 10–11).

For those who were taught sociology and those who practiced it the possibility of a fruitful form of self consciousness was held out. There was something inherently worthwhile and indeed exciting about this. Through the exercise of the sociological imagination we learn new ways of thinking and the capacity for astonishment is made lively again. Mills nailed his colours to the mast. He distinguished between what he termed the personal troubles of the milieu and the public issues of social structure. He offers thumb nail sketches of what he has in mind with reference to unemployment, war, marriage and the metropolis. Whatever our experiences and troubles within any of these contexts, which may well matter deeply to us as individuals, the explanation of the phenomena which they represent cannot be found in the immediate environment of the individual but in the wider institutional nexus – the state, the economy, the range of social institutions that both sustain a society and create difficulties, tensions and conflicts that can be identified as public issues. This is the level at which reason can and should be applied to human affairs.

But for Mills, the promise of sociology as an emancipatory practice was not being fulfilled. He wrote:

> My conception stands opposed to social science as a set of bureaucratic techniques which inhibit social inquiry by 'methodological'

pretensions, which congest such work by obscurantist conceptions, or which trivialise it by concern with minor problems unconnected with publicly relevant issues.

(Mills 1959: 20)

Were there ways of counteracting what he regarded as a crisis in the social sciences? The Appendix of the book, 'On Intellectual Craftsmanship', offered some practical advice to would-be researchers. In this chapter I want to build on that and discuss some of the ways in which the sociological imagination can be stimulated and cultivated. But as a preface to this, we may recall the strong advice of these words:

try to understand men and women as historical and social actors, and the ways in which the variety of men and women are intricately selected and intricately formed by the variety of human societies. Before you are through with any piece of work, no matter how indirectly on occasion, orient it to the central and continuing task of understanding the structure and the drift, the shaping and the meanings, of your own period, the terrible and magnificent world of human society in the second half of the twentieth century.

(Mills 1959: 225)

We can now extend the time period of course. But the thrust of the argument remains the same.

Cross-classification

Mills claimed that 'in many ways cross-classification is the very grammar of the sociological imagination. Like all grammar it must be controlled and not allowed to run away from its purpose' (Mills 1959: 213). Mills saw cross-classification as a technique for dealing with quantitative and qualitative materials. It was a tool which enabled the sociologist to clarify and critique one's own and other people's work and possibly to make innovating conceptual moves as a result:

Charts, tables and diagrams of a qualitative sort are not only ways to display work already done, they are very often genuine tools of production. They clarify the 'dimensions' of the types, which they also help you to imagine and build... When they work, they help you to think more clearly and to write more explicitly. They enable you to discover the range and the full relationships of the very terms with which you are thinking and of the facts with which you are dealing.

(Mills 1959: 213)

I have discussed the usefulness of cross-classification in various places (Eldridge 1985; Cressey et al. 1985; Eldridge 2010).

For example, in offering a framework for the analysis of job satisfaction studies as early as 1948, Mills demonstrates how, by the use of cross-classification and introducing concepts of power and participation, it is possible to move from purely subjective measures of job satisfaction to structural considerations. This involved inventing new categories but also showed the ways in which empirical findings would be shaped and re-shaped by such inventiveness. In such ways conventional thinking in a discipline can be challenged (Mills 1948).

But cross-classification techniques can also be used to throw light on the research process itself. In 1953 Mills wrote about the macroscopic and the molecular as two styles of social research – the large scale and the small scale (Mills 1963). This he cross-classifies against what he terms the problematic (what is the research question?) and the explanatory (what constitutes an explanation?) (Table 1.1).

The research process, he contends, is neither wholly deductive nor wholly inductive. Mills deploys the image of the shuttle to indicate what is happening inside each phase of research both in defining the problem and in explaining it. He expresses it formally in this way:

> We move from macroscopic to molecular in both problem and solution phase (1 to 3 and 2 to 4); then we relate the two on the molecular level (3 and 4); then we go back to the macroscopic (3 to 1 and 4 to 2). After that we can speak cautiously (bearing in mind the shuttles made) of relations on the macroscopic level (1 and 2).
>
> (Mills 1963: 563)

What is interesting about this exposition is that, despite Mills's strictures concerning molecular research in the abstracted empiricist form, he still recognises that work done at that level had potential for sociological work, providing its does not get disconnected from macroscopic concerns. Indeed, just as the macroscopic researcher needs to cultivate a technical imagination, so the research technicians need to develop an

Table 1.1 The research process for Mills

	Problematic	Explanatory
Macroscopic	1	2
Molecular	3	4

Source: Adapted from Mills (1963: 560).

imaginative concern for macroscopic meaning. It is the consciousness of this process at whatever level sociologists are working at any given time which creates a basis for intellectual craftsmanship.

Among other things, then, the technique of cross-classification can inform our understanding of the relationship between theory and method. As it happens, there are parallel observations about this relationship between theory and method in the work of the historian E.P. Thompson, who refers specifically to Mills in his celebrated essay 'The Peculiarities of the English' (Thompson 1978). There Thompson points to Marx and Darwin, giants of social and natural science respectively.

> In both men we can see that exciting dialectic of making and breaking, the formation of conceptual hypotheses, that friction between 'molecular' research and 'macroscopic' generalisation to which Wright Mills often referred. In any vital intellectual tradition this dialectic, this abrasion between models and particulars, is always evident.
> (Thompson 1978: 274)

And when Thompson reflects on the character of historical practice, he sees it as a kind of dialogue

> with an argument between received, inadequate, or ideologically informed concepts or hypotheses on the one hand, and fresh or inconvenient evidence on the other; with the elaboration of new hypotheses; with the testing of these hypotheses against the evidence, which may involve interrogating existing evidence in new ways, or renewed research to confirm or disprove the new notions; with discarding those hypotheses which fail these tests, and refining or revising those which do, in the light of this engagement.
> (Thompson 1978: 43)

It is precisely what Thompson termed the creative quarrel at the heart of cognition that allows intellectual growth to take place. In such ways is the historical and sociological imagination kindled, sustained and disciplined.

Juxtapositions and contrasts

The deployment of juxtapositions and contrasts is of course closely connected with the practice of cross-classification. Here we see the imagination at work in thoughtful, sometimes playful ways. Some of this is now well established and built into the edifice of the sociological tradition. We can think of examples such as culture and society, tradition and modernity, sacred and profane, class and status, elites and masses. In each case some kind of contrast is implied. At the same time we are encouraged to understand one concept by reference to another.

When Max Weber writes about class and status, for example, he wants to show the difference between the two concepts and their potential interconnections. So class is defined in essentially economic terms – the collective standing of groups of people in terms of their property, income, skill and market situation – which shape their life chances. Status is also a collective term which refers to shared life styles between groups of people and may be marked out by matters such as education, occupation, membership of social circles, which may have positive or negative effects on the social standing of people and the social esteem that is accorded to them. Weber, who was a trained economist as well as a sociologist, finds a way of making a distinction between production, which class stratification relates to, and patterns of consumption which lead to specific styles of life and status orders. But he is careful to point out that interrelationships may well exist between life chances and life style. The empirical question is: how do these connections manifest themselves in different situations?

Weber sought conceptual clarity not for its own sake but in order to engage in work that involved wrestling with the big themes of social change. This was strategically done though the extensive use of ideal types. These pure types, or utopian constructs as he called them, were a necessary way for him to gain a sharper sense of the dynamics of social change. The key question for him was: are these types useful? If they were they became part of his conceptual repertoire: types of action, of rationality, of organisation, of bureaucracy, of leadership and of political authority serve as examples. They marked out the ground he was exploring and, in the process, enabled him to grapple with questions of causation in social life and action, together with questions of meaning.

Raymond Aron, still one of the best commentators on Weber, gives us a good sense of how the use of ideal types constitute imaginative acts on the part of the sociologist:

> The ideal type can be used equally well in formulating a problem (how did capitalism, regarded as the achievement of a particular kind of organisation of labour which is only found in the West, originate?),

or in expounding the results, or in research (to what extent does reality conform to the ideal type?).

(Aron 1957: 74)

What is liberating about Weber's approach to ideal type analysis is the recognition that such types can lose their relevance as new problems emerge. He is not therefore insisting that his ideal types are fixed and must be slavishly followed by any budding historian or sociologist. On the contrary:

> there are sciences to which eternal youth is granted, and the historical disciplines are among them – all those to which the eternally onward flowing stream of culture perpetually brings new problems. At the very heart of their task lies not only the transiency of all ideal types but also at the same time the inevitability of new ones.
>
> (Weber 1949: 104)

It is precisely this which constitutes a challenge to the sociological imagination of each generation.

There are quite other ways of looking at juxtapositions and contrasts as ways of illuminating social reality. We may look at the relationship between words and images in a text. Take, for example John Berger and Jean Mohr's *A Seventh Man* (1975), which is about male migrant workers in Europe. The title referred to the fact that at that time in Germany and Britain one out of every seven manual workers was an immigrant. The authors insist that the words and images should be read in their own terms. The pictures, seen as a sequence, are intended to make their own statement rather than as illustrations of the text. And so there are pictures of migrant workers from Turkey, Greece, North Africa and other places. They have mostly come from villages where they worked as peasants. We see them undergoing medical examinations – are they fit enough, capable enough, tall enough? We see them at railway stations, at passport control gates, at reception centres, in their places of work, in their barracks-like accommodation. These are the people who built new buildings and motorways, cleaned the cities, worked on the assembly lines, quarried the minerals, loaded the goods and buried the pipe lines. They came from places of rural poverty to the marginalised existence of migrant labour in the cities of Europe.

It is salutary to read *A Seventh Man* some 40 years on. It anticipates the theme of globalisation now in common parlance. Not only so, but it reminds us of the theoretical relationship between actor and structure in its human dimensions. And of course issues of migration are still very much on the European agenda. At such a time as this we can recall Berger's words:

> To outline the experience of the migrant worker and to relate to what surrounds him – both physically and historically – is to grasp more surely the political reality of the world at this moment. The subject is European, its meaning is global. Its theme is unfreedom. This unfreedom can only be fully recognised if an objective economic system is related to the subjective experience of those trapped within it. Indeed, finally, the unfreedom is that relationship.
> (Berger and Mohr 1975: 1)

Metaphors and similes

Sociology without metaphor is dead or, we might say, impossible. We may well be shocked to realise that the concept of society itself is a metaphor. This, after all, is the concept which, until recently at least, was the defining feature, the very object of sociological study. Bauman points out that the metaphor of society, like all metaphors, was selective. It brought to the surface and made salient the quality of being in a 'company'. He comments:

> Explicitly or implicitly, the metaphor of society uses images of closeness, proximity, togetherness and mutual engagement. 'Society' could be used as a metaphor because the experience which sociologists struggled to grasp and articulate was that of a number of people in the same place interacting in many if not all of their activities, meeting each other often and talking to each other on many occasions. Being united in such a way, the quantity of people faced the prospect of living in close proximity to each other for a long time to come, and for that reason the unity of life setting was capped by the effort to close ranks, to make the co-existence 'harmonious', 'orderly', so that mutual benefits might follow.
> (Bauman and Tester 2001: 101–2)

So here we are offered an image of how to see ourselves and others as social beings. To develop such a concept in the first place is an imaginative act, although today we would scarcely give it a second thought. We take it for granted. But Bauman goes on to point out that there is a paradox at the heart of this inventive moment. Why is this? It is because:

> the kind of experience which sociologists struggled to catch in their conceptual net when using 'society' as a metaphor had become

salient because it was already in a state of disrepair and in need of urgent and close attention, requiring new tools for it to be taught. It was precisely the 'company' that was missing, conspicuous for its absence.

(Bauman and Tester 2001: 101)

There is a somewhat similar reflection on the concept of society to be found in Raymond Williams's *Keywords* (1976). There he traces the origin and development of the term and notes that it enters the English language in the fourteenth century, where it refers to company and fellowship. Gradually the concept becomes more abstract and less intimate, referring to the body of social institutions in which relatively large groups of people live and the social relationships that are formed though them. Other terms come to be used by way of contrast, such as company or community to represent the more intimate sense of being together. Or, at the more abstract level, the term 'state', referring to the apparatus of power, is distinguished from that to which we all belong – society. Again, what came to be described as a central problem of sociology, the problem of order, was addressed by the notion of civil society. The point is, of course, that order comes to be seen and experienced as a problem. Hence the relationship of the individual to society is seen as a problem – the problem of social integration. And the relationship of the different parts of society to one another is also seen as a problem. These 'different parts' could be explored by developing metaphors out of the original metaphor. Thus society could be pictured as a machine in need of repair, or an organism in need of an appropriate environment.

The concept of society then is a crucial example of exercising and stretching the sociological imagination. Here I think Bauman made an insightful comment when he reflected on the circumstances in which the concept emerged

> I wonder: could 'society' be imagined at all, could it become an 'imagined company', were not daily experience already suggesting something quite different – loneliness, abandonment, absence of company? I believe that society became an object of cognition the moment it started making its members into individuals, itself retreating from the realm of the visible (let alone the obvious), from the 'given to hand', and taking a behind-the-scenes position, where it could only be 'imagined' and theorised.
>
> (Bauman and Tester 2001:103)

We can recall that when Marx wrote about alienation, it was to give an account of the ways in which the individual had become separated from others and how society had come to be seen as over and above him or her – a reified thing. And modern society is described in *The Communist Manifesto* as like a sorcerer (note the simile) who has conjured up powers from the nether world that he is not able to control. These are the gigantic means of production and exchange, productive forces that are both marvellous to behold but also the source of continuing instability and crises in modern times. And when Durkheim wrote about anomie it was to express the sense of dislocation, the breakdown of the moral order, the absence of appropriate social norms for the regulation of modern societies, the growth of markets over which individual producers felt they had no control. A society which was in a state of acute anomie was, for Durkheim, a disordered one. The task of repair, of social reconstruction would be difficult, but he was not without hope.

If society is, for the most part, an unnoticed metaphor, there is no question that some labels attached to the term have a much greater explicitness attached to them. Take, for instance, Peter Berger's *Invitation to Sociology* (1963) where he discusses the images of society as prison, puppet theatre, stage and carnival respectively. Each of these gives us a perspective – a way to think about society. They have different emphases: the presence of force and oppression, the techniques of manipulation, the existence of conventions and fictions to define social reality. He sums up the significance of this very well when considering the contrast between the prison metaphor, which focuses on constraint, control and containment with the dramatic one, which allows more active room for agency:

> Stage, theatre, circus and even carnival – here we have the imagery of our dramatic model, with a conception of society as precarious, uncertain, often unpredictable. The institutions of society, while they do in fact coerce us, appear at the same time as dramatic conventions, even fictions. They have been invented by past impresarios, and future ones may cast them back into the nothingness whence they emerged. Acting out the social drama we keep pretending that these precarious inventions are eternal verities. We act as if there were no other way of being a man, a political subject, a religious devotee or one who exercises a certain profession, yet at times the thought passes through the minds of even the dimmest among us that we could do very different things. If social reality is dramatically created, it must also be dramatically malleable. In this way, the dramatic

model opens up a passage out of the rigid determinism into which sociological thought originally led us.

(Berger 1963:138–9)

A metaphor is a way of seeing and a way of not seeing. It enables us to pursue certain ways of thinking at the cost of putting other ways on one side, if only for the time being. But, it is important to remember not only the possibilities but also the limitations this places on us. Erving Goffman reminds us of this in his treatment of the dramaturgical metaphor in *The Presentation of Self in Everyday Life* (1969). There the central interest is in the relationship of the self to society and to do this Goffman uses the image of the individual whose activities constitute a performance. In working this through he draws on a vocabulary – a whole conceptual repertoire we might say – based on the dramaturgical metaphor: role, character, masks, stage, audiences, supporting cast, front and back regions. This allowed him to explore with a wealth of detail and illustration, notions of acting out of character, discrepant roles, talk and gossip, identity and the art of impression management. All this informs our understanding at a micro level of how social order is negotiated, sustained, renegotiated and reordered and the processes and mechanisms that take place when order breaks down: the attempts that are made to repair things and put them right with varying degrees of success or failure. This proves to be a valuable way of showing how trust in social relations is established, the conditions in which it flourishes and the things which threaten its continuance. The richness of the material and the shrewdness of the analysis make this a text that sociologists can revisit with profit.

But there is a sense in which Goffman is also a sociological showman – an impresario. His book is itself a performance and at the end he sharply reminds us of this. He tells us that the use of the dramaturgical metaphor and the language that goes with it was in part a rhetorical manoeuvre. Even while we speak of the world being a stage we know that there are real differences with actual theatres where the action that takes place is a contrived and admitted illusion. In drawing this to our attention Goffman concludes:

> And so here the language and mask of the stage will be dropped. Scaffolds, after all, are to build other things with, and should be erected with a view to taking them down. This report is not concerned with aspects of theatre that creep into everyday life. It is concerned with the structure of social encounters – the structure of those entities

in social life that come into being whenever persons enter into one another's immediate physical presence. The key factor of this structure is the maintenance of a single definition of the situation, this definition having to be expressed and this definition sustained in the face of a multitude of potential disruptions.

(Goffman 1969: 246)

We can see, then, that society as drama can be described as a root metaphor and other metaphors nestle in as the picture of society and social life is filled out. We learn to develop a language and deploy concepts to 'make sense' of the world in which we live.

One other example of the use of metaphor must suffice. In *What is Sociology?* (1978) Norbert Elias argues that a well-chosen metaphor can help us break out of more static ways of thinking about society:

One only needs to compare the imaginative possibilities of such static concepts as the individual and society or ego and system with the imaginative possibilities opened up by the metaphoric use of various images of games and players; the comparison will help us to understand that the models have served to unleash our powers of imagination.

(Elias 1978: 92)

Why does the metaphor of the game prove so fascinating? It is the fact that games are played according to rules (whilst recognising that they can be broken and cheating can take place). When we look at games in all their great variety we see that rules are established for playing. Looked at over time, even rules that are taken for granted may well have been the subject of discussion and argument and from time to time can be changed. There are often issues raised as to whether or not a rule has been broken and what sanctions should be applied if it has. This may call for the judgement of governing bodies, umpires, referees or arbiters. Questions may arise as to what is technically permissible (for example, what type of golf club and how many) and what is 'fair', that is morally permissible. Where there are opponents or competitors in a game they depend upon each other for the game to take place. In other words co-operation and conflict are part of the same process. It was George Simmel who described this Janus-headed relationship as one of 'antagonistic cooperation'. Rules, codes, relationships, roles, expectations, power, control, constraint, cooperation, skills, techniques, strategies, tactics, resources, rituals, outcomes – all of these and other terms we can employ in discussing and analysing games. Herein lies the fruitfulness of the metaphor.

Cicourel has pointed out that specific games – chess, football and so on – have game- furnished conditions, which tell us how the game is played and what the basic rules for playing are (Cicourel 1964), once that is understood we may notice that participants may choose to follow certain rules of preferred play. Thus, in chess, a good many openings are available to the players. The choices that are taken there will there will constrain and enable what is subsequently possible. Moreover, as the game proceeds, some options will no longer be possible. Decisions taken earlier will have irreversible consequences. Some games are intrinsically more uncertain as regards outcomes than others and therefore more difficult to calculate. In exploring the value of the metaphor Cicourel argues that by understanding the conditions and rules of the game we are in a better position to appreciate what is strange or unexpected. It is indeed one way of exploring the significance of cultural meanings in different settings. By the same token, it is also a way of exploring the nature of trust in specific situations and the reasons for the breakdown of trust from time to time.

Improvisation

The musician John Harle has described his experience of conducting the London Symphony Orchestra in a performance of Herbie Hancock's 'Maiden Voyage'. Hancock was the piano soloist. Harle observed that Hancock spent hours the day before the concert practising scales. In the actual performance there was an opening for improvisation with piano and drum. Harle had to count 136 bars before bringing other instruments back in. 'I swear in that whole solo, Herbie never played a single downbeat – which I'm sure he was doing deliberately – so it was a nightmare trying to count it' (Harle quoted in Fordham 2005).

When we consider this kind of improvisation, with all its implied originality and creativity, we cannot fail to notice also that it is tempered by and embedded in the composition itself. This may serve as an illustration of the role of improvisation in sociological work.

There are good examples of improvisation in the work of Raymond Williams. We can see, for example, the improvisation involved in breaking new ground. This was clearly the case in the writing of *Culture and Society* (1961) where he examines the idea of culture as it was to be found in the writings of many authors in Britain from the eighteenth to the mid-twentieth century. As he was to point out many years later to his questioners in *Politics and Letters* (1981), there was no 'culture and society tradition' to which he could relate. Because it was a pioneering study there was a necessary element of improvisation. He captured this very well, when he reflected upon it:

> The whole process of locating the writers who were relevant to my enquiry was a pretty amateur job of reading from one book to another, looking this and that up, and finding always that had to keep revising the formation with which I had originally started.
> (Williams 1981: 99)

The improvising spirit in Williams's work can also be seen in his study *Television, Technology and Cultural Form* (1974). It is there that we find the conceptual innovation of 'flow' as he attempts to pinpoint one of the essential features of television, which marks it off from a book, a play or even a film. In television we are presented day by day with a sequence of programmes that are different from one another and which are marked off in some way to denote that: news, drama, documentaries, current affairs, comedy, natural history, film and so on. This sequence is what might be described as the tele-visual experience. But for Williams it was not enough to discuss the distribution of different kinds of programme. What was required was to work with the more mobile concept of flow. The nature of this flow can be empirically and quantitatively measured and analysed. When Williams did this he was able to show what a planned flow looked like. For him, 'this phenomenon, of planned flow, is then, perhaps the defining characteristic of broadcasting, simultaneously as a technology and as a cultural form' (Williams 1974: 86). The concept of flow enables the researcher to look in general terms at the structured sequence of television programming. But, more than that, one can examine flow in more detailed senses to look at the succession of words and images between different categories of programme (for example, documentary and comedy) and within a programme such as news. Williams's overarching view was that analysis of this kind would enable us to understand the flow of values and meanings within a specific culture. Flow, then, is a dynamic, mobile concept, an example of conceptual improvisation which was not only fruitful for Williams but for others who have subsequently used it.

Improvisation carries with it the notion of risk-taking. Rather than playing safe, like a pianist playing the same old tunes in the same old way, chances are taken. We can hear, say, Keith Jarrett or Brad Mehldau playing the same jazz standard yet, through improvisation, do wonderfully different things with it. We can also hear them produce new and original compositions, which are made possible through their pre-existing musical experience and the development of their expertise.

Consider the work of the French sociologist Alain Touraine. Here is a scholar who, over the years, has wrestled with the concept of social action, who has engaged creatively with Marxist theory and was one of the earliest writers to work with the concept of post-industrial society. He rejected metaphors of society that spoke in terms of machines or organisms, seeing it rather as an arena of conflict in which competing actors struggle for power, influence and authority. For this reason he has given a great deal of attention to the study of social movements, as for example in *The Voice and the Eye* (1981). In a Foreword to this book Richard Sennett pointed out that in some important ways Touraine shares Durkheim's concerns to understand social solidarity. In that sense he is working with an old, well-worn standard tune. But he does new things with it. This is expressed in his finessing use of the concept of structure. Sennett notes: 'For Touraine, structure is a property of activity. People do not act in a social structure, the structure of society is the structure of how a group moves; it has an identity only by virtue of its movement' (in Touraine 1981: x). We might describe this as a theoretical improvisation.

It is this theoretical move which calls for methodological improvisation. In describing this it is important to appreciate that Touraine has an agenda which mirrors his values and sense of what is involved for him in the sociological task. He is clear about this:

> Is it not our main task now – as it always was – to resuscitate social relations, opposition, defiance, struggle and hope wherever they have been crushed, distorted or stifled by order, which is always the order of the state? It is not enough simply to denounce the order; one must show that it is not all powerful, one must rediscover the spring hidden beneath the cement, the word beneath the silence, the questioning beneath the ideology. This is what is at stake, and if we are to lose we shall have to give up believing in social movements and even in what we call society; no longer class actors, only victims. Subjugation and exile are everywhere to be found, but I have undertaken this research into social movements to show that they do exist in spite of subjugation and exile.
>
> (Touraine 1981: 55)

He could not be more explicit. This informs his view of the sociological vocation and permeates his understanding of the methodological task. If, as he argues, sociology's chief problem is to bring social relations to the surface so that we, as citizens, may no longer be dupes to the categories of social practice, then the sociologist should be involved in active intervention. To disclose those social relations and then to analyse them becomes the central purpose of sociology. The method is a form of action, of intervention. Into the social movements being analysed, and with their consent, are interposed an interpreter and a secretary. The secretary essentially charts the nature and substance of meetings that take place. The interpreter is there to aid the group in their self-analysis of the processes they are engaged in. It is another way of coming at the old problem of the relationship between theory and practice. Touraine and his colleagues have worked with a range of social movement groups, including Solidarity, anti-nuclear groups, trade unions, feminist and ecological groups. The process for the social movement group is one of clarification of purposes and learning to reinterpret itself and its political role. We can see that this form of researcher involvement is far removed from the usual understandings of participant observation, where the emphasis is typically on the unobtrusive role of the sociologist. Clearly, this raises a plethora of questions, ethical and political, which take us beyond normal evaluations of methodology.

I think great credit must be given to Touraine for his virtuoso originality. But I find myself reminded of the music hall song about 'the daring young man on the flying trapeze, who flies through the air with the greatest of ease'. We hold our breath at the spectacle and wonder can it really be sustained. Whatever else, Touraine's work stands as a challenge to more deterministic versions of sociology. He is well aware of the high risk taking nature of the activity:

> Thus the many years of efforts that have gone into my attempt to construct a sociology of action... and to invent a research method to fit its orientations, are by no means assured of success. One runs up against the doubt and mistrust of society which scarcely believes any longer in its power to shape the choice of the future through its own social battles and its internal political mechanisms.
> (Touraine 1981: 5)

Here, then, is a sociologist who is not content just to write about risks but is willing to take them in his own research practice.

There is another kind of improvisation: that born of an unexpected opportunity. In 1982, my colleagues in the Media Group obtained a modest amount of funding to study the United Nations Special

Conference on Peace and Disarmament, which was to take place in June 1982. This was to involve looking at all the coverage of the conference on British television news and in the press. The intention was to look at how extensively this conference was covered and how the news was selected, filtered and framed. Since we had access to all the speeches that were delivered at the conference, this provided us with a neat research design: we could compare what was available to the press with what was disseminated to the British public. By the beginning of May we were already videotaping all news programmes. But that was also the time that the British fleet reached the South Atlantic and overt conflict began between Britain and Argentina, which was to end with Britain's repossession of the Falkland Islands.

The Falklands conflict was a very significant political and military event as far as the two countries were concerned, albeit for very different reasons. It soon became clear that there were implications for the Thatcher government and also for relations between the government and the media. In particular the relations between the government and the BBC became highly contentious. As researchers with very limited resources we could have simply proceeded with our original research task. However, we realised that by chance we had the opportunity to undertake to undertake a detailed analysis of media coverage of the conflict. That is what we chose to do. Needless to say, this demanded a great deal of commitment on the part of the researchers in terms of time, energy and analysis. The results were published in *War and Peace News* (Glasgow University Media Group 1985) where it can be seen that the first part of the book is devoted to the Falklands conflict and the second part to the analysis of 'peace news', including the United Nations Special Conference. So it is that improvisation is sometimes a matter of seizing the day. This experience connects with and leads me on to my next way of stretching the sociological imagination: serendipity.

Serendipity

It was Robert Merton, for so long the doyen of American sociology, who was fascinated, even obsessed, with the role of serendipity in scientific research. In his essay 'The Bearing of Empirical Research on Sociological Theory' he refers to 'the serendipity pattern'. He describes this component of research as 'the discovery by chance or sagacity, of valid results which were not sought for' (Merton 1957: 103). One of the most frequently cited examples is Alexander Fleming's discovery of penicillin.

Fleming had not been actively looking for penicillin but was sharp enough to recognise the significance of what he came upon by chance.

Merton referred to three components of the serendipity pattern. The first is its unanticipated quality. Observations give rise to unexpected data which can challenge existing theory and sometimes develop new theory. Serendipity lies in the fact that the findings are a by-product, not the direct intention, of the original research. The second feature is its anomalous character. When the observation is not in line with existing theory, or with already established facts, there is an element of surprise which provokes curiosity in the scientist to explore the matter further. As a result, existing frameworks of knowledge may have to be modified or, in more revolutionary cases, superseded. This links with the third aspect: the unexpected fact must be strategic and the observer must be in a position to see the discovery as strategic. Merton commented that it requires a theoretically sensitized observer to detect the universal in the particular:

> After all, men [sic] had for centuries noticed such trivial occurrences as slips of the tongue, slips of the pen, typographical errors and lapses of memory, but it required the theoretical sensitivity of a Freud to see these as strategic data through which he could extend his theory of repression and symptomatic acts.
>
> (Merton 1957: 105)

The notion of unanticipated discoveries had parallels for Merton in his long-standing interest in the unanticipated consequences of planned human action, which itself had roots in the sociology of Max Weber (Merton 1936). With Elinor Barber he wrote a monograph on serendipity which was a scholarly discussion of the history of the word and the way it has been deployed in the sciences and the humanities (Merton and Barber 2004). In an Afterword to the book he somewhat mockingly referred to Obliterated Scientific Serendipities: the process by which the real messiness of scientific work is tidied up in scientific papers. One way in which this can happen is because the story of scientific accomplishment is told in certain formulaic ways. It does not tell us about the actual processes of scientific thinking and work, not least the uncharted byways of thought. Such byways, as Merton pointed out: 'can be taken to include the hypotheses generated by unanticipated and anomalous observations that one is making serendipitously en route to the solution of the problem in hand' (Merton and Barber 2004: 278). Or again, Merton cited the Nobel Prize winner, Ronald Hoffman, who, in a nicely titled piece 'Under the Surface of the Chemical Article', had written:

> In order to present a sanitised paradigmatic account of a chemical study, one suppresses many of the truly creative acts. (Among these are) the fortuitous circumstances – all of the elements of serendipity, of creative intuition at work.
>
> (cited in Merton and Barber 2004: 278)

There are indeed different ways of telling a story. Not surprisingly, Merton reminded as of the role of serendipity in the discovery of the double-helix model of the molecular structure of deoxyribonucleic acid (DNA). This was truly a momentous scientific discovery with all the developments in bio-technology and the 'new genetics' which have followed from it. James Watson and Francis Crick announced their discovery in a 900-word article in *Nature*, in April 1953. Here, in a standardised presentation, there was no mention of serendipity. Yet when Watson published *The Double Helix* in 1968, there is an abundance of evidence of serendipity at work. Watson, the biologist, and Crick, with a background in physics, were an unlikely combination to begin with. Yet their cross-disciplinary experience proved to be invaluable. Moreover, not only was the Cavendish Laboratory at Cambridge University a supportive environment in which to work, including the provision of necessary equipment, but they had a network of contacts beyond Cambridge, which formed essentially an invisible college. These included Maurice Wilkins and Rosalind Franklin at Kings College, London, and the American crystallographer, Jerry Donohue, who just happened to occupy a desk in their office and put them right on a number of crucial matters. Without this multi-faceted cognitive support Crick and Watson would have remained ignorant of some fundamental matters, as they openly acknowledged. Serendipitous findings of this kind are made more likely in supportive contexts like this and are not purely individual things.

Serendipity, then, can illustrate the imagination at work. In the case of Crick and Watson it is connected with an adventurous spirit, as indeed it was with Freud. Umberto Eco in his book of essays *Serendipities* (1999) offers a number of pleasing examples of serendipity at work. Thus it was that Christopher Columbus, believing he could reach the Indies by sailing westward, 'discovered' America, which, of course, he did not know existed. Moreover, he did it on a mistaken assumption about the size of the earth. Not all projects based on false assumptions end in happy discoveries, but in some cases it is left to those who follow to benefit from the mistakes made. As Eco puts it:

> they are about ideas, projects, beliefs that exist in a twilight zone between common sense and lunacy, truth and error, visionary intelligence and what now seems to us stupidity, though it was not stupid in its day and we must therefore reconsider it with great respect.
>
> (Eco 1999: ix)

It is worth recalling Merton's own experience of serendipity in his sociological research. He was involved in a study of a mainly working class suburban housing community. The research team noted that the participation of residents in voluntary organisations was greater than in their previous place of residence. This included parents with young children. When asked about this, the parents explained that it was that it was easy to find teenage babysitters since there were more here than where they used to live. But empirical enquiry showed that this was not the case. This was an unanticipated finding that had not been part of the original research design and it raised for Merton the theoretical question: what was the source of this illusory belief?

The key to the anomaly was the reported view that, in this community, unlike a big city, people felt more confident in letting teenage babysitters in when they knew the people. Hence, Merton concluded:

> This clearly suggests that the sociological roots of the 'illusion' are to be found in the structure of community relations in which the Craftown residents are enmeshed. The belief is an unwitting reflection, not of statistical reality, but of the community cohesion. It is not that there are objectively more adolescents in Craftown, but more who are intimately known and who, therefore, exist socially for parents seeking aid in child supervision... In short, perception was a function of confidence and confidence, in turn was a function of social cohesion.
>
> (Merton 1957: 103)

Here was an unanticipated and anomalous finding which extended the theory that perception was a product of social framework. The investigator's curiosity was rewarded by a theoretic development which helps us to understand better how norms, standards and judgements are formed in particular social contexts.

Conclusion

Cross-classification, juxtapositions and contrasts, metaphor and simile, and serendipity are ways in which we can stimulate the sociological imagination. No doubt this involves trial and not a little error. But it is also very fruitful in its possibilities for gaining new knowledge and new understandings about the social world. I began with Mills and I conclude with him:

> The sociological imagination... consists in the capacity to shift from one perspective to another, and in the process to build up an adequate view of a total society and its components. It is this imagination, of course, that sets off the social scientist from the mere technician. Adequate technicians can be trained in a few years. The sociological imagination can also be cultivated; certainly it seldom occurs without a great deal of often routine work. Yet there is an unexpected quality about it, perhaps because its essence is the combination of ideas that no-one expected were combinable... There is a playfulness of mind back of such combining as well as a truly fierce drive to make sense of the world which the technician usually lacks.
>
> (Mills 1959: 211)

References

Aron, R. (1957) *German Sociology*. London: Heinemann.
Bauman, Z. and Tester, K. (2001) *Conversations with Zygmunt Bauman*. Cambridge: Polity Press.
Berger, J. and Mohr, J. (1975) *A Seventh Man*. London: Penguin.
Berger, P. (1963) *Invitation to Sociology*. London: Penguin.
Cicourel, A. (1964) *Method and Measurement in Sociology*. New York: Free Press of Glencoe.
Cressey, P., Eldridge, J. and MacInnes, J. (1985) *Just Managing: Authority and Democracy in Industry*. Milton Keynes: Open University Press.
Eco, U. (1999) *Serendipities*. London: Weidenfeld and Nicolson.
Eldridge, J. (1985) *C. Wright Mills*. London: Tavistock.
Eldridge, J. (2010) 'Baldamus's Adventures with Cross-Classification' in M. Erickson and C. Turner (eds.) *The Sociology of Wilhelm Baldamus*. Farnham: Ashgate, pp. 19–33.
Elias, N. (1978) *What Is Sociology?* London: Hutchinson.
Fordham, J. (2005) 'The Untouchable', *The Guardian*, 29 April, http://www.theguardian.com/music/2005/apr/29/jazz.shopping2, date accessed: 23 June 2015.
Glasgow University Media Group (1985) *War and Peace News*. London: Routledge.
Goffman, E. (1969) *The Presentation of Self in Everyday Life*. London: Penguin.

Merton, R. (1936) 'The Unanticipated Consequences of Purposive Social Action', *American Sociological Review*, 1 (6): 894–4.
Merton, R. (1957) *Social Theory and Social Structure*. Glencoe: Free Press.
Merton, R. and Barber, E. (2004) *The Travels and Adventures of Serendipity*. New York: Princeton University Press.
Mills, C.W. (1948) 'The Contributions of Sociology to the Study of Industrial Relations' in Proceedings of the First Annual Meeting of the Industrial Relations Research Society.
Mills, C.W. (1959) *The Sociological Imagination*. Oxford: Oxford University Press.
Mills, C.W. (1963) *Power Politics and People: The Collected Essays of C. Wright Mills*. Oxford: Oxford University Press.
Thompson, E.P. (1978) *The Poverty of Theory*. London: Merlin.
Touraine, A. (1981) *The Voice and the Eye*. Cambridge: Cambridge University Press.
Weber, M. (1949) *The Methodology of the Social Sciences*. Glencoe: Free Press.
Williams, R. (1961) *Culture and Society*. London: Penguin.
Williams, R. (1976) *Keywords: A Vocabulary of Culture and Society*. London: Fontana Press.
Williams, R. (1974) *Television, Technology and Cultural Form*. London: Routledge.
Williams, R. (1981) *Politics and Letters*. London: Verso.

Part I
Sociology of Work and Industry

2
Exploring an Industrial Structure of Feeling: Creating Industrial *Gemeinschaft* in a Twentieth-Century Workplace

Tim Strangleman

Introduction

John Eldridge, and the generation of sociologists of which he is a part, are important for the contemporary discipline in many diverse ways. John's career in particular demonstrates the rich and varied breadth of interests from industrial sociology, through social theory, to cultural and media studies. This scale and scope, this ambition to stretch the sociological imagination, is partly a product of a very different era of academic practice, but is also a function of individual and collective ambition and vision. This vision and ambition is something I think we need to recapture as part of our practice as sociologists. In this chapter I want to explore how this stretching of the sociological imagination might be achieved in my own part of the sociological jungle, that of the study of work. I want to reflect briefly on John's writing and research in that subfield, but then make the argument that the development of his interests into theoretical and cultural areas has to be understood as an extension rather than break with his earlier work. In the remainder of the chapter I use my research on the Guinness Brewery at Park Royal to show the kinds of ways in which John's ideas and broader vision have informed my own thinking – one that combines classical approaches and ideas with cultural questions and approaches.

John Eldridge and industrial sociology

In many ways John Eldridge's writing on work is less well known in sociology than other later aspects of his career. This stems in part, I think, from the fact that it forms part of his earlier career but also that it is labelled 'industrial sociology'. This relative neglect is based on a prejudice against what is often caricatured as an unreflective period of the sociological study of work where the focus of research was around white working-class men in traditional industries. From the mid-1970s onward and especially the 1980s the context of such a study was rapidly being eroded by recession and industrial closure. However, it is important to understand that John's vision of the study of work was not to produce plant studies which simply described specific and general aspects of manual labour. Rather, if one revisits *Industrial Disputes* (Eldridge 1968), for example, what the reader gets is a far clearer sense that this is the work of a sociologist first who happens to be examining social forms in the context of a particular type of work. Perhaps some contemporary readers will not be able to see beyond the book's title or the chapters in it, but if they do venture behind the cover and especially the contents page what one is still rewarded with is a working sociologist who manages to combine a richly ethnographic eye for detail with a more formal sociological account of the form and content of workplace interaction. Importantly, in his essay on demarcation disputes John is alert to the way in which workplace and occupational culture are present but shifting in response to wider forces – in the local and regional labour market, but also at the macro level of the economy. When we read this account, then, we are confronted with a nuanced understanding of the interplay between structure and agency and the way that particular instances are played out on a very particular terrain. We see the way in which tradition, custom and workplace rules of law are upheld, shaped, bent and reproduced in dynamic ways and played out in real time. My point here is that John's writing is informative not just of the immediate workplace studied but because he tells us important and transferable things about any workplace, and further that these insights can be applied to other forms of social interaction outside the workplace milieu. This vision, I think, is not unique to John, but rather is reflective of many of those centrally involved in post-war British sociology who combined a commitment to a broader discipline and its development alongside often multiple specific areas of specialisation (see Strangleman 2005).

John has continued throughout his career to be interested in work, but again importantly his interest has shifted alongside changes in the wider political economy. His writing and research in the 1980s, for example, looks at what later would be called deindustrialisation and plant closure. These studies link micro and mezzo changes with wider macro shifts in political and economic regulation associated with neo-liberalism. Later still John wrote a series of articles on important but often neglected figures in the development of work sociology, such as Gi Baldamus, Joan Woodward and Reinhard Bendix (Eldridge 1998; 2007; 2011). These writings highlight the importance of understanding the historiography of a particular discipline, how frames of reference, of foci interplay with the personal biography of the researcher. I became very aware of this in John's contribution to a special issue of *Sociology* edited by myself and Susan Halford (Halford and Strangleman 2009). John's ability to tell a fascinating story of sociological development alongside personal recollection of the individuals involved is a masterclass of its type (Eldridge 2009).

However, before moving on I want to stress that the other aspects of John's writing are important for understanding his thinking about and contribution to the study of work. For example, his media work includes industrial subjects and examines the way journalists shape, play up and occlude certain aspects of industrial production in their coverage – most obviously in the case of the 1984–85 miners' strike. His writing on theory obviously has major implications for the study of work and reminds us that the founding fathers were rooted in an understanding of the transition of society from traditional to modern forms through political economy and economic life. John's interest in the work of Raymond Williams is also, I think, rooted in the economic (Eldridge and Eldridge 1994). He understands working-class culture and the idea of structure of feeling as shaped by, and in turn shaping, the changing nature of work. This, then, is a far broader way of thinking about work and economic life. John's work gives licence to those of us who wish to study work in a broader way and who want to think about the wider sociological implications of one particular workplace. In the rest of the chapter I want to use some of the ways of seeing work that have animated John's approach and apply these to my research carried out at the former Guinness Brewery at Park Royal in West London.

Guinness at Park Royal

In 2004 I found myself at the Guinness Brewery at Park Royal. I was leading a project that sought an understanding of the experience of older men in the contemporary workplace and wider labour market. The brewery was a good place to do such research as successive waves of restructuring had restricted recruitment over the years, and therefore with the passage of time most of the vastly slimmed down production crew fitted the age range sought. The closure of the brewery had been announced some time before and it was obvious it preoccupied all of those working on the site. During a project meeting I suggested to the manager we were dealing with that Diageo, the owners of the Guinness brand, might like to fund a small piece of research to record the last six months of production and the subsequent closure in words and pictures. I had been inspired to do this by Bill Bamberger and Cathy Davidson's (1998) *Closing: The Life and Death of an American Factory*, a beautifully poignant book combining images and words from the last six months of a North Carolina furniture factory. The idea was that I would work with a photographer who would try and capture visually the spirit of the people who worked on site as well as the built environment and material culture found there. My task was to record oral history interviews with as many workers as could be obtained in the time we had available to us before closure the following summer. The immediate 'output' was the production of a DVD which was to combine the images with the oral accounts; it was to act as a family album for those losing their jobs after, in some cases, four decades of work there. In discussions with workers it became apparent just how much history haunted the site itself, and one worker suggested that we visit the archive in Scotland where the records, including photography, of Park Royal were kept.

I will never forget that first occasion as the incredibly helpful archivist welcomed me into the wood-panelled front room of the Diageo archive at Menstrie some ten miles outside Stirling in central Scotland. Housed in the former manager's house of a whisky distillery owned by the Diageo group, the building contained archives belonging to the various brands subsumed into the wider holding company. Apologetically she hoped that we had not wasted our time as there were *only* four archive boxes of Park Royal photographic material. Opening the first lid revealed an amazing visual record of this one site from its beginnings in the 1930s. In just those initial hours in the archive it became apparent that there was a far larger project to be done, a far richer and more complex story to be told. For this small collection was simply the tip of an enormous iceberg: on later visits I discovered that there were not four archive boxes of images but 59, masses of material taken for all sorts of reasons over the years to record different types of brewery history for a range of audiences. Through a doorway off the ground floor the archivist led me to a vast subterranean vault holding the bulk of the archive. The space reminded me of a Bond villain's lair, the type of place that housed the submarine/spaceship which will ultimately be destroyed in the film's denouement. In the racks there was a complete three decade run of the brewery staff magazine *Guinness Time*, begun in 1947. There were masses of other material including written documents of various shapes and sizes, oral histories carried out by the company over the years, film and videos of the site as well as a fish on a bicycle, but that is a different anecdote!

The story of why Guinness decided to build their English brewery is a fascinating one. In 1932 the Arthur Guinness Company of Dublin decided to open a new brewery to serve its British market. What lay behind this move was a complex story of diplomatic intrigue and Irish nationalist politics. In 1929 Éamon de Valera and his Fianna Fáil party had been elected in what was then the Irish Free State, a contested political space created out of a compromise between the British government and senior Irish politicians (Foster 1988; Lyons 1973). The election of de Valera meant that agreements made under the Anglo-Irish treaty of 1921 would be reneged upon. In particular de Valera and his colleagues sought to place import tariffs on British goods. The British threatened to do the same and warned the Guinness Company of the retaliation. This move set in train the events which would see the opening of the Guinness Brewery at Park Royal in 1936 (Guinness 1997; Wilson 1998). The British market was a crucial one for Guinness since Britain represented the largest single export outlet for this brand of stout. The company already produced four-fifths of the total beer drunk in Ireland, so its potential to expand further at home was limited (Wilson 1998:200). The company's search for a suitable site briefly settled on Manchester before the focus of attention turned towards London, which in itself was the largest market for the stout on the mainland. The acquisition and construction of the site was kept secret, as the company did not want to alert the Irish government of its plans nor inflate land prices in the Park Royal area. In a cloak-and-dagger operation company directors set about identifying a suitable site within 25 miles of Charing Cross, the assumed centre of the capital. The directors later reflected on the needs for the site:

> We laid down for ourselves all sorts of ideals and objectives, minimum transport facilities, a site that would lend itself to publicity, reasonable amenities, plentiful water supply, room for expansion
> (*Guinness Time* Spring 1957:4)

Figure 2.1 Construction of an office block, *c*. 1935
Source: Diageo Archives.

Eventually they settled on the then semi-rural location of Park Royal, the former Royal Agricultural Society showground, as a later commentator described it:

> ... [former] home of the Queen's Park Rangers and when we came the abode of gipsies, ponies and still a few rabbits
> (*Guinness Time* Spring 1957:5)

Guinness purchased a large part of the available land in the area on which they constructed the brewery buildings on a substantial plot, while simultaneously creating a much larger area as a business park.

The company employed one of the premier architects of the day, Sir Giles Gilbert Scott, who could count Liverpool's Anglican cathedral and Cambridge University library among his many achievements, to work on the design of the building alongside consulting engineers Sir Alexander Gibb and Partners. The building was a dignified and restrained piece of design and echoed Scott's other industrial work at Bankside and Battersea power stations in London. As a later staff magazine noted:

The Board decided that it would wish to have a building that would outlive the taste of the moment, something that would not attempt to hitch on to the latest mode or to set a new pattern, that would not try to seem anything else than a large and efficient factory; built firmly and solidly to last a century or two as the company itself had already lasted

(Hugh Beaver on the architect Sir Giles Gilbert Scott in *Guinness Time*, 13/2/1960:8)

The main buildings were finished in 1936 and brewing began the same year, with the site supplying the company's stout to pubs and clubs all over the UK mainland.

The brewery was an excellent example of modern organisational integration and scientific management; practically everything that the brewery required to support production was done on site by its own employees. Hops and barley were delivered by rail, and from then on the whole production process was carried out at Park Royal. Not only did the

Figure 2.2 Park Royal Brewery, looking south, *c.* 1960
Source: Diageo Archives.

company employ all its own staff on its core business of brewing but it also employed vast numbers in countless trades and occupations including builders, scaffolders, caterers, laundry workers, engineers, laboratory technicians and mechanics. The site had its own power station and fire brigade and could even boast its own ambulance station and crew. The Guinness Company was noted for its strong paternalist traditions. Park Royal was seen as a desirable place to work with relatively high wages mixed with good conditions of service and staff facilities such as sports and social clubs, amateur drama groups and company welfare provision. The company also provided some housing both on the site and in the immediate vicinity of the brewery on newly constructed estates. Many firms were attracted to this part of West London in the interwar years because of relatively cheap and abundant land available for industrial development along with good transport and communication links and labour. Companies locating operations in this area included Heinz, Hoover, EMI and J. Lyons and Co. (see Glucksmann 1990).

This situation remained the case largely until the 1980s, when Guinness like many other companies underwent profound, far-reaching industrial change. Guinness merged with other companies first into Grand Metropolitan, before forming a brand within Diageo (see Griffiths 2005; Guinness 1997; Wilson 1998). During the 1990s the site at Park Royal underwent a wave of restructurings and job redesign as was the case with other parts of the brewing industry in the UK (see Pike 2006). The announcement that the brewery was to close was made in 2004, and the last brew was completed in June 2005. By the time of closure there were fewer than 100 Guinness workers employed on site where once there had been well over a thousand. The horizontal and vertical integration of the works' staff had been replaced by a series of outsourcing contracts for functions such as cleaning, catering and power supply. At closure only the core brewing and quality control processes were carried out by Guinness workers. Despite being the most profitable production site in the Diageo group, Park Royal was victim of a declining market for beer, the company deciding to concentrate operations at its original St James' Gate Brewery in Dublin.

One reading of this history is to say that this is just another example of a plant closure or the wider story of deindustrialisation in the UK, a narrative that is echoed in the rest of Europe, the USA and other parts of the world. What makes the Guinness story so important is I think the fact that its history, the narrative arc from pre-cradle to post-grave, allows us access to wider shifts within capitalism during this time. Guinness at Park Royal represents a privileged occasion, or more accurately a series of such occasions in which we can study work and organisations in the twentieth and early twenty-first centuries. Guinness's story is both special, in that it is an unusually well-documented example of an integrated plant with many of the features that US scholars would associate with what is known as Welfare Capitalism. But at the same time it has elements within it that are mirrored by, or aspired to, many other companies at the time. Guinness, then, is a good place to rethink the era of the long post-war boom, what the French describe as The Glorious Thirty, alongside its decay and eclipse beginning in the 1970s. Importantly, to do justice to this story sociologically we need to draw on a wide range of evidence and approaches (see Strangleman 2010; 2012b).

For the purposes of this chapter I want to explore what happens at Guinness in the wake of the Second World War. What I want to argue is that the company makes a conscious effort to evoke a sense of industrial community at the site and, as we will see, talked of creating 'Guinness Citizens'. While this purpose and desire could be seen as an extension of older forms of paternalism which companies such as Guinness were renowned for there is a shift here that goes beyond those forms of management. How do we attempt to reconstruct management intention and desire? In my research on this project I have used a selection of company documents housed in the archives but also made extensive use of the company's staff magazine for Park Royal, *Guinness Time*. This was created in 1947 and edited by Edward Guinness, a family member who was a little later to become the personnel manager at Park Royal and later still a senior company executive (Guinness 2014). *Guinness Time* is a beautiful time capsule of the long post-war boom, running as it does from 1947 through to the early 1970s. While many large and medium-sized firms and undertakings at this time produced in-house magazines, a few combined both the very high production values and the sheer range of topics considered that we can find in *Guinness Time*. Of course there are the usual aspects of corporate journalism one would expect, such as the reports on sports and social clubs, the birth, marriages, retirements and deaths. But in addition there are two aspects that I think really set what Guinness were doing apart from their peers. Firstly, each edition of the magazine had an editorial piece of two or so pages. These are almost poetic in the way they reflect on life in the brewery, but especially on issues concerned with work and working life. The second aspect I want to discuss is the inclusion of a photo-essay alongside text looking at a particular aspect of the division of labour at Park Royal.

34 *Sociology of Work and Industry*

Figure 2.3 Worker purchasing the *Guinness Times*, 1947
Source: Diageo Archives.

The tone of the *Guinness Time* editorials was set early on, where there was talk of 'life returning after the social hibernation of the war years', and it went on:

> Again most of us are now returned from the Services and are no longer just ships passing in the night. Gradually we are anchoring ourselves to this noble community, and any community that is worthwhile has a natural curiosity about the doings of its fellow members. Actual acquaintance is best achieved in the Social Club, but we need to expand that by a wider survey than can be there achieved. Thus it is with these objects in view that we have attempted to portray life at Park Royal
>
> (*Guinness Time* 1 (1):3)

The editorials are a clear statement of a desire to build bridges and to develop community at the site. But there is also a recognition that this is something that needs deliberate action on the part of both management and workers to achieve. In a slightly later edition, an editorial makes clear intent behind the design of the magazine:

> ...in the passage quoted at the head of this page Aristotle gives his solution to this problem – to find happiness in one's work, whatever

that work may be. To do this it is necessary to have an interest in that work and to understand how one's own job fits into the general scheme. *Guinness Time* hopes to help towards both these ends, for we do not believe in the Shavian pin-maker, who, while tending the machine that makes the heads, neither knows or cares about the man who sharpens the points. We hold that men and women who spend half their waking lives working together must be interested in the results of their labours, and our pages are designed to foster this interest. We are proud of the organisation for which we work, and of the product which we produce and our stories and pictures help to make them better known to ourselves, and to others

(*Guinness Time* 3 (3):3)

Figure 2.4 Washing casks
Source: Diageo Archives.

Each issue of the magazine included one of these photo-essays combining words and pictures. Each describes the work of a particular aspect of the brewery beginning with production-orientated staff such as the brewers and coopers but extended to virtually every aspect of the brewery's vertically integrated workforce including cleaners, laundry workers, bricklayers and builders, security guards, groundsmen and farmers. The pieces, though driven by the images, included background to the departments as well as a fairly detailed account of the type of work undertaken.

How, then, can we think of these narratives of post-war work? What do they tell us about how work was thought about and how the problem of economic life was conceptualised? In the limited space I have here I want to pull out two related themes – the problem of the division of labour and industrial citizenship. One way to read the work

Figure 2.5 Steaming metal and wooden casks
Source: Diageo Archives.

Figure 2.6 The Maltstore at Park Royal, *c*. 1950
Source: Diageo Archives.

photo-essays and by extension the entire run of *Guinness Time* is to see them as attempts to confront and offer solutions to the post-war problem of work. Though the phrase *anomie* is not deployed in the staff magazine's pages this is what is being hinted at.

Book Three of Durkheim's *Division of Labour* concerns itself with 'Abnormal Forms of modern Industrial Specialisation'. Here Durkheim is at pains to try and understand how workers in more narrowly defined roles accept and embrace their place in a hierarchy. He tackles this head on, suggesting that this has to emerge organically out of the division of labour itself, predicated on a meritocratic allocation of task and position; but that such an acceptance is itself rooted in an intelligibility of the overall division of labour. As he puts it:

> For, normally, the role of each special function does not require that the individual close himself in, but that he keep himself in

constant relations with neighbouring functions, take conscience of their needs, of the changes which they undergo, etc. The division of labour presumes that the worker, far from being hemmed in by his task, does not lose sight of his collaborators, that he acts upon them, and reacts to them. He is, then, not a machine who repeats his movements without knowing their meaning, but he knows that they tend, in some way, towards an end that he conceives more or less distinctly. He feels that he is serving something

(Durkheim 1964:372)

It seems to me that the Guinness company at Park Royal, or to be more precise an element within the management there, understood this insight in their own, non-sociological and lay manner. They conceived of the role of their staff magazine, *Guinness Time*, as a way of conveying the organic linkages between people who worked in the brewery. In addition to this awareness at least in the 1940s and 1950s it is also possible to read into what was going on at Park Royal through another aspect of Durkheim's writing around the role of morals and ethics in the workplace. At various points in the run of *Guinness Time* it is possible to detect a concern with the role of work in modern society and what this type of work was doing to the workforce. In one editorial reflecting on the success of Roger Bannister in breaking the four-minute mile, the editor ponders the role of sport in work.

For sport is a wonderful medium for good international relations and equally is it important on the home front. If we were asked to comment on one aspect of this, we would say that in an age of increasing mechanisation it does give a most valuable outlet to young workers who are so often beset with the monotony of industrial life. No more awful picture of the present day can be given than of the young worker watching different products of the industrial machine go past him all day and then watching motion or television pictures go past him all evening. Yet we know it happens

(*Guinness Time* 7 (3):3)

The pages of *Guinness Time* are full of reflections on work and its role and meaning in the modern age, and it is clear that management at Park Royal attempted to build what T.H. Marshall referred to as industrial citizenship (see Strangleman forthcoming). Indeed at various points the actual term 'Guinness citizenship' is used in articles on brewery life. In his relatively neglected *Professional Ethic and Civic*

Morals (1992), Durkheim recognised the importance of moral regulation as an emergent property of the group if it was to have traction over both the group as a whole and the individuals who constituted it. As he put it:

> A system of morals is always the affair of a group and can operate only if this protects them by its authority. It is made up of rules which govern individuals, which compel them to act in such and such a way, and which impose limits to their inclinations and forbid them to go beyond. Now there is only one moral power – moral, and hence common to all – which stands above the individual and which can legitimately make laws for him, and that is collective power. To the extent the individual is left to his own devices and freed from all social constraint, he is unfettered too by all moral constraint
>
> (Durkheim 1992:6–7)

This quote I think cuts to the heart of Durkheim's vision of work groups and their potential power. Far from being a conservative theory of the social there is a really radical aspect to his writing and vision of the potential of the collective moral order and the implications that has for the practice of individuality.

Now I am not trying to suggest that Guinness at Park Royal during the 30 years after the Second World War was some kind of industrial Shangri-La; like any work site it had its industrial conflict and tensions. There is a tension, for example, between Durkheim's conceptualisation of the autonomy of work groups and the paternalism of the Guinness Company. But what attracts me to John Eldridge's writing has always been his desire to think about the world he encounters in a critical but open way. There has been a tendency within the sociology of work to be dominated by Marxist approaches to the subject, and perhaps even more narrow has been the dominance of Labour Process Theory, to the extent that that type of writing comes to stand for work sociology. While John's writing has made use of Marxist perspectives, he has also always been a champion of the insights to be found in Weberian and Durkheimian traditions. As he put it in 1971:

> We are not so far removed from the founders or from the practical and theoretical problems they confronted that we can afford to forget them. Neither for that matter is it clear that sociologists have assimilated all that the founding fathers have to teach.
>
> (Eldridge 1971:9)

It is this essential openness to the potential and possibility of other alternative ways of reading that I find attractive for my own work. Like John I have used Marxian insights in my own writing, but I am frustrated by the reductive nature of some who take a more fundamentalist line, one that seems to me unnecessarily narrow and simplistic when one is attempting to understand the complexity of human social interaction. This generosity of spirit extends to the way John broadened out his interests later to include Mills's work as well as that of Raymond Williams. John alerted me to the value of Williams's writing – particularly his *Country and the City* (Williams 1973) – and the issue of nostalgia when he acted as my external examiner for my doctoral viva. Since then I have used Williams's notion of the structure of feeling in various aspects of my writing, and in my current project on Guinness at Park Royal I have used it to think in terms of the way an industrial culture shifts from being a vibrant, self-confident outlook to one eroded or even eclipsed by deindustrialisation and closure.

Raymond Williams talked about *emergent*, *dominant* and *residual* structures of feeling, and I think the value of this is that it allows us to think of the ways in which workplace cultures are always in transition and are contingent. Many of the types of workplaces that were the object of study in the golden age of industrial sociology demanded attention in part because they enjoyed strong autonomous cultures – the workers in them were embedded in their work, and enjoyed a dominant structure of feeling towards it. David Byrne (2002), using Williams's concept has talked about an 'industrial structure of feeling', an industrial sensibility common across many industrial workforces in the post-war years. I think what Byrne is describing is that self-confidence that comes from being embedded and knowledgeable about one's work and by extension life. In much of my work on industrial change and deindustrialisation I think it is possible to witness or hear testimony to this industrial structure of feeling being made residual, the process by which a culture is being gradually erased (see Strangleman 2012a; Strangleman and Rhodes 2014).

Some of the most interesting work on deindustrialisation pays serious attention to the voices of those who are caught up in industrial change and are trying to make sense of a half-revealed process. To listen and really hear what is being said about work requires a historically informed humanistic sociology. This is a type of sociology that to be sure is critical, but at the same time is one that seeks to understand the complexity of the social world explored. This is equally a sociology that seeks to understand the values of people from their own point of view – from their own world view.

Concluding remarks

What I have tried to do in this chapter is reflect on John Eldridge's writing in thinking about my own work on Guinness as well as the wider sociology of work. Such a reflection needs to consider the different interests and phases of John's career, but in doing so we need to acknowledge the organic way in which insights gained from previous projects are applied in the understanding of the new. John's interest in economic life is a case in point. His earlier work on industrial culture and interaction may look dated if viewed superficially but it is a magnificent example of the exercise of the sociological imagination. His writing on traditional cultures stands the test of time precisely because it asks a variety of sociological questions about social forms. John's writing and research is embedded in a profound respect for the continuing relevance of classical sociology. This respect is not an excuse to see the writing of the founding fathers as sacred texts but rather to see them as providing a range of insights and clues as to how we might shed new light on the social in our own times. Later still John's focus turned to the consequences of industrial change, what has come to be seen as the process of deindustrialisation, and here again John's work asks bigger questions about this process, beyond the immediate problem of individual closure. These approaches, taken together with his interest in the media, Mills and Williams, illustrate the richness of a sociological career. They offer a powerful model for an open inquiring sociology. This breadth of approach to economic life has been an inspiration to me to follow a broader way of thinking about work. John's work offers a wonderful model of how to extend the sociological imagination around and beyond the world of work.

Acknowledgements

All photos are copyright Guinness Diageo Ireland and are reproduced with their kind permission.

References

Bamberger, B. and Davidson, C. (1998) *Closing: The Life and Death of an American Factory*. New York: Norton.
Byrne, D. (2002) 'Industrial Culture in a Post-Industrial World: The Case of the North East of England', *City*, 6 (3): 279–89.
Durkheim, E. (1964) *The Division of Labour in Society*. New York: The Free Press.
Durkheim, E. (1992) *Professional Ethics and Civic Morals*. London: Routledge.

Eldridge, J. (1968) *Industrial Disputes: Essays in the Sociology of Industrial Relations*. London: Routledge and Kegan Paul.

Eldridge, J. (1971) *Sociology and Industrial Life*. London: Nelson.

Eldridge, J. (1998) 'A Benchmark in Industrial Sociology: W. G. Baldamus on *Efficiency and Effort* (1961)', *Historical Studies in Industrial Relations*, 6: 133–61.

Eldridge, J. (2007) 'A Tract for the Times: Joan Woodward's Management and Technology (1958)', *Historical Studies in Industrial Relations*, 23: 181–207.

Eldridge, J. (2009) 'Industrial Sociology in the UK: Reminiscences and Reflections', *Sociology*, 43 (5): 829–45.

Eldridge, J. (2011) 'Work and Authority in Industry: The Research Strategy of Reinhard Bendix', *Historical Studies in Industrial Relations*, 31–32: 155–79.

Eldridge, J. and Eldridge, L. (1994) *Raymond Williams: Making Connections*. London: Routledge.

Foster, R. F. (1988) *Modern Ireland, 1600–1972*. London: Penguin.

Glucksmann, M. (1990) *Women Assemble: Women Workers and the New Industries in Inter-War Britain*. London: Routledge.

Griffiths, M. (2005) *Guinness is Guinness: The Colourful Story of a Black and White Brand*. London: Cyan.

Guinness, E. (2014) *A Brewer's Tale: Memoirs of Edward Guinness CVO*. Croydon: CPI Group.

Guinness, J. (1997) *Requiem for a Family Business*. London: Pan.

Halford, S. and Strangleman, T. (2009) 'In Search of the Sociology of Work: Past, Present and Future', *Sociology*, 43 (5): 811–28.

Lyons, F.S.L. (1973) *Ireland Since the Famine*. London: Fontana.

Pike, A. (2006) 'Shareholder Value versus the Regions: The Closure of the Vaux Brewery in Sunderland', *Journal of Economic Geography*, 6 (2): 201–22.

Strangleman, T. (2005) 'Sociological Futures and the Sociology of Work', *Sociological Research Online*, 10 (4): http://www.socresonline.org.uk/10/4/strangleman.html, date accessed: 30 March 2015.

Strangleman, T. (2010) 'Food, Drink and the Cultures of Work: Consumption in the Life and Death of an English Factory', *Food, Culture and Society*, 13 (2): 257–78.

Strangleman, T. (2012a) 'Work Identity in Crisis?: Rethinking the Problem of Attachment and Loss at Work', *Sociology*, 46 (3): 411–25.

Strangleman, T. (2012b) 'Picturing Work in an Industrial Landscape', *Sociological Research Online*, 17 (2): http://www.socresonline.org.uk/17/2/20.html, date accessed: 30 March 2015.

Strangleman, T. (forthcoming) 'Rethinking Industrial Citizenship: The Role and Meaning of Work in an Age of Austerity', *British Journal of Sociology*.

Strangleman, T. and Rhodes, J. (2014) 'The "New" Sociology of Deindustrialisation?: Understanding Industrial Change', *Sociology Compass*, 8 (4): 411–21.

Williams, R. (1973) *The Country and the City*. Oxford: Oxford University Press.

Wilson, D. (1998) *Dark and Light: The Story of the Guinness Family*. London: Orion.

Other material

Guinness Time, Park Royal Brewery staff magazine.

3
John Eldridge's Adventures with Cross-Classification in the Sociology of Work

Tony Elger

Introduction

One of John Eldridge's recent publications explored 'Baldamus's Adventures with Cross-Classification' (Eldridge 2010), and John has also had his own adventures with this technique. His comments on cross-classification also link his long-standing interests in the sociology of employment relations and social theory, especially through discussions of C. Wright Mills and Gi Baldamus. In this essay I will consider the scope for further adventures of this sort, first by examining the advocacy of Mills, Baldamus and Eldridge; then by exploring a few classic studies that deploy two-by-two diagrams; and finally by comparing two extended applications of cross-classification, one by John and his colleagues.

Advocates of adventurous cross-classification: Mills, Baldamus and Eldridge

Cross-classification is central to Mills's influential essay 'On Intellectual Craftsmanship' (in Mills 1959a; 1980/1952 is an earlier version, prepared for teaching at Columbia), and inspired later work by Baldamus and Eldridge (Eldridge 2010:20). Mills emphasises the importance of keeping a file – a running repository of experiences and ideas, covering everyday observations, personal feelings and analytical ideas – to focus and stimulate the exercise of intellectual craftsmanship. This material should be actively and playfully mixed and re-sorted to discover 'unforeseen and unplanned linkages' (Mills 1959a:212–14). His discussion of cross-classification offers detailed guidance on using explicit and systematic criteria to develop fresh distinctions and permutations, probing beyond common-sense categories and identifying 'new types as well as criticising and clarifying old ones' (Mills 1959a:213). This includes unpacking the different levels of generality involved in such analyses, working up and down through these levels to explore the dimensions in play. Such cross-classification facilitates both the private exploration of observations and arguments and the public presentation of such work, as 'charts, tables and diagrams of a qualitative sort are not... only ways to display work already done; they are very often genuine tools of production' (Mills 1959a:213, quoted in Eldridge 2010:20). 'Little cross-classification[s]' are scattered across his files and drafts, though he 'do[es] not always or even usually display such diagrams' and 'most of them flop in which case you have still learned something' (Mills 1959a:213). Mills also qualifies his initial distinction between private and public uses, as ideas in unpublished files are discussed with colleagues while diagrams for public presentation 'become[s] a new context of discovery' (Mills 1959a:222).

As Eldridge (2010:20) notes, Mills saw cross-classification as 'a way of dealing with [both] quantitative and qualitative materials'. But Mills's discussion also suggests he prioritised *qualitative* two-by-two cross-classification in the primary creative processes of reconceptualisation, before registering the likely pertinence of more quantitative assessments of categories and typologies later in the research and publication process. 'Often you get the best insights by considering extremes... you can then sort out the dimensions in terms of which the comparisons are made', and only then seek 'to gain and to maintain a sense of proportion – to look for some lead to the frequencies of given types' (Mills 1959a:213–14), often through quantification. This process is exemplified in the longest excerpt from his private files, which maps the conceptual terrain of *The Power Elite* (Mills 1959b). This starts with 'four Weberian variables' – class, status, power and occupational skills – chosen to 'define analytically and empirically the upper circles' (Mills 1959a:207–8). For each he contrasts the top 2 per cent with the remainder, generating a diagram which identifies 16 possibilities through cross-classifications of all four variables. Finally he highlights the fruitfulness of this cross-classification in both qualitative and quantitative terms: it helps to clarify definitional and substantive issues (for example, overlap or separation between top groups; significance of mobility between 'boxes'), and to specify relevant empirical data, not least quantitative indices, which allow mapping and weighting of the range of possibilities. But finally he emphasises that thoughtful conceptualisation and cross-classification must drive the empirical research:

> I don't have the data, and I shan't be able to get it – which makes it all the more important that I speculate about it, for in the course of such reflection, if it is guided by the desire to approximate the empirical requirements of an ideal design, I'll come upon important areas on which I might be able to get materials that are relevant as anchor points and guides to further reflection.
> (Mills 1959a:209)

This underlines how his private file was characterised by experiments in cross-classification (here multiplying up beyond two-by-two), combining both qualitative and quantitative thinking. This represents the detail behind Mills's formula, that 'in many ways, cross-classification is the very grammar of the sociological imagination. [But] like all grammar, it must be controlled and not allowed to run away from its purposes' (Mills 1959a:213, quoted more fully in Eldridge 1983:39, and 2010:20).

But in his published work overt diagrammatic cross-classifications appear quite rare. *White Collar* (Mills 1956) includes a rich range of typologies and dimensions, with some tabular quantification of the rise or decline of specific categories of white-collar workers, while *The Power Elite* (Mills 1959b) deploys multiple typologies and dimensions, usually given quantitative weight in the text, but neither presents basic conceptual two-by-two diagrams. Perhaps this underlies Baldamus's view, paraphrased by Eldridge (2010:20), 'that Mills somewhat obscured the significance of what he was pointing to because the actual examples he gave were quantitative – the cross-tabulation of statistical data – rather than theoretical'. But, as Eldridge (1983:39) also suggests, this contrast between statistical and theoretical categories can be overdrawn, as cross-tabulation of statistical data necessarily 'carries with it conceptual implications and views about possible relationships'. It would be fairer to say Mills prioritised theoretically driven conceptualisation which could then frame both qualitative and quantitative research, though the basic cross-classificatory intellectual scaffolding that he developed in his private files often became submerged in his publications by presentations and analyses which built upon these typologies.

This may explain why Eldridge (1983:39–40; 2010:21) used an early paper (Mills 1948/1970) to illustrate Mills's analytical use of cross-classification (Figure 3.1). This considers *objective structures of power* and

	Participation in Objective Structures of Power	Non-participation in Objective Structures of Power
Subjectively Cheerful and Willing	Unalienated worker	Manipulated pseudo-morale
Subjectively Uncheerful and Unwilling	Malcontent/ unadjusted worker	Alienated worker

Figure 3.1 Participation and worker responses
Source: Adapted from Mills 1948/1970:24 and Eldridge 1983:39.

subjective conditions of the individual in a way that resonates with his later arguments, that the sociological imagination must locate biographies and milieu within historically changing social structures, and should challenge the ideological and institutional 'drift' which translates public issues into private troubles (Eldridge 1971:193–5, reviews Mills's treatment of these themes, and briefly but powerfully reprises his critical appreciation in Eldridge 2003:327–9). Mills uses the distinction between objective participation and non-participation in the exercise of workplace power to generate fresh categories that were suppressed in the human relations discourse on 'morale', which concentrated entirely on the transformation of the subjective feelings of (non-rational) workers by the exercise of the organised capacities of (rational) managers. Mills (1948/1970:24) understands those 'cheerful and willing' employees who genuinely participate in objective structures of power as unalienated workers, a category rooted in specific historical conditions of self-managing craftsmanship or, perhaps, workers' control. Meanwhile 'cheerful and willing' non-participants are seen to manifest 'manipulated pseudo-morale', and practitioners of human relations are regarded as complicit in generating this pattern; though 'to explain the different types of people who fall into this category'. Mills (1948/1970:25) also registers the possible impact of co-worker expectations *and* a persisting psychology of craftsmanship even in alienating large-scale industry. Workers who are not cheerful or willing also form two contrasting categories: those without power are classic 'alienated workers', whilst those who can actually participate constitute 'malcontents'.

Eldridge (1983:39–40; also 2010:20–1) uses this example to underline how 'new types are formulated which also serve the purpose of criticising and clarifying old ones', highlighting how Mills 'essentially invents two new categories', the 'unalienated worker' and the 'unadjusted worker' (and, we could add, *reinvents* the other categories). Such insights influence how we handle data (such as apparently objective indices of job satisfaction) and also offer scope to develop 'an alternative ideology about preferred outcomes' (by highlighting non-alienation, not simply apparent satisfaction). Eldridge makes three further points. The resulting reconceptualisation poses fresh empirical questions:

> [First,] the chart in itself does not tell us anything about mechanisms whereby workers move from one category to another, but it does provide us with new ways of thinking about the nature of such changes and therefore is a stimulus to research activity.
> (Eldridge 1983:40)

Second, we can move through different levels of cross-classification, probing into the details of one of these boxes (say the 'unadjusted worker') or locating existing possibilities within a wider typology (say varieties of industrial society). Finally a crucial implication is that Mills's 'own alternative has a greater explanatory power in principle', revealing a commitment to a realist ontology notwithstanding 'the relativistic foundations of Mills's own sociology of knowledge' (Eldridge 1983:40, and for discussion, 21–3; 45–50).

Eldridge drew explicit inspiration from Mills when he used cross-classification in his own research, whereas Baldamus was cited for his substantive ('neo-Marxist') theorising of power relations and the effort bargain (Cressey et al. 1985:126). But Eldridge also encountered Baldamus's ideas on cross-classification during the 1970s (Baldamus 1971; 1976), and his later discussion of these ideas reveals long-standing intellectual engagement. Eldridge (2010:20–1) emphasises that Baldamus believed Mills's overall treatment was 'remarkably insightful', especially in illuminating the value of playful innovation, but also undersold the centrality of systematic theoretical analysis in cross-classification. However, Mills and Baldamus were probably closer in their emphasis on analytical distinctions than the latter recognised, as both stressed cross-classification should yield conceptual clarification and innovation. Indeed, the arguments of Mills and Baldamus often ran in parallel, not only in advocating cross-classification but also in broader interpretations of the malaise (and remaining potentials) of sociology. Baldamus's emphasis on the dangers of trivialisation identified failings similar to those highlighted in Mills's critique of grand theorising and abstract empiricism (especially divorce between macro and micro analyses, emphasis on static models, decontextualisation of subjective orientations, and loss of social and political relevance), and Eldridge

(2010:25) registers some of these parallels. However, Baldamus added more detailed discussion of the sorts of insights that could be developed using cross-classification, especially through the generation of 'paradoxes' and 'pleonasms', though Eldridge (2010:29–31) also suggests the pleonasms 'are probably not so fruitful' as the paradoxes.

In some ways, however, Baldamus was more pessimistic than Mills, because he saw trivialisation/attenuation as 'to some extent the unintended product of disciplined social enquiry' (Eldridge 2010:25 quoting Baldamus) – its sources embedded in such standard features of scholarship as 'progressive complexification', alongside the theoretical incommensurability which besets attempts to combine disciplines. Thus much was at stake in Baldamus's (1976:208) identification of cross-classification as *the* pivotal 'counter-trivialisation device' available to sociologists. We may not wish to increase the stakes in this way, and several commentators on Baldamus (such as Turner 2010:84–5) have argued convincingly that his emphasis on a single appropriate sociological method is too narrow, indefensible even in terms of his own work. But if Baldamus claimed too much in this regard, he did highlight another crucial potential of cross-classification more clearly than Mills, namely its linkage to a realist ontology which envisaged analytical engagement with real social structures and relations – a theme forcefully underlined at several points in Eldridge's commentary. This linkage is registered in Eldridge's (1983; 2003) discussions of Mills, but he implies that Baldamus provided a more explicit and persuasive treatment. Thus Baldamus's adventures with word play and creativity also involved a 'growing conviction that the methods of cross-classification and post-factum interpretation provide the means of discovering something about the nature of social reality' (Eldridge 2010:26). More specifically, Baldamus saw cross-classification as a process of coming to terms with 'stubborn facts' and 'recalcitrant anomalies' through a trial and error process:

> The most interesting aspect for anyone who has tried this technique of progressive conceptual articulation seems to me the certainty – amidst overwhelming confusion – which one experiences in respect of discrepancies and disharmonies. It is only the negative experience of 'bad fits', the frustration of recalcitrant discordances in the overall system, which keeps the never-ending process of outer-inner double fitting going, rather than the satisfaction derived from occasional 'good fits'.
>
> (Baldamus 1971, quoted in Eldridge 2010:28)

Baldamus's position cannot be assimilated to more recent realist philosophies of social science, but there are interesting points of convergence with 'critical realism' (Elger 2010), which advocates theoretically informed 'retroduction' rather than reliance on testing predictive covering-law models. Eldridge seeks to encourage engagement with Baldamus's arguments 'whatever our overall judgement on the endeavour' (Eldridge 2010:33). But he remains strongly positive in his celebration of the dual character of Baldamus's approach to cross-classification – as a creative and imaginative technique characterised by 'serious playfulness', and as one way of developing an analysis of underlying social structures and relations – and pursues both features in his substantive work with Cressey and MacInnes.

Classic examples of published cross-classifications: Mars, Crouch and Burawoy

Both Mills and Baldamus portrayed cross-classification primarily as a procedure for the informal development of concepts and analyses, while recognising its role in communicating with wider audiences. We rarely have access to private files and working notes, making it difficult to investigate cross-classification in that context, but there *is* scope to consider its uses in published literature. Two caveats are necessary. Firstly, cross-classifications form a small subset of published diagrams, and other formats predominate even among enthusiastic users. In Cressey et al. (1985), 18 other figures and tables accompany the three cross-classifications discussed below, while only five of Littler's (1982) 25 figures and tables are two-by-two diagrams. Secondly, my selection of three published examples is inevitably idiosyncratic rather than representative; just a glimpse of the variety of usages in both procedural and substantive terms.

Turner's (2010) systematic discussion of diagrams in sociological theory offers valuable pointers for assessing their value. He distinguishes between different types of diagram (cross-classifications being just one variant), but also registers differences in the purposes they are intended to serve, the importance attached to them and the levels of abstraction at which they operate. This leads him to

> construct a sliding scale of diagrammatic weight. At one end would be diagrams that are central to a theory, at the other, diagrams that are there for purposes of illustration alone, or, while sincerely meant, so misleading/ineffective as to be redundant...there is something

unsatisfactory about diagrams at each end of the scale, since they are either so heavy that they burden the inquiry as a whole, or so light that they add nothing to it. Somewhere in between are diagrams that have the chance of acting as a genuine cognitive tool, going beyond mere illustration by doing something the text cannot do, taking the reader to places he or she would not otherwise have explored, having a life of their own yet without leading the reader to believe that by knowing the diagram he or she thereby knows the social world

(Turner 2010:115)

Turner borrows the phrase 'pictorial work space' to characterise such productive diagrams; those with a 'sophisticated relationship between text and diagram, in which the diagram really can do work which the text cannot, or in which there is...a continual movement from text to diagram to text' (Turner 2010:117). In registering varied uses of cross-classification I will bear these evaluative points in mind.

My main examples date from the early 1980s, but illuminate the different roles cross-classification can play at different stages in an argument and also indicate the range of subject matter addressed in this way. Mars's analysis of *Cheats at Work* (1982) considers the organisation of workplace discipline and effort bargaining, focusing specifically on 'workplace crime'. His cross-classification is one of just two figures, comes early in his text and frames his whole analysis by generating a typology of contrasting occupations characterised by distinctive 'fiddles' (Figure 3.2). Later chapters then discuss each job type, before an analytical stocktaking which considers broader implications for conceptions of crime, industrial relations and political economy. Mars's cross-classification uses two strongly theorised but quite abstract dimensions, *grid* and *group*, drawn from Douglas's (1970/2003; Turner 2010) classification and mapping of different cultures. 'Grid' addresses the extent to which social norms and categories are shared within an (occupational) culture, represented as a dichotomy between strong and weak imposition of such categories, but also as variations in 'autonomy', 'insulation', 'reciprocity' and 'competition'. 'Group' concerns the extent to which mutual obligations are shared by members of a collectivity, presented as a dichotomy between strong and weak obligations, but also variations in 'frequency', 'mutuality', 'scope' and 'boundary'. This provides the basis for Mars's memorable characterisation and comparison of distinctive occupational situations, types of work and characteristic fiddles in terms of 'hawk', 'donkey', 'wolf' and 'vulture' jobs.

	Weak 'Group'	Strong 'Group'
Strong 'Grid'	'Donkey' jobs involving isolated subordination (e.g. checkout workers)	'Wolf' jobs involving tight work groups (e.g. dockers)
Weak 'Grid'	'Hawk' jobs involving individual 'entrepreneuriality' (e.g. small businessmen)	'Vulture' jobs involving loose work groups (e.g. salesmen)

Figure 3.2 Occupational controls and workplace fiddles
Source: Adapted from Mars (1982:29).

Mars reflects explicitly on the strengths and weaknesses of this procedure and the categories it generates, commenting that:

> They represent 'ideals'. Many occupations straddle more than one type, while others may be between types. Their characteristics are not, therefore, as clearly defined as the schema might suggest... No occupation is static. Some indeed possess a considerable dynamic and their members periodically move from one quadrant to another... the scorings of different strengths both within and between occupations are obviously amenable to greater sophistication than has been used here... [and] there may be reason to dispute the somewhat arbitrary way that the occupations... have been scored.
>
> (Mars 1982:28, 36, 38)

Despite such qualifications he provides a robust defence of his typology as a powerful heuristic device. Furthermore 'it is the extreme [occupational] cases that are the most interesting and the most informative', while the focus is on the *average* experience of people in such occupations, rather than internal variations within it (Mars 1982:28, 38). Reminiscent of Mills, he also suggests the model can be scaled up and down, moving between societies, occupations and workgroups. And apparent weaknesses may become strengths: the scope for occupations to move across categories suggests the typology 'can be used dynamically... as an aid to understanding change and its effects at work' (Mars 1982:37). Most importantly, he claims, 'this schema allows us to differentiate between the superficial similarities shared by some occupations and provides a basis for rational comparison... between occupations that is... more meaningful and fruitful than previous attempts in the field' (Mars 1982:37–9). His critical target is 'class typologies created solely by reference to prestige, ownership and control', against which he advocates 'a focus on the structural bases of jobs' (Mars 1982:39). Comparisons in these terms

> do more than merely point to the relation between the nature of occupations and their fiddles. It emphasises that there is a link... between the social environment of jobs and what might be called their cosmology... the ideas, values, attitudes and beliefs that are appropriate to them
>
> (Mars 1982:34)

Mars's analysis has been widely appreciated (see Ackroyd and Thompson 1999:37–8; Edwards 1986:253; Edwards and Wajcman 2005:102–4), but some have also challenged the way his 'grid' and 'group' framework abstracts from, rather than being integrated with, more standard analyses of the class dynamics of employment relations. Thus Edwards (1986:255) contrasts 'hawk fiddles' with the other categories, 'because they do not stem from relations of domination and subordination in employment but instead reflect the exploitation of uncertainty in market transactions by autonomous people', and also suggests the coherence of the remaining occupational categories is significantly compromised by the scope for occupations to fall across or shift between categories. For him these comparisons lack a sufficiently explicit and dynamic treatment of evolving relations between management controls and workers' counter-controls within specific occupational settings, where wider collective organisation may transform individualised and vulnerable fiddles into more robust collective fiddles or even jointly legitimated accommodations, while management offensives may reverse this sequence (Edwards makes this assessment while developing his own theory of conflict in employment relations, which also experiments with cross-classification).

While Mars presents his theoretically derived typology as a starting point for framing his substantive discussion, Crouch (1982:201) presents his cross-classification of strategies in the politics of industrial relations in a final chapter, explicitly as an emergent product of earlier chapters (and books). It follows a narrative account of British industrial relations from 1945 and analyses of the strategic options and dilemmas of the state, 'capital' and 'labour' respectively. Crouch's fundamental concern is to address the implications of strong *trade union*

	Strong Unions	Weak Unions
Liberal Polity	Free collective bargaining	Neo-laissez-faire
Corporatist Polity	Bargained corporatism	Corporatism

Figure 3.3 Alternative politics of industrial relations
Source: Adapted from Crouch (1982:201).

organisation for the operation of two *models of the political economy*, liberalism and corporatism, which 'can work only in their pure form if labour is subordinated' (Crouch 1982:201). His left-hand boxes, populated respectively by 'free collective bargaining' and 'bargained corporatism', represent departures from these pure models; and 'bargained corporatism', in particular, constitutes a fruitful paradox and a distinctive conceptual innovation (introduced in Crouch 1977:263, and developed further in Crouch 1979/1982), despite overlaps with other analyses of 'neo-corporatism'.

Crouch uses Figure 3.3 to explore the distinctiveness, internal tensions and conditions of existence of each of these types, though he also registers short-term overlaps between the contrasting forms of corporatism and laissez-faire (Crouch 1982:211). His dominant comparison is between a neo-laissez-faire politics exemplified by Thatcherism and a recuperated 'bargained corporatism'; the first projected as 'a major force to be reckoned with as a likely future development' despite 'distinct costs and certain snags', while 'bargained corporatism' (if embracing moves towards industrial democracy) offers a 'chink of light' for a more attractive alternative, despite clear recognition of the persistent tensions and challenges it would face (Crouch 1982:209 and 212–22).

This analysis made a significant contribution to broader debates about neo-corporatism and neo-liberalism by addressing the wider conditions and the contradictory and dynamic features of these strategies. In wider comparative and historical studies Crouch later worked with four comparable variants of the relations between organised labour and capital, but also moved down a level and modified the cross-classification ('the power of organized labour' versus 'the level of organizational articulation of both capital and labour') to identify four distinct, though unequally viable, variants of 'bargained corporatism' itself (Crouch 1993:38–47; also Crouch 1999:355–60). Meanwhile 'bargained corporatism' gained wider currency in analyses of the politics of industrial relations in other countries, including South Africa, Holland,

Ireland and Malaysia, though the character of the 'bargain' and the strength of the protagonists remained contentious.

Numerous later cross-classifications (such as Kristensen and Morgan 2007 or Vincent 2011) deserve similar scrutiny, but I have chosen Burawoy's (2003) discussion of case study revisits (that is, later study of the same site or organisation by the same or another researcher) because it shifts attention from substantive analyses to methodological reflections (see also Elger 2013:253–7). Burawoy, a prolific user of two-by-two diagrams, is particularly explicit about the conceptual issues he faces, especially in defining boundaries between the contrasts that form the axes of his cross-classification. One axis contrasts those revisits that emphasise access to a changing social reality with those that focus on ethnography as social construction, but Burawoy adds 'there is no transcendence of this dilemma – *realist* and *constructivist approaches* provide each other's corrective'. His other axis contrasts *internal* and *external explanations* of differences between initial and revisit case studies: while he regards this as a robust contrast he admits that

> the distinctions are far from watertight... if there is bleeding across the constructivist-realist dimension, the boundary between internal and external is a veritable river of blood... [but] however fluid and permeable the line between internal and external, the distinction itself is nonetheless unavoidable.
> (Burawoy 2003:668)

Burawoy uses this matrix to illuminate four distinctive tendencies in the anthropological literature on ethnographic revisits and to reassess his own research at Roy's (1954) earlier site/case in these terms, but finally recommends that all revisits (and perhaps we could extend this to all comparisons between cases, even when they are not strictly revisits) should address all four aspects in explaining differences in findings (though ultimately he gives priority to reconstructing theory).

These classic examples provide ample demonstration that simple, qualitative two-by-two cross-tabulations have played an important role in the intellectual armoury of economic sociology; have been used to address a wide range of substantive and methodological issues; and in different ways meet some of the criteria identified by Turner to become genuine 'pictorial work spaces'. One apparent contrast – perhaps reinforced by positioning diagrams earlier or later in the text – is between those diagrams where the dimensions are heavily theorised at the outset (Mars, Burawoy?) and those where they appear primarily to crystallise earlier substantive analysis (Crouch). Each alternative has strengths and weaknesses as a basis for productive diagrams: heavily theorised versions may capture pivotal contrasts but can gloss over features other analysts deem central, whilst substantive summaries may highlight critical issues with wider salience or remain rather bald re-descriptions. But such a contrast should not be overdrawn, as redrafting will have involved an implicit interplay of theorising and substantive re-sorting (as envisaged by Mills) or, in Baldamus's terms, a process of 'double fitting'.

Another issue flagged by these cases concerns the definition of category boundaries, or alternatively the relationship between sharp qualitative contrasts and graded continua. Mars addresses this explicitly by registering (multiple) continua while highlighting the productiveness of comparisons between extremes, while Burawoy combines an emphasis on necessary conceptual distinctions with a willingness to reassess boundaries for differing purposes, a possibility also hinted at by Crouch. A related issue concerns the extent to which the boxes embody internal tensions and instabilities, a feature Crouch emphasises in his treatment of alternative industrial relations strategies characterised by different sources of dynamism and crisis, and implicit in Burawoy's project of both mapping and transcending one-sided explanations of differences in ethnographic findings. This concern with internal tensions and limitations feeds into questions about the relationship between static classifications and attempts to grasp movement or dynamics. Crouch, in particular, uses his diagram to identify lines of probable constraint and continuity but also of potential openness and change. These considerations indicate some of the different ways in which cross-classifications can be construed and worked with, though a fuller assessment of the contribution of such formal properties to conceptual innovation and analytical insight must await wider comparisons.

Two styles of serial cross-classification: Edwards and Eldridge (and their colleagues)

Many two-by-two diagrams stand alone, though some are produced by frequent cross-classifiers and a few form cumulative sequences addressing specific themes. This section considers two instances where authors explicitly pursue a strategy of serial cross-classification, though in rather different ways. One (Edwards et al. 2006) involves a cumulatively elaborated diagram designed to categorise and analyse a wide array of case study findings on forms of worker participation and patterns of management–worker compromise. The other (Cressey et al. 1985) exemplifies a 'serious playfulness' in deploying several different cross-classifications to illuminate their own case-studies of 'authority and democracy in industry'. The strong affinities in the substantive interests and forms of research embraced by these research teams would merit more consideration elsewhere, but here they throw into relief contrasting approaches to serial cross-classification, with different strengths and weaknesses.

Paul Edwards has used cross-classification many times in his published work, pushing both the use of this technique and its critical assessment further than most (see Elger 2013:253–7, for fuller discussion). In particular he identifies several key criteria for assessing such diagrams, namely the analytical significance of the distinctions used; the coherence of the categories; the absence of empty boxes; and scope for empirical investigation to 'test' the model (Edwards 2003:350). Such diagrams, he argues, are not ends in themselves but 'useful devices', bringing 'discipline into analysis by forcing us to identify in what respects one situation differs from another' (Edwards 2003:348, 352), but he also complicates his assessment by noting scope to multiply dimensions beyond two by two, and by emphasising each box may involve underlying tensions, not just stable entities. Recently he and his collaborators (Bélanger and Edwards 2007; Edwards et al. 2006) have developed an elaborate analysis of varied forms of 'compromise in the workplace' informed by these criteria. They combine two two-by-two cross-classifications to generate a 16-cell diagram which hinges on the extent to which employers on the one hand and workers on the other prioritise their leverage over existing production arrangements (control concerns), prioritise the further development of such 'productive forces' (developmental concerns) or are committed to both (or neither) of these priorities. They then locate many published case studies within this matrix, though four unoccupied cells are deemed unsustainable *within capitalism* (Figure 3.4). Edwards and Bélanger (2008) link this substantive theorising to a methodological argument for comparing case-studies holistically, rather than disaggregating them into clusters of variables, precluding some forms of quantification but allowing quantitative assessments of the frequency with which particular cells (and trajectories across them) are occupied. This ambitious project suggests scope for using systematic comparisons to address substantive questions in fresh ways, especially if these comparisons gain a dynamic aspect by tracing the movement of cases across cells. However, it also raises

		Labour: High Development		Labour: Low Development	
		Labour: High Control	Labour: Low Control	Labour: High Control	Labour: Low Control
Capital: High Development	Capital: High Control	Volvo	'Choc Works'	Subaru Isuzu	'Kay'
	Capital: Low Control	Standard in heyday	GM Austria	Standard in decline	'ISE'
Capital: Low Development	Capital: High Control	*Non-viable*		CAMI	'Pyramid'
	Capital: Low Control	*within capitalism*		'Presswork'	Textiles in decline

Figure 3.4 Patterns of compromise in workplace case studies, cross-classifying both 'concerns' and control capabilities of labour and capital
Source: Adapted from Edwards et al. (2006:133, figure 4).

questions about how far we can push such cumulative complexification by combining multiple cross-classifications.

Cressey et al. (1985:128–33) explore three different cross-classifications across six pages of a pivotal comparative chapter, following chapters on each of their six in-depth studies. Having justified their use of case studies to probe organisational process and change, they outline their realist aspirations. While all research involves an 'inescapable element of interpretation', they want to develop 'ways of analysis which recognise both the reality of actors' perspectives and of structural constraints', stressing that 'the problem of control in organizations is not an imagined fiction but an experienced reality' (Cressey et al. 1985:125–6). They then draw explicitly on Mills (and implicitly on Baldamus) to justify using ideal types and cross-classification as tools for a realist comparative analysis of their case studies, to 'suggest fresh ways of thinking about the relations between power, control, participation and democracy' (Cressey et al. 1985:126). The sequence of diagrams is then interwoven with textual commentary and, when we translate the textual location of their case-studies into the diagrams themselves, their role as 'pictorial work spaces' becomes clear.

Their first diagram (Figure 3.5) uses influential contrasts developed by earlier students of organisation to cross-tabulate contrasting

	Mechanistic Organisational Structures	Organic Organisational Structures
Unitarist Ideology	Hierarchical control by rational elite; 'participation' limited to informing workers when necessary; devolution/resistance/opposition deemed pathological (but may require concessions)	
Pluralist Ideology		Enterprise as community of interests; decentralised 'responsible autonomy' to address organisational challenges; but problems of incoherence, constraints and conflicting interests (evoking ultimate management control)

Figure 3.5 Authority and democracy in industry: First move (organisational structures x ideologies) and second move (exploring quadrants)
Source: Adapted from Cressey et al. (1985:128–30).

'mechanistic' and 'organic' *organisational structures* (Burns and Stalker 1961) and contrasting 'unitarist' and 'pluralist' *corporate ideologies* (Fox 1966). Their second analytical move registers the relative coherence of the configurations in the top left and bottom right boxes compared with the other two quadrants and considers the tensions and pressures which nevertheless beset these configurations. This suggests that the underlying realities of managerial prerogatives, conflicting interests and imposed authority create pressures across all quadrants, summarised in the key argument that top managements that face problems of control tend to drift towards the upper left quadrant in the form of 'last resort unitarism' (Cressey et al. 1985:127, 132).

Figure 3.6 results from their third move, which is to utilise a fresh set of analytical distinctions to cross-classify *explicit* versus *implicit managerial ideology* against *explicit power* (authority plus coercion) versus

	Explicit Managerial Ideology	Implicit Managerial Ideology
Explicit Power	*Box 1* LIFTCO 2 Intervention by HQ underlines managerial prerogatives but erodes management legitimacy NORSTEEL 2 Active management invokes team cooperation within parameters of managerial prerogatives BEERCO 2 Paternalism combined with explicit management power but legitimacy relatively sustained	*Box 3* NORSTEEL 1 Active management engagement in collective bargaining without strong ideology
Implicit Power	*Box 2* COMCO 1&2 Decentralised and informal 'human relations' approach in prosperous conditions WHISCO Autocratic unitarism with participation designed to foster enterprise consciousness BEERCO 1 Explicit paternalism framing participation initiatives	*Box 4* LIFTCO 1 Decentralised consultation in benign environment SCOTBANK Participation sustained, though NT and reorganisation presage more explicit management power (3) and possibly management ideology (1)

Figure 3.6 Third move (charting different strategies of legitimation and control) and fourth move (locating cases in matrix)
Source: Adapted from Cressey et al. (1985:131–2).

implicit power (authority plus manipulation), and on this basis to unpack some of the implications of their first cross-classification. Their diagram merely identifies the four quadrants, but the text populates them with specific case-studies and traces migrations between them over time, since 'individual companies moved their positions as circumstances changed' and 'insofar as companies could be discerned to be moving towards box 1 as difficulties and uncertainties...were encountered, this illustrates what we mean by last-resort unitarism' (Cressey et al. 1985:131–2). Furthermore some cases exhibited clear-cut changes, but others revealed tensions associated with incipient but as yet incomplete tendencies for change:

> Scotbank, while its interest in participation shows some movement in the direction of making its ideology more explicit, remains essentially in box 4. Yet it was facing problems concerning mergers and new technology, which could be moving it in the direction of box 2 and possibly box 1 since the need to justify actions with extensive implications for the workforce provides that kind of momentum.
>
> (Cressey et al. 1985:132)

Here the diagram is more evidently a pictorial workspace, though the workings are embedded in the text more than the diagram itself.

Their next moves, involving Figure 3.7, develop a critical evaluation of an earlier typology of organisational political systems and forms of participation (Thurley 1984). The authors recognise that 'cross classifying the extent to which a company is highly integrated or fragmented with the dimension of implicit-explicit power' generates a sophisticated typology, which identifies several different forms of pluralism (boxes B,

	Explicit Power	Implicit Power
Highly Integrated	A. Dominance: Top management power deploying sanctions to enforce control; participation via consultation LIFTCO 2 WHISCO (primarily) SCOTBANK (primarily)	C. Organic integration: Tasks pursued by knowledgeable project teams; participation integral to team activity COMCO (primarily)
Fragmented	B. Bargained solutions: Lateral bargaining between [equivalent?] interest groups; participation through formal joint decision-making committees LIFTCO 1 NORSTEEL (primarily) BEERCO (primarily)	D. Détente: Power balance between contending interests with difficult issues side-lined; committee participation underwrites status quo via non-decision and veto

Figure 3.7 Fifth move (Thurley's matrix of organisational structures and forms of power) and sixth move (mapping cases into boxes)
Source: Adapted from Cressey et al. (1985:130–4).

C and D) associated with different types of participation, and serves as 'an orienting device to trace the circumstances in which an enterprise moves from one position to another' (Cressey et al. 1985:133). However, when Cressey, Eldridge and MacInnes locate their own cases within this framework they are led to question how far Thurley's cross-classification can be regarded as analytically productive. One issue is that only one of their cases occupies the right half of his diagram (though we might also ask why more cases are characterised by implicit power in Figure 3.6). More crucially, locating their cases often involves the qualifier 'primarily', highlighting how different aspects of each enterprise appear to fall in different boxes. Their research suggests such 'mixed situations' could even characterise the operations of a single committee, where 'the ostensible position of the bargained solution was permeated with elements of détente and dominance', while 'if this kind of slippage can occur in one such committee, the empirical variations in a large company can well be imagined' (Cressey et al. 1985:133–4).

This might suggest that complexity inevitably overwhelms such cross-classificatory exercises, as

> The coexistence of different kinds of system, with varying implications for our understanding of participation, is likely to be part of organisational reality. At the same time the mix may well vary at different levels in the organisation in relation to different kinds of decision.
>
> (Cressey et al. 1985:134)

Their dominant criticism, however, is more specific since 'however varied the scene in individual enterprises, where different ensembles are mixed with different ideologies, they are all permeated with relations of dominance' (Cressey et al. 1985:135). This suggests the crucial weakness of Thurley's cross-classification arises from overlooking this feature in all three variants of pluralism. By comparison their previous cross-classification remains more productive, even if their application may need to be nuanced in relation to different organisational settings. Figure 3.6, combined with its textual unpacking, provides tools to address the tensions within each of the different boxes (characterised by the persistence of both 'relations of dominance' and 'antagonistic co-operation' across all cases), but also hierarchical and spatial variations in dominant tendencies within firms and their related movement across these boxes. These themes are developed further in later comparative chapters, addressing 'crisis management' then implications for wider debates about industrial participation and democracy.

Here, then, are two distinctive (but not necessarily mutually exclusive?) styles of serial cross-classification. That of Eldridge and colleagues is a rather playful serial experimentation with different bases of cross-classification, to sort, compare and reconceptualise the character and implications of a panel of case studies. That of Edwards and colleagues is a more systematic interweaving of multiple cross-classifications to generate one large matrix of closely specified categories within and across which to map case studies. The first approach has the strength of drawing on a variety of possible classifications, but it is less evidently systematic and cumulative. The second approach has the latter strengths but may be less open to innovative ideas and confronts limits to cumulative complexification.

Conclusion

I hope this discussion has not only demonstrated John Eldridge's engagement with cross-classification but also vindicated his advocacy of the adventurous use of this procedure. It has certainly demonstrated that cross-classification can be pursued in a variety of ways even in published work, using more or less heavily theorised categories, for example, or stand-alone versus cumulative diagrams. It also suggests that the best diagrams offer distinctive insights in interaction with their text, possibly becoming genuine 'pictorial working spaces'. Several examples highlighted questions about the demarcation of contrasting categories, and scope to redraw boundaries at different points. One response is to translate polar contrasts into continua. Closer to the spirit of cross-classification, though, is recognition that researchers will rework such boundaries through conceptual experimentation *and* engagement with empirical investigations, and might also refine their analyses by moving levels or interweaving fresh distinctions with existing ones. As Edwards and Bélanger (2008) imply, this might then combine an ability to address distinctive configurations of social relations with quantitative treatment of their occurrence, without dissolving those configurations into clusters of variables – perhaps a reason for the apparent affinity of this procedure with case study research. Finally, in many of the diagrams discussed above it is notable that the identification of distinctive configurations or types is associated with an appreciation of persistent tensions and sources of change, which in turn serve to animate movement across those types. This is not an *inherent* property of cross-classification, which sometimes appears to freeze the types it identifies, but it may be an important feature of its most successful applications.

Acknowledgements

Thanks to Rachel Cohen, Chris Smith and the editors for comments, and *Historical Studies in Industrial Relations* for permission to draw on Elger (2013).

References

Ackroyd, S. and Thompson, P. (1999) *Organizational Misbehaviour*. London: Sage.
Baldamus, W. (1971) 'Cross-Classification', *Discussion Paper 16, Series E*. Faculty of Commerce and Social Sciences: University of Birmingham.
Baldamus, W. (1976) *The Structure of Sociological Inference*. London: Martin Robertson.
Bélanger, J. and Edwards, P. (2007) 'The Conditions Promoting Compromise in the Workplace', *British Journal of Industrial Relations*, 45 (4): 713–34.
Burawoy, M. (2003) 'Revisits: An Outline of a Theory of Reflexive Ethnography', *American Sociological Review*, 68 (5): 645–79.
Burns, T. and Stalker, G. (1961) *The Management of Innovation*. London: Tavistock.
Cressey, P. Eldridge, J. and MacInnes, J. (1985) *Just Managing: Authority and Democracy in Industry*. Milton Keynes: Open University Press.
Crouch, C. (1977) *Class Conflict and the Industrial Relations Crisis*. London: Heinemann.
Crouch, C. (1979/1982) *The Politics of Industrial Relations*. London: Fontana.
Crouch, C. (1993) *Industrial Relations and European State Traditions*. Oxford: Clarendon.
Crouch, C. (1999) *Social Change in Western Europe*. Oxford: Oxford University Press.
Douglas, M. (1970/2003) *Natural Symbols: Explorations in Cosmology*. New York: Routledge.
Edwards, P. (1986) *Conflict at Work: A Materialist Analysis of Workplace Relations*. Oxford: Blackwell.
Edwards, P. (2003) 'The Future of Industrial Relations', in P. Ackers and A. Wilkinson (eds.) *Understanding Work and Employment: Industrial Relations in Transition*. Oxford: Oxford University Press, pp. 337–58.
Edwards, P., and Bélanger, J. (2008) 'Generalizing from Workplace Ethnographies: From Induction to Theory', *Journal of Contemporary Ethnography*, 37: 291–13.
Edwards, P., Bélanger, J. and Wright, M. (2006) 'The Bases of Compromise in the Workplace: A Theoretical Framework', *British Journal of Industrial Relations*, 44 (1): 125–45.
Edwards, P., and Wajcman, J. (2005) *The Politics of Working Life*. Oxford: Oxford University Press.
Eldridge, J. (1971) *Sociology and Industrial Life*. London: Nelson.
Eldridge, J. (1983) *C. Wright Mills*. London: Tavistock.

Eldridge, J. (2003) 'Post-Modernism and Industrial Relations', in P. Ackers and A. Wilkinson (eds.) *Understanding Work and Employment: Industrial Relations in Transition*. Oxford: Oxford University Press, pp. 325–36.

Eldridge, J. (2010) 'Baldamus's Adventures with Cross-Classification', in M. Erickson and C. Turner (eds.) *The Sociology of Wilhelm Baldamus: Paradox and Inference*. Farnham: Ashgate, pp. 19–34.

Elger, T. (2010) 'Critical Realism', in A.J. Mills, G. Durepos and E. Wiebe (eds.) *Encyclopedia of Case Study Research*. London: Sage, pp. 253–7.

Elger, T. (2013) 'The Legacy of Baldamus: A Critical Appreciation', *Historical Studies in Industrial Relations*, 34: 229–61.

Fox, A. (1966) *Industrial Sociology and Industrial Relations*. London: HMSO.

Kristensen, P.H. and Morgan, G. (2007) 'Multinationals and Institutional Competitiveness', *Regulation and Governance*, 1: 197–212.

Littler, C.R. (1982) *The Development of the Labour Process in Capitalist Societies*. London: Heinemann Educational Books.

Mars, G. (1982) *Cheats at Work: An Anthropology of Workplace Crime*. London: George Allen and Unwin.

Mills, C.W. (1948/1970) 'The Contribution of Sociology to Studies of Industrial Relations', *Berkeley Journal of Sociology*, 15: 11–32. Originally published in 1948 in M. Derber (ed.) Proceedings of the First Annual Conference of the Industrial Relations Research Association, Urbana: IRRA.

Mills, C.W. (1956) *White Collar*. Oxford: Oxford University Press.

Mills, C.W. (1959a) *The Sociological Imagination*. Oxford: Oxford University Press.

Mills, C.W. (1959b) *The Power Elite*. Oxford: Oxford University Press.

Mills, C.W. (1980/1952) 'On Intellectual Craftsmanship', *Transaction*, January/February: 63–70.

Roy, D. (1954) 'Efficiency and the "Fix": Informal Group Relations in a Piecework Machine Shop', *American Journal of Sociology*, 60 (3): 255–66.

Thurley, K. (1984) 'Comparative Studies of Industrial Democracy in an Organisation Perspective' in B. Wilpert and A. Sorge (eds.) *International Yearbook of Organisational Democracy*, Vol. 2, London: Wiley, pp. 171–82.

Turner, C. (2010), *Investigating Sociological Theory*. London: Sage.

Vincent, S. (2011) 'The Emotional Labour Process: An Essay on the Economy of Feeling', *Human Relations*, 64 (10): 1369–92.

4
'When All Hell Breaks Loose': Striking on the British Coalfields 1984–85

Huw Beynon

Introduction

Strikes are complicated phenomena, and the miners' strike that began in 1984 is no exception. Its complexity defies simple generalisations. It has changed the lives of many people and its consequences are still being experienced after 30 years. It is, however, possible to evaluate. In doing so it is useful to remember the words of Warner and Low (1947:1) who wrote of 'the great busting-open' that a strike involves, 'when all hell breaks loose' and people do their best and worst and when 'the powerful forces which organise and control human society are revealed'. In a strike things appear more markedly for what they are. So clear did they become for one young miner in Durham that he expressed the view, quite forcibly, that 'we could do with one of these every two years and then people would really see what this system is like'.[1]

After three decades the strike remains real in popular memory. In South Wales the lodge secretary of the Celynen South colliery describes it as 'the best year of my life'; his counterpart in Cynheidre saw it as the worst. Situated in Newbridge, the Celynen strikers were supported by a 'Miners' Wives' group that helped maintain the strike until its end. These women remember the strike for the way it changed them and opened up new experiences. Dorothy Phillips saw herself as an 'ordinary housewife', yet she was one who had spoken at a large meeting at Exeter University as part of their fund-raising activities. She was able to overcome her nerves with the anger she felt over the injustice of it all;

especially the state withholding welfare payments in lieu of supposed (but non-existent) strike pay:

> What the government did was to take away benefits from people on strike [they] would normally have been entitled to and this made some of them feel guilty, almost that if they were eating something, they were taking food off the tables of their wives and children. We set up a soup kitchen... and we started making meals so the men could eat and their families could eat.
> (Turner 2014; see also Jones and Novak 1985)

In Newbridge the strike held together. Further west in the Gwendraeth valley on the anthracite field, there was a 'back to work' campaign at the Cynheidre colliery – a mine drawing on miners from two villages – where 90 men returned to work. Here, the memories are more bitter. As one man put it, 'there are people I'll cross the road to avoid looking at their faces'. Another took 'pride in the fact that we stood for what we believed in and know that we made the effort... for some things there is no forgiveness – ever'. The men who returned to work – who scabbed – felt that 'no-one gained anything' (S4C 2014).

Different places, different memories, but in all accounts the police have a powerful presence. After visiting Newbridge during the strike, Martha Gellhorn, the war correspondent, came to refer to the police as 'storm troopers', reflecting the way in which the power of the state was being used against the people (Devine 2012). This view was shared by one young man at the Nantgarw colliery. He had just completed his apprenticeship at the time of the dispute, he became actively involved, was arrested, beaten while in jail and travelled to Orgreave for the mass picket on 16 June. His most powerful memory is of 'the violence that was inflicted upon me and the violence I witnessed fellow miners received [it] will stay with me for the rest of my days'. However, he concluded that he 'would probably do it all over again'(Price and Butts-Thompson 2014:113).

There is perhaps enough in these few paragraphs to elaborate into a chapter, but there is more to deal with for the strike has also been remembered and represented in more formal and organised ways. For example, there have been five feature-length films, including the most recent and acclaimed *Pride*, and these interpretations colour the memory (Alderson 2011). *Brassed Off*, for example, viewed the aftermath of the strike though the experiences of the local colliery band and in 2014 was developed into a theatrical production with an opening planned in

Darlington. The organisers rang up the office of the National Union of Mineworkers (NUM) in Durham to ask for the union's support. To his surprise the union Secretary Dave Hopper learned that the music in the play would be provided by the band of the Durham constabulary. He rang to tell me:

> something that you will find hard to believe. The police band! I've never heard of anything as ridiculous in my life. We were going to have the men who truncheoned us down and destroyed our communities now playing music for us

The arrangements were changed.

Any strike that lasts a year, located in a critical industry and directly involving over 200,000 workers and their families is likely to be a complex affair. The more so, as in this one, when it is overlaid with deep political divisions, animosities and support played out with the active engagement of the various apparatuses of the state. During the strike over 20,000 miners were arrested or hospitalised. Two were charged with murder.[2] Over 200 miners served time in custody, including the President of the Kent miners who spent two weeks in jail. A total of 995 miners were victimised and sacked.[3] Two miners were killed on picket lines, two died on their way to the picket lines and three teenage children died in Yorkshire foraging for coal (National Justice for Mineworkers Campaign 2015). In the coalfield areas convoys of police vans –40 or 50 at a time with motorcycle outriders-became regular features of the roads and motorways. There was a powerful and deep sense of oppression: the unnerving upset of liberal sensibilities. Mining villages were cut off by the police. People talked of having their 'backs against the wall' as they stayed on strike to save their pit. At the time of the strike there were 174 working collieries in the National Coal Board (NCB) with a labour force of 230,000. In 2015, the last two mines of the privatised industry were on the edge of closure, leaving the resurrected Hatfield Colliery in Doncaster as the last of the NCB mines. Meanwhile, coal (imported from abroad) remained central to electricity supply (Beynon 1984).

In reflecting on this event and considering the ways in which it has impacted upon British society and the labour movement it is helpful to turn to the writings of Raymond Williams. Williams was of course the leading left theoretician of the 1980s who had, with others, launched the *May Day Manifesto* in the 1960s arguing for the development of new forms of democratic socialism (Eldridge and Eldridge 1994). As the strike came to its bitter end he wrote a short and reflective piece in the *New Socialist* magazine entitled 'Mining the Meaning: Key Words in the Miners' Strike'. In this he argued that the issues raised in the dispute required debate that went beyond the persistent questioning of the tactics of the NUM. Drawing on a metaphor with the coal-mining process, he wrote of 'the dust and stone of confused, short term and malign argument' (Williams 1993:120),[4] and went on to identify four 'key words' raised by the dispute: *management, economy, community* and *order*.

Using the thematic structure provided by these key words this chapter explores some of the empirical detail of the strike, drawing upon my own field notebooks, the work of other researchers and data from The National Archives at Kew (TNA). In the run up to the strike a miscellaneous cabinet committee (MIC101) met to discuss the coal industry. This was transformed into the Cabinet Ministerial Group on Coal (CMGC) on 14 March chaired by the Prime Minister.[5] The minutes of these meetings were digitalised and since their release under the 30 year rule have been carefully analysed (Phillips 2014; Williams 2014). While there is nothing here that comes as a complete surprise, there is confirmation of previous understandings and suspicions. In its detail it reveals the continuous and direct involvement of Mrs Thatcher and the extent to which senior policy advisers and civil servants became positively engaged in the strategy to defeat the NUM. In this way, as Paul Mason has observed, 'the truth on paper still has the power to shock' (Mason 2014).

Real economy – real communities

It is hard to exaggerate the impact of the years of the first Thatcher government. At the time it had become commonplace for people to open conversations with the phrase 'if you had told me five years ago that [such and such had happened or such a plant had closed] I would have thought that you were off your rocker'. In the short space of three years, 3 million manufacturing jobs were made 'redundant', another key word. The steel industry followed with major plant closures, achieved under the direction of Ian MacGregor who, in 1983, was appointed by Mrs Thatcher as Chairman of the NCB. As one miner commented, speaking for many, 'the first time that I realised that what Arthur Scargill was saying was right was when Margaret Thatcher appointed Ian MacGregor. Then I knew we were in for a bad time.'

In June 1983, the Monopolies and Mergers Commission had produced a report on the National Coal Board (Cmnd 8920), identifying a tail of heavy loss-making collieries, and these, along with the communities associated with them, became a source of concern. For Macgregor the report was 'the Bible'. It provided Williams with an example of 'isolated accounting', an approach that had removed 'economy' from its social and geographical setting, and in this case took no account of the long-term consequences of colliery closures upon mining areas and their accumulated social capital. Coal, he argued, echoing an earlier dispute in 1972, was indeed a special case: 'it is a deep economic resource of this island and any reasonable economic calculation of its mining has to include not only current trading calculations but long term and interrelating calculations of general energy policy' (Williams 1993:123). To this he added the impact on the local mining communities, which he saw as 'the implacable logic of the social order which is now so strongly coming through: the logic of a new nomad capitalism which exploits actual places and people and then (as it suits them) moves on' (Williams 1993:124). For Williams this 'nomad capitalism' was a particularly virulent form, being quite detached from 'any settled working and productive activity'. The consequences he finds in the

> Inner cities and the abandoned mining villages, [where] real men and women know that they are facing an alien order of paper and money which seems all powerful... For what lies ahead of us, within that alien order, is a long series of decisions in which one industry after another will declare more and more people redundant.
> (Williams 1993:124)

This implied a need for a new economic policy that would 'begin with real people in real places that would be designed to sustain their continuing life'. He is clear that this would require a significant shift in political thinking, but argued that it was one which the miners 'in their arguments about pits and communities – their refusal to separate economics from a people and society' had initiated (Williams 1993:124).

The miners had of course gone a long way in this process. Through their union and though the work of its industrial relations, education and research departments they had spearheaded a major campaign throughout 1983. This was styled *Campaign for Coal* – not Campaign for Jobs – and was in many ways an example of how a trade union engages in broader political and social issues. The NUM's campaign contained seven information pamphlets put together in a maroon folder covering the major themes of 'Unemployment', 'Privatisation' and 'The Attack on the Industry'. These were supported by pamphlets on 'Nuclear

Power' and 'New Ways of Using Coal'. Two other papers dealt with ways in which work in the industry could be reorganised, looking at 'New Technology' and 'The Incentive Scheme'.[6]

This package formed the basis of extensive discussions in night classes, day schools and trade union and political party meetings. Armed with these packs, several of us led discussions across the coalfields throughout the autumn and winter of 1983. Later, when James Fox talked with miners' pickets in South Wales during the strike, he expressed astonishment at their capacity to engage in debate on the widest range of issues relating to both the dispute and the future of the industry (*The Observer* 16 September 1984). The campaign, however, was not restricted to coal miners. In Easington district, for example, it led to the formation of a community group called SEAM – Save Easington Area Mines – and similar organisations appeared in other coalfields. SEAM was chaired by a local woman, who was also a district councillor. It organised meetings, lobbies and discussions, and once the strike had begun became the main focus for coordinating the daily support for coal miners' families, involving people across the communities.

In his discussion of 'community' Williams considered two of its meanings. The first related to the places where the miners 'have lived and want to go on living, where generations not only of economic but also of social care have been invested and which generations will inherit'. Clearly in 1984 the coal industry contained a variety of such places, and the examples from South Wales (where support for the strike was probably most uniform) show that the community experience could differ greatly. More significant perhaps was the division that appeared between communities in different coalfields; between those where the majority of the miners were on strike and those (mainly in Nottingham) where the majority worked. This division *between* communities can be rooted in historical social processes and also in the sustained and *federal* nature of the miners' union with the different associated forms through which the local communities were organised. This was revealed to me dramatically in 1982 when I was invited by Hywel Francis to speak to a group of South Wales miners about changes taking place in the North East. In the discussion it became clear that while the miners had similar viewpoints there were significant differences, exacerbated by the fact that none of the miners in the school had visited Durham or knew and had regular contact with lodge activists in the North. Here there was a great contrast with the development of combine committees in engineering, where shop floor representatives had built close links with their opposite numbers in other factories. Within the structure of the NUM, the regions were very separate and contact across them was mainly achieved through the union's National Executive Committee (NEC), which was almost entirely the domain of the full-time officials.

Williams had written in 1983 of a weakening of the ways in which the politics of reflex, which had linked workers to the Labour Party, had been eroded by a variety of different social changes. This process was also at work within the miners' union, exacerbated by the different ways in which the industry had developed across its various regions, emphasising the ways in which 'community' is made and remade. Facing the complex question of mine closures, with the inevitably skewed regional effect, alliances of solidarity between different communities of coal miners could not be assumed but needed to be *constructed* and could not easily be resolved though a national ballot.

Here Williams introduced his second idea of community, with a wider definition which could include all coal miners or at its broadest 'a people or a nation' and one that has to include 'all its actual and diverse communities'. He noted the danger, apparent in 1985, of this *wider* community and its interests being used against the *particular* local community in a way that would be 'evil and false' (Williams 1993:124). Here he raises as problematic the route through which 'an injury to one' could become seen as 'an injury to all'. This was at the root of an article the NUM President Arthur Scargill wrote for the *Morning Star* at the beginning of the strike. It was entitled 'The Miners' Battle for Britain' and it referenced the riots of the previous years, the rising poverty and unemployment and the rule of the rich. Affirming the miners' action therefore to be in the *general* interest, he described the situation as a 'social powder keg in which the present miners' explosion has taken place'. He went on to explain the need to understand 'one supreme point':

> The miners cannot win this dispute alone. The forces opposing us, though wobbling, are strong. To defeat them it will take people and cash on a massive scale. Every sinew in every factory, office, dole queue, docks, railway, plant and mill will need to be strained to the maximum. Not tomorrow or the next day but now... What is urgently needed is a rapid and total mobilisation of the labour and trade union movement to take positive advantage of a unique opportunity to defend our class.
>
> (Scargill 1984)

Here, community is extended to another general level – the level of class. In 1981 Williams had written of the ways in which apparent sectional interests could directly appeal to a general class interest, but he had warned that 'it can no longer be taken for granted that so absolute a link is inevitably present' (Williams 1993:250). This was to prove the case in 1984, and in no small part this was due to the way in which Mrs Thatcher coordinated her campaign against the NUM. The CMGC minutes reveal the government's fear of solidarity action and of the strike extending both to other mining communities and to other industries. When this seemed likely, as with the railways and especially the docks in July when the movement of coal was threatened, the government directly intervened to ease the settlement of disputes (Jones 2014; Phillips 2014). Of greatest importance was the power supply industry, and when pay negotiations began there the view was that 'although a high settlement would have damaging repercussions, there would be much to be said for getting it out of the way quickly and quietly' (CMGC 27 March).

The right to manage

Williams saw nationalisation to be one of the great achievements of the socialist movement over decades based on the belief that 'the major industries and services would be nationalised so that instead of embodying a capitalist interest in profit, they would embody a national or public interest' (Williams 1993:121). These same industries were, in the mind of the Conservative government, a major obstacle to economic progress, needing to be managed by people who understood the bottom line. While in opposition Nicholas Ridley had chaired a committee for the Party concerned with the future of the nationalised industries. In its view these industries had been 'run for the benefit of those who work in them. The pressures are for more jobs for the boys, and more money for each boy' (Economic Reconstruction Group 1977:5). The resolution of the problem lay in regaining the 'right to manage', which would be difficult because:

> There would be trade union objection and opposition. It would need dedicated top management to carry it through. The civil service would resist it. The motivation of all concerned – from worker to board chairman to Permanent Secretary – is to do the opposite. The key to doing it lies with top management... We should start now to recruit chairmen who will be sympathetic to our objectives.
> (Economic Reconstruction Group 1977:17)

Here we see the beginning of a process that would confirm Williams's claim that 'the Coal Board, instead of representing the most general public interest has become, in practice, a corporate employer with political and financial relations only to the state' (Williams 1993:121).

In 1985 I interviewed Norman Siddall, who had retired as head of the NCB in 1983. While he wouldn't be drawn to openly criticise the appointment of MacGregor, he remarked wryly that 'I thought that I was too old and given my health couldn't do another five years, but they brought in someone six years older who lasted for two years'. Siddall had spoken at the NUM Conference in 1982, explaining the difficulties that the industry faced, with coal being stockpiled and demand low. He clearly felt in 1985 that the difficult situation had been exacerbated by the government, and in this he was undoubtedly correct (Beynon 2014). With Siddall out of the way, the government still needed to establish the conditions that would allow management to impose its economic plan.[7] This meant sustaining a major dispute with the NUM, a union guaranteed by statute, together with its enshrined rights for negotiation and conciliation. In this the central aim was to safeguard electricity supply.

Under the direction of the Department of Energy and MISC 101, and at enormous cost to the Exchequer, land was purchased to extend the capacity of the coal stocking sites around power stations, some coal stations were converted to accommodate oil and the publicly owned Central Electricity Generating Board was briefed on the need to increase the use of 'oil-burn' during a major stoppage (Beynon and McMylor 1985). This was all understood by government as assisting 'endurance', and this became a key word in their discussions once the strike had begun. On 30 March, Peter Walker (a Tory wet) reported that the government must ensure that: 'moderate miners have correct perception of endurance; the police operation ensures continued working and movement of coal; we are confident about the endurance of power stations'. In his view 'the situation also provides an excellent opportunity to accelerate pit closures and to maximise opencast operations'; moreover (referring to Arthur Scargill's article in the *Morning Star*) the government had 'a unique opportunity to break the power of the militants in the NUM' and ensure that 'industrial relations reflect economic reality'.

Here we see how 'rational economic management' becomes linked to the control and manipulation of people's ideas and beliefs. Ridley's committee had written of the need for 'stealth' to be the watchword, something that Peter Oborne (2005) would call lying, and the operation of this principle was most clear in the way the closure programme was established, denied and implemented.

In September 2013, with MacGregor in place and the coal stocks accumulated, the government was prepared to implement its policy. A

MISC101 meeting was held on 15 September 1983, which (like others around this time) was enveloped in deep secrecy, with no copies kept of the minute which read:

> Closures produce considerably greater economies than the results of practicable pay moderation. Mr MacGregor had it in mind over the three years 1983/85 that a further 75 pits would be closed... There would be no closure list but a pit by pit procedure. The manpower at the end of that time in the industry would be down to 138,000 from 202,000. The Secretary of State noted that there would be considerable problems in all this. The manpower reductions would bite heavily in particular areas: two-thirds of Welsh miners would become redundant, 35 per cent of miners in Scotland, 48 per cent in the North East, 50 per cent in South Yorkshire and 46 percent in the South Midlands (which included the whole of the Kent coalfield)

This, of course, was suspected by the NUM but repeatedly denied by the NCB and government. So much so that in June, 1984 when the struggle for advantage between the two sides was at its height and when the possibility of extending solidarity beyond the mining communities still existed, the NCB intervened. In a meeting of CMGC Thatcher agreed the draft of a letter to be sent to all miners from MacGregor. No-one who was around the coalfields in those days failed to see a copy. It said simply that the union was lying over the scale of pit closures. In sympathetic tone it explained that the NCB was not planning to butcher the coal industry and make over 70,000 men redundant as the NUM was claiming: 'If these things were true I would not blame miners for getting angry or for being deeply worried. But these things are absolutely untrue. I can state categorically and solemnly that you have been deliberately misled.'

While these solemn words were most generally viewed with scepticism, they had their effect and were referred to by miners in the autumn when the strike began to break. All this of course was assisted by the popular press, picturing the miners' leaders as the 'Three Wise Monkeys', identifying them and other trades union officials as 'bosses' or 'barons' and sometimes openly linking them with near-feudal practices as they defended the rights that Williams had identified as central to the development of a better kind of society. As Andrew O'Hagan noticed as a teenager from his home on the Ayrshire coalfield:

> Suddenly there was a turn in the conversation, not locally, but on the TV news: the union men were now corrupt, evil, violent criminals.

To us they were hardworking men who made half decent wages in terrible conditions, people who lived in modest houses and had holidays on the English seaside. But on the news they were tyrants and Mrs Thatcher was going to bring them down.

(O'Hagan 2013)

The history of this change of tone still needs to be written, but it is clear that the issue of trade union officials regularly appeared on the agenda of the Conservative Party in the 1970s especially within its influential 'Stepping Stones' group (Dorey 2014). Examining the need to make 'a sea change in Britain's political economy' and one which restored management's right to manage, at the expense of workers' rights and employment, the group saw *trade unions* as the stumbling block 'because they are the only group whose leaders' political convictions and lack of economic understanding could pit them against any government which dares to do what has to be done' (Hoskyns 1978:2). The group's full report went to considerable (and at times absurd) lengths to consider discursive interventions capable of driving a wedge between these leaders and the rank and file, emphasising the supposed tyranny that underpinned solidarity and contrasting it with notions of 'concern, self-respect, maturity' (Hoskyns 1977). In complex ways these ideas fed into the media and the whole of the body politic in the 1980s.

Law and order

In 1979, while she was leader of the opposition, Margaret Thatcher entered into a detailed correspondence with the Home Secretary, Merlyn Rees. The occasion for the correspondence was the road haulage dispute and the advice given by the Minister to chief constables in relation to picketing. Merlyn Rees made it clear that in his view 'It is not the task of the Home Secretary to give advice to the police about the day to day conduct of their job'.[8] Mrs Thatcher disagreed, and in this had the support of Ridley's committee, which had recommended that a Conservative government needed 'a large mobile squad of police equipped and prepared to up hold the law against violent picketing. Good non-union drivers should be recruited to cross picket lines with police protection' (Economic Reconstruction Group 1977:26). As such, it was no surprise that in the first weeks of the strike the Prime Minister asserted that:

Helping those who volunteered to go to work was not sufficient; intimidation had to be ended and people had to be free to go about their business without fear. It was essential to stiffen the resolve of Chief Constables.

(CMGC 14 March)[9]

Leon Brittan, the Home Secretary, was pressed to ensure that they undertook a 'more vigorous interpretation of their duties'. This stiffening of resolve is addressed by Raymond Williams in his discussion of law and order which, he says, should be treated as one word. For him the

> real problem is *order*... Listening to some ministers, it is easy to pick up their real sense of order. Which is command; obedience to lawful authority; indeed when combined with the 'right to manage', obedience to all authority.
>
> (Williams 1993:125)

Against this he posits another view: the actions of the government, taken together, amounted to 'the dislocation of our habitual social order and the destruction of specific communities' (Williams 1993:125). That it was in effect class warfare (Miliband 1980).

Certainly the scale of the police power used in 1984 would support that view. It was a major, even decisive, influence upon the outcome of the dispute, with arrests depleting the miners' union of its key activists (Fine and Millar 1985). Of those arrested, only 8 per cent were charged with the use of violence. By far the largest number were charged under Section Five of the Public Order Act of 1936 – 'threatening, abusive or insulting words and behaviour likely to cause a breach of the peace'. This charge, which accounted for 40 per cent of all arrests, was laid in a highly arbitrary manner, often relating less to what the picket did than to the circumstances in which he did it. Added to this, the flexibility afforded the police by the Public Order Act (later allied with the near-medieval charge of 'watching and besetting') was critical. This was made most obvious on 18 June at the Orgreave coke works near Rotherham.

The works produced coke for the steel works at Scunthorpe, and the workers there were sympathetic to the miners but concerned to protect their jobs and those in the steel plant. When coke production was increased the NUM organised a picket on 30 May attended by the national president. In a letter written to the Independent Police Complaints Commission on 21 November 2013 Arthur Scargill noted that:

> upon my arrival at Orgreave on 30 May, I was arrested within approximately 15 seconds – by Chief Superintendent Nesbit, who admitted

in Court on 13 December 1984 I was the only person he had arrested in his position as Chief Superintendent. It was obvious then and it is obvious now that decisions were taken at the very highest level to arrest me – apparently on any charge – immediately I arrived at Orgreave Coking Plant on 30 May 1984.

The picket continued and escalated to the one full-scale nationally coordinated picket of the strike, scheduled for 18 June. The police were very well aware of Orgreave as a flash point, and on that day seemed to change their established policy of stopping on the highway any miners travelling to such events, and turning them back. At Orgreave the coaches and cars were ushered into the throat of the valley in which the coke works was sited. Here the miners were confronted by a battle line of police in riot gear. Behind the line, police mounted on horses were visible, while over to the right stood teams of dogs with their handlers. First-hand accounts by miners there spoke of how 'you actually felt that you were penned in – literally'. One man who stood up against the police line felt a truncheon crack into his head, opening his forehead. But apart from that it was uneventful until the afternoon, when the police decided to clear the field and began to use horses. At that point one of the pickets described how 'it was set out like a military campaign' and one in which the normal rules no longer seemed to apply. A local reporter from Radio Sheffield remembered

> looking up and suddenly seeing two lots of horse sweeping in from the left and right simultaneously on the pickets. It was like a scene of war, a battle. They swept, the police went forward. The miners obviously didn't realise what had hit them
>
> (quoted in Waddington et al. 1989:91)

This was followed by four aggressive advances by the riot police with the customary banging of their shields with truncheons. Pickets were chased 'across railway lines, up the streets of a nearby village, and into private gardens' (Waddington et al. 1989:87). Encouraged by the union president to turn back, one miner from Durham responded: 'I'm not going back down there, Arthur – it's murder down there'. While the Chief Constable was later to assure the press that the police truncheon 'is not aimed at people who run away', those who felt many of the blows would challenge that view. As one commented, 'it shouldn't have been us who were charged with riot, it was them'.

The experience of Orgreave left a mark on the miners who were there, and upon the general morale of the pickets. Ron Stoate, lodge secretary of the Penallta colliery, remembers that the scale of the force and organisation that had been brought against them left him with the thought that: 'if they want it this bad they could have it!'. The events also hung heavily over the heads of the 39 men who were arrested, charged with rioting and facing lengthy prison sentences. However the trial of the first 15 collapsed in the face of highly dubious police evidence, illustrated by 31 officers from 14 different forces using the same complex phases. Vera Baird acting for the defence described the police action as 'perverting the course of justice'.[10] However in the view of the prosecution, the miners

> came in fleets of coaches. Their aim was force and violence. No miner could say that they went to Orgreave not anticipating violence. It was mob rule... The defendants committed the offence of Riot... 'a common purpose which they intend to achieve through force'. The police were there to keep the peace.

He continued with reference to 'our democratic system' and to the need to defend society form 'the rule of the bully boy' (The Battle for Orgreave 1984).

Here then is the emphasis on 'order' and one that reappears consistently in the discussions of the CMGC. In this John Redwood, head of the party's Policy Unit, was centrally involved in calling for speedier use of stipendiary magistrates and of legal processes so that pickets could see their comrades being prosecuted and punished quickly for criminal offences. Throughout the summer the cabinet group pushed for speedier convictions and the need to sack picketing miners. It also raised the possibility of conspiracy charges being brought against union officials. In this way, as one lawyer working for Thompson's Solicitors explained to me at the height of the conflict, 'there is no doubt that the law was used in a very strategic way. It was used *strategically* to break the union.'

There is also more than a suspicion that the security services were directly involved and that they had penetrated the administrative hierarchy of the union (Milne 1994:201). In September 1984, when I organised a weekend school for 350 men and women from the coalfield in Durham University, I was advised by one of the porters (an ex-policeman) to 'be careful because Special Branch are in tonight'. Here the National Archives are of little help. Nicholas Jones was informed by the Archive staff that 'all files relating to the advice and activities of the

Security Service... had been removed and are not being made available to the public' (Jones 2014).

The legacy

The great functionalist sociologist Lloyd Warner had no doubt about the significance of strikes as 'human dramas' and also of what 'behavior in such crises tells us of the meanings and significance of human society' (Warner and Low 1947:1). Coming from a different, Marxist, tradition Raymond Williams brought a similar awareness to his writings on the miners' strike, something which he unravelled around the key words of community, the right to manage and order. For him, the deep meaning of the strike for *human society* lay in the fact that 'In a period of very powerful multinational capital... virtually everyone is exposed or will be exposed to what the miners have suffered' (Williams 1993:122).

In an important way this prediction has been borne out, with the processes established in the early 1980s continuing. Manufacturing employment has continued to decline as more and more jobs have been off-shored (Urry 2014). A new term 'precarity' has been developed to explain changing employment conditions (Standing 2011). Williams wrote of the way in which 'our protection hitherto has been in our unions and the idea of public service' (Williams 1993:122), and the attack on both of these has continued. Both Conservative and New Labour regimes have adapted to corporate styles of governance in the public sector as new management techniques, outsourcing and privatisations have gone further to establish his claim that ' "management" of a supposedly professional operation has become a simple cover word for the will and calculation of a *de facto* employer' (Williams 1993:121). All this threatens the very idea of a public service. Meanwhile the police forces have mastered the art of crowd control through kettling, and the undercover operations of Scotland Yard's Special Documentation Squad have been revealed to have included protest groups and trade unions. Government reaction to rioting that followed the disturbance in Tottenham in 2011 once again involved the use of stipendiary magistrates and exemplary punishments. Many have suffered in the ways that Williams feared.

Perhaps his other main conclusion is more problematic. He claimed that 'the miners' strike is being represented as the last kick of the old order. Properly understood, it is one of the first steps towards a new order' (Williams 1993:123). Certainly there has been little sign in the last 30 years of the radical shift in political thinking that he was looking for, and the emergence of Thatcher-lite in the guise of New Labour would have depressed him deeply. Hope would have to be found outside the main political parties. Certainly in the deep involvement of the women through the 'Miners' Wives' groups and community-based organisations such as SEAM there was a suggestion of a new way of organising within trade union action that has been influential. This was seen in the strike by ambulance workers in 1989 which successfully built links with, and concern for, the patients into the conduct of the dispute (Williams and Fryer 2011:487). Moreover, the principles that underpinned the Campaign for Coal have appeared in various campaigns to protect public services that are under attack. At a time when opinion polls indicate significant support for taking privatised utilities and railways under public ownership, it is possible to see hope for the trade unions and the values that Williams wrote about so passionately in 1984. In no small part that is because of the way in which the coal miners and their families resisted mine closures and endured what is now recognised as a prolonged government attack. The various outpourings that accompanied the 30th anniversary of the strike were evidence of this, as was the way the country divided over the death of Mrs Thatcher. With this thought in mind, I wrote to one of my ex-mining friends in Durham and received a typically sophisticated and optimistic reply.

> Yes 30 years on. I often think how poorer out lives would have been without that year. If we had just faded away without a fight I am sure there would now be no Gala to boost our sense of wellbeing each year. But more importantly it has become a symbol of resistance and a rallying point which is quite extraordinary. The whole question of the state is looked on differently now.

Notes

1. Unless referenced otherwise all quotations come from the field notes of the author.
2. Dean Hancock and Russell Shankland, miners in the Merthyr Vale colliery in South Wales, dropped a concrete block from a bridge onto the taxi that was taking a miner to the colliery. The taxi driver, David Wilkie, was killed. The men were convicted of murder and sentenced to life imprisonment. At the announcement of the verdict in May 1995, the 700 miners at the Merthyr Vale colliery walked out. On appeal the convictions were reduced to manslaughter with an eight-year sentence.
3. This was the figure provided by the NCB to the Select Committee on Employment on 22 May 1995. The Committee's report argued that the NCB's procedures amounted to 'summary treatment' that should be reviewed.

4. The piece was reproduced as part of his *Resources of Hope*. All future references are to this edition.
5. Meetings took place usually twice a week from the start of the strike in March until the end of October, when NACODS, the union of pit deputies and safety officers, agreed a revised system for consultation and agreement on pit closures with the NCB. The CMGC met just once a week thereafter. Its membership makes clear how centrally concerned the government was with the detailed management of the strike. It included the Prime Minister, who usually chaired its meetings, and ministers responsible for each of the key departments of state: Walker, Lawson, Tebbit, Ridley, King, Brittan, Heseltine, Havers and Younger.
6. There was little awareness of global warming at the time and this environmental issue is entirely absent from Williams's account. The miners were aware of developments in clean coal technology, though, and of the work of the NCB's research establishment at Bretby which was closed along with the mines.
7. The NCB's area managers had quite different perspectives on this, with South Wales nearer to Siddall's viewpoint and Scotland MacGregor's.
8. This correspondence is included in the minutes of CMGC on the instigation of Sir Brian Gubbon, Permanent Secretary at the Home Office in the context of 'the current posture'.
9. Although couched in the language of freedom, there was clearly a strategic aim here, confirmed in the handwritten note of the Prime Minister on 27 March to the effect that 'it is important to distinguish between endurance with Notts and without. Endurance is significantly higher indicating the value of the police operation.'
10. This was revealed first in a major investigative documentary, *Inside Out*, shown in the Yorkshire and Lincolnshire area on 22 October 2012 and discussed in Williams (2014).

Bibliography

Alderson, D. (2011) 'Making Electricity: Narrating Gender, Sexuality, and the Neo-Liberal Tradition in *Billy Elliot*', *Camera Obscura*, 25 (3): 1–27.

Beynon, H. (1984) 'The Miners' Strike in Easington', *New Left Review*, 1 (148): 104–15.

Beynon, H. (2014) ' "Still Too Much Socialism in Britain" The Legacy of Margaret Thatcher', *Industrial Relations Journal*, 45 (3): 214–33.

Beynon, H. and McMylor, P. (1985) 'Decisive Power: The New Tory State Against the Miners', in Beynon, H. (ed.) *Digging Deeper: Issues in the Miners' Strike*. London: Verso, pp. 29–46.

Devine, D. (2012) 'Martha Gellhorn at Newbridge', *The Western Mail*, 28 November.

Dorey, P. (2014) 'The *Stepping Stones* programme: The Conservative Party's Struggle to Develop a Trade Union Policy, 1975–79', *Historical Studies in Industrial Relation*, 35: 89–116.

Economic Reconstruction Group (1977) *Final Report of the Nationalised Industries Policy Group*, http://www.margaretthatcher.org/document/110795, date accessed: 3 May 2015.

Eldridge, J. and Eldridge, L. (1994) *Raymond Williams: Making Connections*. London: Routledge.
Fine, B. and Millar, R. (eds.) (1985) *Policing the Miners' Strike*. London: Lawrence and Wishart.
Hoskyns, J. (1977) 'Stepping Stones', *Conservative Party*, http://www.margaretthatcher.org/document/111771, date accessed: 3 May 2015.
Hoskyns, J. (1978) 'The Stepping Stones Programme', *Conservative Party*, http://www.margaretthatcher.org/document/109848, date accessed: 3 May 2015.
Jones, C. and Novak, T. (1985) 'Welfare Against the Workers: Benefits as a Political Weapon', in H. Beynon (ed.) *Digging Deeper: Issues in the Miners' Strike*. London: Verso, pp. 87–100.
Jones, N. (2014) 'The Cabinet Papers: Thatcher and the Police' in G. Williams (ed.) *Settling Scores: The Media, The Police and the Miners' Strike*. London: CPBF.
Mason, P. (2014) 'Thatcher vs. the Miners', *Channel 4 News*, http://blogs.channel4.com/paul-mason-blog/thatcher-miners-official-papers-confirm-strikers-worst-suspicions/265, date accessed: 3 May 2015.
Miliband, R. (1980) "Class War Conservatism", *New Society*, 18 June. Reprinted in R. Miliband, *Class War Conservatism and Other Essays*, London, Verso, 2015.
Milne, S. (1994) *The Enemy Within: The Secret War Against the Miners*. London: Verso.
National Justice for Mineworkers Campaign (2015) *Justice for Mineworkers*, http://www.justiceformineworkers.org.uk/, date accessed: 3 May 2015.
Oborne, P. (2005) *The Rise of Political Lying*. New York: Simon and Schuster.
O'Hagan, A. (2013) 'Maggie', *New York Review of Books*, http://www.nybooks.com/articles/archives/2013/may/23/maggie/, date accessed: 3 May 2015.
Phillips, J. (2014) 'Containing, Isolating and Defeating the Miners: The UK Cabinet Ministerial Group on Coal and the Three Phases of the 1984–5 Strike', *Historical Studies in Industrial Relations*, 35: 117–41.
Price, D and Butts-Thompson, N. (eds.) (2014) *How Black were Our Valleys*. Bargoed: BBTS.
S4C (2014) *Y Streic: Cyscoed Cynheidre*, 12 March.
Scargill, A. (1984) 'The Battle for Britain', *The Morning Star*, 16 March.
Standing, G. (2011) *The Precariat: A New Dangerous Class*. London: Bloomsbury.
The Battle for Orgreave (1984) 'Film Transcript', *Journeyman Pictures*, http://www.journeyman.tv/?lid=10025&tmpl=transcript, date accessed: 3 May 2015.
Turner, R. (2014) 'The Women who Joined the Pickets of the Miners' Strike', *Western Mail*, 19 March.
Urry, J. (2014) *Offshoring*. Cambridge: Polity Press.
Waddington, D., Jones, K. and Critcher, C. (1989) *Flashpoints: Studies in Social Disorder*. London: Routledge.
Warner, W.L. and Low, L.O. (1947) *The Social System of the Modern Factory: The Strike: A Social Analysis, Yankee City Series*. Vol. 4, New Haven, CT: Yale University Press.
Williams. G. (ed.) (2014) *Settling Scores: The Media, the Police and the Miners' Strike*. London: CPBF.
Williams, R. (1993) *Resources of Hope*. London: Verso.
Williams, S. and Fryer, R.H. (2011) *Leadership and Democracy: the History of the National Union of Public Employees. 1928–1993*, London: Lawrence and Wishart.

5
False Self-Employment
Howard Davis

When John Eldridge was pioneering the field of 'industrial sociology' in the UK with his studies of industrial conflict and the sociology of economic life (Eldridge 1968; 1971) I was a research student in Edinburgh, supervised by Tom Burns and Frank Bechhofer. My project explored the theme of class and consciousness and empirically it followed some of the traditions of 'plant sociology' by comparing workers at three sites in Scotland (Clydebridge steelworks, Grangemouth oil refinery and an Edinburgh insurance company) (Davis 1978). Like most industrial sociology at that time it was framed in terms of large employers, institutions, bureaucracy, trade unions and collective action. It seems appropriate in the context of this Festschrift to return to the field of economic life to find a perspective on one aspect of the current transformation in work relations.

Only a decade after the publication of *Sociology and Industrial Life* (Eldridge 1971) the question was being asked 'Whatever happened to industrial sociology?' (Hyman 1981). This concern reflected the theoretical fragmentation of the field between functionalist, neo-Weberian, Marxist and phenomenological approaches, as well as new developments in the organisation of work and employment which we now associate with de-industrialisation, globalisation and 'new capitalism'. In my own search for theoretical inspiration I found the work of the French sociologist Alain Touraine to be particularly helpful, especially his early writings on the *Sociologie du travail* and his later work on social movements, the economic crisis and liberal democracy (Touraine 1965; 1974; Touraine et al. 1965; and see Davis 2015). John Eldridge and his colleagues used the following quote from Touraine in the conclusion to their book *Industrial Sociology and Economic Crisis*:

> When we speak of crisis, we are looking at society from the point of view of the ruling forces; when we speak of transformation, we

imply that we are studying the formation of a new cultural field, new relations and new social conflicts. This directs our attention not only to the birth of new social movements but also to the shaping of new forms of power

(Touraine 1981:339 cited in Eldridge et al. 1991:220)

And, true to his emphasis on action and the subject, Touraine states in the same text: 'we are being threatened with the loss of our capacity to imagine, prepare, and build the future. A crisis is not a situation; it is an incapacity to act' (Touraine 1981:340).

The context is now a much deeper and more extensive global crisis, but we can use Touraine's idea to focus on the task of the sociology of work relations as they are today. My aim is to take this dynamic notion of transformation and consider the development of one specific form of work relationship and the possibilities it contains for imagination and action. This is a piece of work in the original spirit of *Sociologie du travail* using the results of a small-scale empirical study.

Self-employment and flexibility

The wider context for this research is the changing nature of employment, and the relationships through which it is organised in the UK as a result of the globalisation of industrial production, the de-industrialisation of the West and the neo-liberal economic response to these changes (Bauman 1998; Beck 1992; 2000; Crouch 2011; Gorz 1999; Harrison 1997; Harvey 2005; Layard et al. 2005; Noon and Blyton 2002; Rifkin 1995; Sennett 1998; 2006; Standing 2009; 2011; Strangleman and Warren 2010). One consequence of the neo-liberal promotion of competitiveness in business and flexibility within the workforce has been the emergence of 'non-standard' and 'contingent' forms of employment such as part-time contracts, temporary contracts, zero hours contracts, outsourcing of recruitment to agencies and temporary contracts for services with self-employed persons (Benner 2002; Beck 2000; Beynon et al. 2002; Felstead and Jewson 1999; Felstead et al. 2004; McGovern et al. 2004; Muehlberger 2007; Nolan 2002; Pollert 1998; Purcell et al. 1999), and the associated insecurities (Beck 1992:143; Standing 2011).

The category of self-employment (those in the working population who directly provide services and do not have a contract of employment) is becoming more significant. In recent years, self-employment in the UK has risen to a level higher than at any point over the past 40 years. The often-cited advantages of self-employment include the freedom to choose what work to do and when, where or how to do it, increased job satisfaction, as well as the tax advantages of being able to charge certain items as deductible business expenses. According to the ONS, in 2014, 4.6 million people in the UK were self-employed in their main job, accounting for 15 per cent of those in work (ONS 2014). An additional 356,000 employees had a second job in which they were self-employed. Self-employment is the category which has contributed most to the rise in total employment since 2008. The sector is highly diverse, including directors and consultants as well as manual trades. The four most common occupations for self-employment are taxi drivers, construction trades, carpenters and joiners and farmers. Many commentators draw attention to the diversity of the self-employed category and their low average income (Dellot and Reed 2015). There is a close but not direct relationship between rates of self-employment and rates of employment. For example, one response to redundancy in an economic downturn is to seek an alternative in self-employment, but the same circumstances work against those who start from a position of self-employment and wish to be employed.

Of particular interest here is how the growth of self-employment and greater flexibility have resulted in a 'grey area' in relation to employment status, whereby official classifications are no longer adequate. Freedman (2001), writing for the Tax Law Review Committee of the Institute for Fiscal Studies, questioned the utility of the classification of workers into the categories of either 'employed' or 'self-employed'. Workers cover a broad spectrum from the unequivocally self-employed at one end to the unequivocally employed at the other. The problem of classification arises with workers who do not fit either of these two categories precisely but sit somewhere between the two ends of the spectrum. Within this area of flexible, 'contingent' and 'non-standard' employment are workers who may be deemed 'falsely self-employed' (FSE).

Although FSE or 'bogus self-employment' is not an official classification, it is used by researchers (Burchell et al. 1999; Harvey 2001) and is recognised by Her Majesty's Revenue and Customs (HMRC), the Trade Unions Council (TUC) and others to refer to a category of worker identifiable by a discrepancy between the employment classification allocated to them by an engager and which they self-certify on their tax returns, and their 'actual' employment conditions which should warrant their classification as 'employees'.[1] The phenomenon has been particularly well known in building and construction, where the fragmented nature of the industry and complex relationships between end clients, employment intermediaries and workers blur the distinction between self-employed and employee status. The situation occurs because there are distinct financial advantages to the 'engager'. If workers are self-employed the engager is not responsible for National Insurance payments, pension contributions, paid sick leave, holiday pay, overtime rates or redundancy pay. Furthermore, a self-employed building worker does not qualify for Statutory Sick Pay if he is injured on site, nor does a self-employed cleaner qualify for Statutory Maternity Pay if she becomes pregnant. From the worker's point of view the situation may promise independence and rewards for an entrepreneurial spirit, but the risks are high. Typically, in cases of FSE, there is no way for the worker to choose between being employed or self-employed if he or she is to take the work.

The invidious and contradictory position of the 'falsely self-employed' is afforded by several institutional factors. Firstly, engagers are not required to make officially accountable their decisions to employ persons in the different categories pertaining to employment status; an employer may simply ask a worker to be 'self-employed' and he or she can either agree or refuse. Secondly, there is a potential contradiction between government 'tests' for the different categories of employment status and the practice of self-certification of employment status on HMRC self-assessment tax returns; there is no HMRC 'check' to decide if a self-categorised 'self-employed' person is in fact self-employed or employed according to government tests for employment status. These institutional factors provide a loophole through which false self-employment may occur unchecked.

False self-employment

A small-scale study, conducted with the support of WISERD,[2] reviewed existing data sources, previous research literature and professional bodies' interest in the topic. The dimensions of the sociological problem became apparent from interviews with engagers and workers. As with previous research which focused on the occurrence of FSE in the construction industry (Harvey 2001; Harvey and Behling 2008), we found discrepancies between HMRC employment status guidelines and actual conditions of work. There are good reasons to believe that FSE occurs widely beyond the construction industry, and increasingly so, in other sectors of the UK economy.

One of the earliest, and somewhat unexpected, examples in our study was in a local café, where it was found that all of the staff were engaged as self-employed even though they were, for all practical purposes, employees. This led to an attempt to find a sample of FSE workers across the catering sector. A number were identified, including a catering sales representative and coffee machine maintenance manager who had access to a wide number of catering establishments, an ex-cook and two baristas. The interview with the sales representative suggested that FSE was becoming increasingly common in those parts of the catering sector involved in such catering services as deliveries, wholesales, and coffee and other catering equipment maintenance. However, a survey of 20 hotels and cafes in one local town found no cases of FSE. This demonstrates the fact that FSE is distributed unevenly across the sector and may be most prevalent in service companies.

Further research made use of internet recruitment sites, both public (Jobcentre Plus) and private, indicating that job advertisements for 'self-employed' workers ranged across numerous sectors. Random samples of car valets drawn from an internet listing of car valet franchise owners, delivery drivers drawn from phone book listings of logistics companies, and home carers drawn from internet listings of care agencies indicated that self-employment in these sectors is not only common but is often likely to fall into the category of FSE. We estimated that every one of 20 car valets, the majority of drivers in four large delivery companies and three-quarters of live-in home carers recruited via four large home care agencies were falsely self-employed. Further research would be needed to confirm the accuracy of these estimates. The demise of the City Link delivery firm in late 2014 highlighted the plight of what the company described as 'Service Delivery Partners' (owner drivers) responsible for deliveries. Self-employed, they were responsible for a delivery round and were paid per delivery stop (without guarantee of work). Drivers leased their vehicle from the company, paid for their uniform, fuel, insurance and replacement cover for holiday periods or sickness absence, and had no entitlement to redundancy pay. Other cases came to light in the media. For example, a hairdresser told a *Panorama* programme that he had made a number of his staff self-employed to avoid paying holiday and sick pay and PAYE tax. 'It's almost like a legal way of avoiding the high overheads that come with the minimum wage' (BBC Panorama 2011). The Employment Appeal Tribunal upheld the case of a dancer in a London club who, although self-employed, was bound by club rules on attendance and other working conditions and could therefore be considered an employee and be protected from unfair dismissal

(Employment Appeal Tribunal 2011). Highly skilled occupations are also affected. A report (Jorens et al. 2015) on types of employment among civil airline pilots highlights the trend towards atypical (other than open-ended employment) contracts following the liberalisation of the European aviation market. They include what the authors term 'bogus self-employment', which occurs when an individual pilot is registered as being self-employed but is de facto bound by an employment relationship with one airline in terms of their remuneration, working time, holidays and place of employment (Jorens et al. 2015:39).

It seems timely to deepen our understanding of this phenomenon, which raises a number of challenges for sociological research. There is, firstly, the uncertainty surrounding the extent of FSE. Secondly, there is the dimension of personal experience, the risks and rewards to individual workers. Thirdly, there is the role of institutions, especially the HMRC and the Employment Tribunal system in creating and maintaining a classification system. Finally, there are questions about the culture and apparent normalisation of new forms of employment.

How common is FSE?

Given the problem of classification, there is no direct source of quantitative data on the extent and distribution of FSE. The alternative is to make inferences from available sources in datasets relating to employment and self-employment. Questions in the Labour Force Survey (LFS), European Working Conditions Survey (EWCS), the Workplace Employment Relations Study (WERS) and other sources help to give a disaggregated picture of self-employment. For example, the LFS has an indicator of self-employment under the INECAC05 Economic Activity variable as well as questions on employment status, methods of payment other than wages or salary from an employer, and who is responsible for paying NI and tax. The LFS can thus be used to estimate the numbers of 'dependent' (Muehlberger 2007) or 'ambiguous' (Burchell et al. 1999) self-employed workers by defining a dependent self-employed as a self-employed worker who has no employees and only one customer. This measure does not precisely capture the phenomenon of FSE. The EWCS asks the self-employed about the numbers of clients they have, where they do their work and issues surrounding the determination of working arrangements. The WERS gathers information about the size and composition of the workforce at a workplace and has included questions on the use of freelance staff and independent contractors in areas of work that were previously done by employees. Data from these surveys provide only a general indication of the scale and distribution of FSE. The rapid growth in the number of recruitment and employment businesses or 'intermediaries' is another useful indication, since they facilitate false self-employment by exploiting weaknesses in the existing legislation. According to HMRC, 'Around 200,000 workers in the construction sector, and 50,000 in other sectors, are reckoned to be engaged with and through onshore employment intermediaries'. A conservative estimate of the loss to the Exchequer in 2014–15 is £520m (HMRC 2013). Although the HMRC has targeted certain other fields of work because the proportion of workers claiming to be self-employed is much higher – up to three times higher – than average, there are no reliable estimates for other sectors. However, it is likely that the rate of increase in self-employment overall is matched by the rate of increase in the category of workers who are falsely self-employed.

Experiences of 'Falsification'

What are the characteristics of the 'process of falsification' whereby workers are engaged in terms of one classification of employment status (self-employed) but are then treated in terms of another (employees) which contradicts the first? It is often assumed that workers will correctly certify their self-employed status, driven only by their desire to choose a particular type of work relationship. Our research suggests that this is not the case at all but rather that self-certification as self-employed is a product of interaction between worker and engager in the course of which the engager requires the worker to register as self-employed, often under the pressure to take such work as is available or under the threat of dismissal in the event of non-compliance. This process consists of two stages: the stage of the job offer, when workers are informed that they will have to be self-employed as a condition of their engagement; and after they have commenced their engagement, when they discover that they are not self-employed at all but are in fact employees. Whilst this appears to be the broad outline of the process, we know little of its detail. The intermediaries (recruitment businesses) that are often involved do not necessarily bring clarity to the contractual arrangement. In the case of direct recruitment via internet advertising, companies present the advantages of being self-employed in glowing personal terms. Are you enthusiastic, determined and ambitious? Do you want to be your own boss? Our findings suggest that some workers do not realise at the point of engagement that it is a false classification. They learn what their employment classification means over time. It is a process whereby discrepancies and contradictions are revealed with respect to employment status classification on the one hand and to the organisation of the engager/worker relationship on the other. Some workers described their growing awareness that their engagers were denying them rights and imposing conditions of work which were inconsistent with what they took to be the meaning of the employment classification category allocated to them.

It might be supposed that the allocation of self-employed status is the product of a struggle or negotiation involving the interests of the engager on the one hand and those of the worker on the other, with the more 'powerful' engager succeeding in imposing their interests on the worker. Indeed, the sample of workers we interviewed uniformly reported that they felt powerless to withstand the demands of their engagers and a sense of frustration at having no institutional recourse once they found themselves in the position of FSE. However, the invocation of concepts such as 'power' and 'economic interest' does not indicate how they are actually manifested in social interaction. Our evidence from some sectors of the economy where FSE is present shows that conditions of crisis and limited opportunities to work meant self-employment was experienced as necessity rather than opportunity. The meanings of the traditional categories of employment status were obscured by a sense of ambiguity, indeterminacy and a lack of autonomy, in spite of the promised attraction of working on one's own account.

Institutional categorisation

The distinction between being an employee and being self-employed is determined by the contractual terms of an engagement, based on a number of tests laid down over the years by the courts. The tests take account of factors such as the level of control over the content, location and conditions of work, whether the worker is able to send someone else to do their work and whether the worker provides their own equipment. HMRC provides an online tool, the Employment Status Indicator, to allow checks on the employment status of an individual or group of workers to see if they are employed or self-employed. But a noteworthy aspect of our interviews was workers' reports of the lack of protection provided by employment law. It is clear that HMRC provides no such protection and does not see it as their role or responsibility to do so. Most workers did not know of their right to take their disputes with engagers to an Employment Tribunal.

On the face of it, judging from the criteria included in the government's tests for categories of employment status, it should not be difficult for a worker to establish the category which fits his or her particular circumstances. The HMRC considers that certification as employed or self-employed is a matter for the worker to decide. A tax inspector interviewed in our study confirmed that:

> it is the taxpayer, not HMRC that categorizes the status. The registration is taken at face-value as declared...In short, there is no questionnaire or test that is applied at registration with HMRC, and no decision made by HMRC as to status at that stage.

Falsely self-employed workers who wish to contest their employment status may take their case to an Employment Tribunal (for a fee). But this is not a simple matter, as one HMRC tax inspector in our study acknowledged: 'If a worker wanted to take issue, then in my view he or she is in an uncomfortable position, as doing so might cost them a job.' If there is a problem of classification with respect to the contract of engagement, then there is also one at the level of Employment Tribunals, where the ambiguities and contradictions in employment status are exhibited in disputes over employment status in particular cases. In these tribunals, the classification problem involves a dispute over the allocation of 'self-employed' status by an engager upon a worker, and its contestation by a worker who seeks classification as an 'employee'. Our investigation showed that contestations typically concerned whether a worker had a 'contract for services' (and therefore was self-employed) or had a 'contract of service' (and was therefore an employee).

Burchell et al. (1999) and Harvey (2001) describe the four tests for employment status which have been widely used in the Tribunal system, each consisting of a number of factors which are taken into consideration. These are (1) Control: the extent to which the employer decides what tasks the worker does and how he or she does them; (2) Integration: the extent to which the worker is a part of the organisation; (3) Mutuality of obligation: the extent to which the employer is required to offer work to the worker and whether the worker is expected to do it; (4) Economic reality: the extent to which the worker bears the financial risk. These 'tests' do not, however, mean that the classification problem can be unambiguously and definitively resolved through their application. For example, the control test does not automatically resolve the issue because it can be argued that control is consistent with both an employment contract and a business contract. The HMRC guidelines caution that 'this is for guidance only and a definitive answer can only be given by an Industrial Tribunal or court' and that:

> there is no one thing that completely determines your employment status. If there is a dispute about your status between you and the person or company that you work for, an Industrial Tribunal will make its decision based on all the circumstances of a case

According to Harvey (2001:29), the tests as they stand lead to considerable confusion, often countering each other. For example, a person may, under the test of 'control', be clearly an employee in that they 'obey orders', 'have little or no discretion on hours of work' and are under supervision in their work. On the other hand they may be 'poorly integrated' into the business, with no disciplinary or grievance procedures, and they may not be included in occupational benefit schemes. On these criteria, the person may be more 'self-employed' than employed. These contradictions have to be weighed: what counts most, control or integration? The contrast between a 'contract of service' as opposed to a 'contract for services' is the heart of the matter, but the meaning of these items appears to be contingent and flexible, a product of decisions with respect to considerations taken 'in the round'.

Many of these problems have been recognised in government and the HMRC. The issue was debated in Parliament in March 2011. The question of Employment Intermediaries and False Self-Employment was the subject of a wide-ranging consultation by the HMRC (2013; 2014). The Office of Tax Simplification (OTS) launched an Employment Status project in July 2014 and the HMRC has conducted an Employment Status Review. The OTS terms of reference explain that:

> the boundary between employment and self-employment has not kept pace with changing work patterns, especially in recent years. Many people work for more than one business and can be classed as employed for one job and self-employed for other work. The growth of freelancing as a way of conducting business had led some to suggest this is a 'third way' between employment and self-employment.

All of this activity supports the conclusion that the juridical demarcation between direct employment and self-employment is based on case law and that changing work patterns have created the need for new approaches to classification for employment and tax purposes.

Classification decisions are typically made at an institutional level without much engagement with workers' common-sense knowledge of work relationships. It suggests that there is a neglected topic for sociological investigation: the capacity of these workers to contest their employment status and challenge their dependency.

Normalisation of new forms of employment

Our study opens up three further avenues of inquiry which should contribute to our understanding of the falsification process. Firstly, it suggests that in their accounts of the reasons for offering engagement on the basis of self-employment, and their reasons for maintaining FSE in the face of workers' questions about and resistance to their employment classification, engagers invoke wider contextual factors. They blame the 'current economic climate', for example. Such accounts provide an opportunity to investigate how employers who adopt the practice of FSE understand their economic circumstances, including the constraints that they face, such that the use of falsely self-employed labour is a reasonable and sensible practice as far as they are concerned.

Secondly, it raises questions concerning 'who' is selected or self-selects for employment under this classification. We have already considered the quantitative aspect of the distribution of FSE. From an ethnographic point of view, the distributional question is whether, and if so how, age, gender and ethnicity and other characteristics are taken into consideration by engagers who to take on workers on the basis of FSE. In the case of a car valet company in our research sample, the engager only selected East European workers, both male and female, on a word-of-mouth basis. We also know that many other car valeting companies advertise their positions as not requiring criminal record checks and therefore as being 'ideal' for ex-offenders. We do not know, however, whether such selective practices are operated in other sectors or what the reasons for these selective practices may be.

Thirdly, with respect to the other side of the relationship – the falsely self-employed worker – relatively little is known. Harvey (2001) indicated that FSE is a long-standing 'tradition' in the construction industry, and this may well be one of the reasons why construction workers accept FSE as normal practice. However, the extent to which such a tradition is prevalent or has been adopted in other sectors is less clear, nor whether 'constraints of tradition' are key features of workers' acceptance of FSE in other sectors. Some patterns may be explained by relatively short-term developments in technologies, markets and changes in demand.

Home delivery and courier businesses may be one such example. In parallel, then, to addressing engagers' understandings of their economic circumstances and conceptions of engager/worker relationships, a sociological approach should investigate workers' experience and views of the contractual relationship of FSE. As is the case with the employers, the unanswered questions here centre on the cultural and interpretive dimensions of acceptance, accommodation and – sometimes – resistance to FSE.

Current critical interpretations of change in employment practices (such as Standing 2011) emphasise the loss of rights which had been accumulated over generations, leading to new types of insecurity.[3] Specifically, the case of FSE denotes a shift in conceptions of engagers, workers and their relationship, towards an individualised, 'irresponsible' engager and an individualised and unprotected worker. This category of 'individualised worker' is one which serves the logic of the flexibilisation of labour and promotes the interests of employers at the expense of workers. This category may signify a wider change in conceptions of what 'workers' are in the post-industrial economy, how they may be treated and what rights they may or may not be entitled to. To the extent that FSE is more prevalent or growing faster in some sectors of the economy than in others, we can identify the factors which contribute to this spread. It may be that the sectors in which the opportunities for FSE are especially taken up and exploited have particular characteristics, that businesses within them have particular problems and that engagers within them share a particular cultural attitude to workers, work and enterprise. It may also be that in some sectors of the economy where FSE is operative, the meaning of employment and self-employment is less clear, and specifically that some of the particular features traditionally tied to these categories are neither taken for granted nor seen as relevant in the era of the flexibilisation of labour. For a worker, the convenience of finding work through an employment agency may obscure the reality and risks involved in the complex relationship between the main contractor, agency and worker.

Alongside the state's recent interest in employment status and taxation, growing attention is being given by civil society organisations to the place of the self-employed in the economic and political landscape (e.g. Royal Society of Arts 2014). While this attention is directed towards the reasons for the recent growth and the motivations behind it, and issues such as the living standards of the self-employed (rather than FSE), there is also some discussion of the political implications of the self-employed becoming a group 'for itself'. For example, there are advocates of collaboration between the self-employed and trade unions, recommending policies for recruitment of such workers into union membership. This is an alternative to views of the self-employed as either reluctant victims or thrusting entrepreneurs, a positive response to what these commentators see as a structural shift in economy and society, not a short-term reaction to austerity.

Conclusion

The earliest forms of industrial sociology, like most other areas of sociology, were based on the tacit assumption that the basic institutions in which workers had to operate and the essential roles for which they had to be prepared could be taken as given. Self-employment was a small and generally neglected category apart from some studies of the petty bourgeoisie. This orientation was largely overtaken by a sociology which placed collective, essentially institutional, conflict at its core. The origins and impact of industrial conflict became central problems of the discipline. Self-employment remained a marginal topic. Today, neither approach will serve because institutions, whether firms or unions, can no longer provide a stable framework or the capacity to steer collective action. They have been hollowed out, and the state of many workers is individually precarious. Returning to Touraine, in his latest contribution to the critique of modernity, he writes of this process in the following terms.

> If Society describes the use of resources according to a particular cultural pattern or orientation, shaped by social institutions such as the welfare state, the 'end of society' refers to the hollowing out of key institutions, a process that is marked by the loss of capacity for integration and control of the relationship between the system and actors.
>
> (Touraine 2013:38)

The case of FSE appears to fit this description perfectly in terms of the loss of capacity for integration between the economic system and the action of the employers and workers. However, Touraine is no pessimist. He remains committed to social and political action that can serve to increase the capacity of subjects to act with freedom and solidarity as they make their own history. His argument is also that under these conditions of the social void, the key to action is the awareness of rights, not as a universal given but as the outcome of struggles which express the creative power of the subject and lead to the growth of freedom. In the context of work relations, the principle refers to practical conduct and imagination which reinforce the individual's consciousness of being a worker over and above the particularities of their engagement, and a participant in the wider relations of production. The final sentences of the volume by Eldridge and colleagues cited earlier read: 'To show what possibilities may exist for political choices in an active democracy is to exercise the sociological imagination. If this is so, then industrial sociology itself is only in crisis when it fails this challenge' (Eldridge at al. 1991:220). The challenge of false self-employment is to imagine how to act to ensure that the rights and responsibilities of the working relationship are first made transparent and then made subject to principles of fairness and mutuality of obligation.

Notes

1. For example, HMRC (2014) describes FSE as a situation 'where someone whose engagement terms would dictate [they] should be treated as an employee falsely presents their terms and conditions as though they would be self-employed' (p. 20).
2. Wales Institute of Social & Economic Research, Data & Methods. WISERD is a collaborative venture between the universities of Aberystwyth, Bangor, Cardiff, University of South Wales and Swansea. The research was funded by the ESRC (grant number RES-576-25-0021) and the Higher Education Funding Council for Wales. Dr Sally Hester conducted the fieldwork.
3. In our own sector, the ongoing marketisation of higher education in the UK has led to the casualisation of larger numbers of workers, but we did not find examples of FSE in Higher Education in our pilot study. Where self-employment or freelance working occurs among research or teaching staff it appears to be a freely chosen option. The University and College Union campaign against casualisation is a useful point of reference for understanding these trends.

References

Bauman, Z. (1998) *Work, Consumerism and the New Poor.* Milton Keynes: Open University Press.
BBC Panorama (2011) *All Work and Low Pay,* BBC One, broadcast 3 October 2011.
Beck, U. (1992) *Risk Society: Towards a New Modernity.* London: Sage.
Beck, U. (2000) *The Brave New World of Work.* Cambridge: Polity Press.
Benner, C. (2002) *Work in the New Economy: Flexible Labour Markets in Silicon Valley.* Oxford: Blackwell Press.
Beynon, H., Grimshaw, D., Rubery, J. and Ward, K. (2002) *Managing Employment Change: The New Realities of Work.* Oxford: University Press.
Burchell, B., Deakin, S. and Honey, S. (1999) *The Employment Status of Individuals in Non-Standard Employment.* London: Department of Trade and Industry.

Crouch, C. (2011) *The Strange Non-Death of Neo-Liberalism*. Cambridge: Polity Press.
Davis, H. (1978) *Beyond Class Images: Explorations in the Structure of Social Consciousness*. London: Croom Helm.
Davis, H. (2015) 'Alain Touraine', in *International Encyclopaedia of Social and Behavioural Sciences*, 2nd ed. Oxford: Elsevier, pp. 459–64.
Dellot, B. and Reed, H. (2015) *Boosting the Living Standards of the Self-Employed*. London: Royal Society of Arts.
Eldridge, J. (1968) *Industrial Disputes: Essays in the Sociology of Industrial Relations*. London: Routledge and Kegan Paul.
Eldridge, J. (1971) *Sociology and Industrial Life*. London: Nelson/Joseph.
Eldridge, J., Cressey, P. and MacInnes, J. (1991) *Industrial Sociology and Economic Crisis*. Hemel Hempstead: Harvester Wheatsheaf.
Employment Appeal Tribunal (2011) 'Quashie vs. Stringfellow Restaurants Ltd', 05/07/2011 UKEATPA/1861/10.
Felstead, A. and Jewson, N. (1999) *In Work, At Home: Towards and Understanding of Homeworking*. Oxford: Routledge.
Felstead, A., Jewson, N. and Walters, S. (2004) *Changing Places of Work*. Basingstoke: Palgrave Macmillan.
Freedman, J. (2001) *Employed or Self-Employed? Tax Classification of Workers and the Changing Labour Market*. IFS Working Papers (DP1), London: Institute of Fiscal Studies.
Gorz, A. (1999) *Reclaiming Work: Beyond the Wage-Based Society*. Cambridge: Polity Press.
Harrison, B. (1997) *Lean and Mean: The Changing Landscape of Corporate Power in the Age of Flexibility*. New York: Guilford Press.
Harvey, D. (2005) *A Brief History of Neoliberalism*. Oxford: University Press.
Harvey M. (2001) *Undermining Construction*. London: Institute of Employment Rights.
Harvey, M. and Behling, F. (2008) *Self-Employment and Bogus Self-Employment in the European Construction Industry*, http://www.academia.edu/311458/Self-Employment_and_Bogus_SelfEmployment_In_the_European_Construction_Industry, date accessed: 7 January 2015.
HM Revenue & Customs (2013) *Onshore Employment Intermediaries: False Self-Employment Consultation document*, HMRC Consultation document 10 December.
HM Revenue & Customs (2014) *Onshore Employment Intermediaries: False Self-Employment. Summary of Responses*, HMRC 13 March.
Hyman, R. (1981) 'Whatever Happened to Industrial Sociology?', in D. Dunkerley and G. Salaman (eds.) *International Yearbook of Organisation Studies, 1981*. London: Routledge & Kegan Paul, pp. 84–104.
Jorens, Y., Gillis, D., Valcke, L. and De Coninck, J. (2015) *Atypical Forms of Employment in the Civil Aviation Sector*. Brussels: European Commission: European Social Dialogue; available online at: https://www.eurocockpit.be/sites/default/files/report_atypical_employment_in_aviation_15_0212_f.pdf
Layard, R.G., Nickel, S. J. and Jackman, R. (2005) *Unemployment: Macroeconomic Performance and the Labour Market*. Oxford: Oxford University Press.
McGovern, P., Smeaton, D. and Hill, S. (2004) 'Bad Jobs in Britain: Nonstandard Employment and Job Quality', *Work & Occupations*, 31 (2), 225–49.

Muehlberger, U. (2007) *Dependent Self-Employment: Workers on the Border Between Employment and Self-Employment.* Basingstoke: Palgrave Macmillan.

Nolan, J. (2002) 'The Intensification of Everyday Life', in B. Burchell, D. Ladipo and F. Wilkinson (eds.) *Job Insecurity and Work Intensification.* London: Routledge, pp. 112–36.

Noon, N. and Blyton, P. (2002) *The Realities of Work.* London: Palgrave.

Office for National Statistics (2014) *Self-Employed Workers in the UK – 2014*, http://www.ons.gov.uk/ons/dcp171776_374941.pdf, date accessed: 6 January 2014.

Pollert, A. (1998) 'The "Flexible Firm": Fixation or Fact?', *Work, Employment and Society*, 2 (3): 281–316.

Purcell, K., Hogarth, T. and Simm, C. (1999) *Whose Flexibility? The Costs and Benefits of Non-Standard Working Arrangements and Contractual Relations.* York: Joseph Rowntree Foundation.

Rifkin, J. (1995) *The End of Work: The Decline of the Global Labour Force and the Dawn of the Post-Market Era.* New York: Putnam.

Royal Society of Arts (2014) *Salvation in a Start-up?*, http://www.thersa.org/__data/assets/pdf_file/0004/1543855/Salvation-in-a-start-up-report-180714.pdf, date accessed: 8 January 2015.

Sennett, R. (1998) *The Corrosion of Character: The Personal Consequences of Work in the New Capitalism.* London: W. W. Norton.

Sennett, R. (2006) *The Culture of the New Capitalism.* New Haven, CT and London: Yale University Press.

Standing, G. (2009) *Work after Globalization: Building Occupational Citizenship.* Cheltenham: Edward Elgar.

Standing, G. (2011) *The Precariat: The New Dangerous Class.* London: Bloomsbury Academic.

Strangleman, T. and Warren, T. (2010) *Work and Society: Sociological Approaches, Themes and Methods.* London: Routledge.

Touraine, A. (1965) *La conscience ouvrière.* Paris: Seuil.

Touraine, A. (1974) 'Towards a Sociology of Action', in A. Giddens (ed.) *Positivism and Sociology.* London: Heinemann, pp. 75–100.

Touraine, A. (1981) 'The New Social Conflicts: Crisis or Transformation?' in C.C. Lemert (ed.) *French Sociology.* New York: Columbia University Press, pp. 313–31.

Touraine, A. (2013) *La fin des sociétés.* Paris: Seuil.

Touraine, A., Durand, C., Pecaut, D. and Willener, A. (1965) *Workers' Attitudes to Technical Change: An Integrated Survey of Research.* Paris: O.E.C.D.

Part II
Social Theory

6
On the (Alternative) Worlds That We Have Lost: *Sociology and The Third Way* Revisited

Matt Dawson

This chapter is inspired by a paper, entitled 'Sociology and the Third Way', published by John Eldridge in 2000. Written at the height of Anthony Giddens's fame as 'Blair's Brain', Eldridge traced the history of sociologists engaging in public debate by drawing upon ideas of 'third' ways. Taking in Durkheim, Hobhouse, Mannheim, Dahrendorf and Giddens, Eldridge argued that 'the history of sociology is replete with examples of sociologists who want to make academic and political contributions to their societies' and that, in doing so, 'what the sociologists offer is not a sociological theory as such, but an interpretation of where we are and where we might go which is sociologically informed' (Eldridge 2000:143).

In the years since this paper was published its argument remains true as a historical statement about sociology, especially in Britain, but increasingly sociologists have stopped engaging in debates on social reconstruction. In short, sociologists have stopped offering sociological alternatives. To demonstrate this I will first highlight some of the alternatives offered by sociologists; this will include a Third Way to add to the list from Eldridge, that of Patrick Geddes and Victor Branford. The second part of the chapter will then consider reasons for the decline in sociologists offering alternatives. In the conclusion I will turn to Ruth Levitas and her conception of sociology as a utopian activity.

Before this, some definition of my key term is needed: what exactly counts as a 'sociological alternative'? Here I partly refer to what was previously spoken of as social reconstruction, most famously in the book series founded by Mannheim on sociology and social reconstruction (Eldridge 2000:136). However, I also mean something more all-encompassing. To be exact, a sociological alternative has three components: the critical (a statement concerning 'problems' with society as currently constituted), the vision (an outline of a policy or model of society) and a justification (why this normative vision would solve the problems identified in the critique). So, to take one of the protagonists from Eldridge's chapter, we could argue that Durkheim had a clear sociological alternative since he formed a critique (the 'malaise' plaguing industrial society due to a lack of economic regulation), provided an alternative vision based upon occupational corporations and justified these as able to provide both the economic regulation and functional differentiation needed in modern society (see Dawson 2012). Durkheim provided a sociological view of where we are, as well as where we might, and should, go; therefore he offered a sociological alternative. It is this practice which I see as having declined in contemporary sociology.

The basis for claiming sociological alternatives

The tradition of offering 'sociologically informed' alternatives discussed in Eldridge's chapter is a notable one. In addition to the names mentioned above, if we see a sociological alternative as drawing upon a sociological conception rather than the scholar explicitly identifying as a 'sociologist' (though many also did), we can identify others, such as George Herbert Mead in his work on 'rational democracy' in Chicago (Cook 1993:99–114) in which he often collaborated with Jane Addams, most notably in the Hull House social settlement (Deegan 2013). It can be found in the work of W.E.B. Du Bois, both in his early focus on ways of developing the 'Talented Tenth' (Du Bois 1986) and later work on black economic cooperation (Du Bois 1984:173–220). Feminist sociology has also made a distinguished contribution to this field, whether it be Selma James (1975) advocating wages for housework, Angela Dworkin (1989) campaigning for the banning of pornography or work from scholars such as Sheila Rowbotham (1973) promoting consciousness-raising and revolutionary forms of action. Even Marxism, despite Marx's quip that he would not be 'writing recipes for the cookshops of the future' (Marx 1996:17), has a tradition of outlining forms a communist alternative could take, including from Marx himself, as well as from scholars such as Henri Lefebvre in his work on *autogestion* (1966) and Herbert Marcuse's call for the 'autonomy of the imagination' in a society based upon the 'aesthetic sensibility' (1969).

Another alternative is one within the lineage of Third Ways: the so-called 'Third Alternative' (Branford 1919a) offered by Patrick Geddes and Victor Branford. For them, sociology was central in offering alternatives since it had an empirical focus rather than being based on 'abstraction'; it was 'not only retrospective, but prospective' (Branford and Geddes 1919:15). This allowed it to develop the necessary practically orientated ideas since 'before we can really reconstruct we must have a definite vision of what we desire' (Branford 1919a:62). For Branford and Geddes, it is essential that sociologists do this, since other social sciences tended to 'put their faith in the primacy of money over goods and life', following the lead of university management who are 'an institution well adapted to a financial age' (Branford 1919b:144).

The alternative offered by these two sociologists was, like all Third Ways, defined in opposition to capitalism and socialism – notably in opposition to the distributionist and guild socialist ideas prominent on the left at the time (Scott and Bromley 2013:191–4) – and had three key elements. The first, drawing on knowledge from Branford's day job in finance, advocated a system of 'social credit', whereby credit was made available to small businesses and organisations on social rather than financial grounds. The second element was the expansion of cooperatives. Cooperative banks should be encouraged since they can provide this social credit at the direction of their members, who will then set out to produce 'goods and services valued by the community as equivalent to the given credit' (Branford 1919b:149). Furthermore, there should be a greater use of consumer cooperatives because of their 'practical' and everyday orientation. Indeed:

> If [co-operatives] come about, as we trust it may, our modern tragic antagonism – of capitalism, with its sadly unideal practice, and socialism with its sadly unpractical ideals – must alike steadily rise and merge into a truly practical – yet nobly idealised – everyday life of true, that is, full and developed, Co-operation.
>
> (Geddes 1888:308)

The third and final element was what led Geddes and Branford to link their third alternative to the school of sociology as civics (Geddes 1904): the use of 'conservative surgery' to remake cities which would be the recipient of a devolution of power away from nation-states and their 'war capitals' (Geddes and Slater 1917). Geddes' plans for city rebuilding tended to have two key elements: one was the greater availability of public spaces for meetings and civic activity; the second was a greater link between universities and their surrounding communities. While Geddes' most detailed plans for conservative surgery were developed during his time in India (Scott and Bromley 2013:118–23), the principles of his ideals can be seen on the streets of Edinburgh's Old Town where the Outlook Tower, now the Camera Obscura, was purchased by Geddes and turned into the 'world's first sociological laboratory' (Zueblin 1899). Geddes then went about replanning parts of the wynds off the Royal Mile, including the building of co-ed student housing and the improvement of housing generally recognised as 'slums'; a label Geddes set out to challenge by moving in. Geddes' sociological alternative can be seen on the streets of Edinburgh, where you can now take the 'Patrick Geddes Heritage Trail' to see his work (Johnson and Rosenberg 2010).

Therefore, Geddes and Branford demonstrate the breadth and visionary element of sociological alternatives as well as how these manifested themselves in Third Ways. In their case they hoped such changes would provide the balance between the 'temporal' (money and industry) and 'spiritual' powers (collective good and the relation to the natural environment) in modern society (see Scott and Bromley 2013).

Sociological alternatives today

It is difficult to identify the same utilisation of sociological alternatives in the discipline today. The detailed construction of alternatives, the visionary element, has largely disappeared from the field. Instead, what has become dominant is the first part of sociological alternatives: critique. The idea of sociology as a 'critical' activity has become central to the point of ubiquity, such that to accuse sociological work of being uncritical is 'a criticism verging on the insulting' (Levitas 2013:99). This critical approach is central to recent attempts to reimagine the discipline found in public sociology (Burawoy 2005), live sociology (Back 2012), punk sociology (Beer 2014), experiencing sociology (Fraser 2009) and lyrical sociology (Abbott 2007), among others. This idea of sociology being 'critical' would have been anathema to many of the aforementioned sociological alternative scholars. For example, in Mannheim's Third Way, while sociology is useful since it can outline the rules of social interaction, the outcome and content of these rules is irrelevant since 'to the sociologist the social conditions which produce a gangster are as relevant as the social conditions which make for the development of a good citizen' (Mannheim 1943:136). This was why Mannheim advocated the universal teaching of sociology; not to create critical, enlightened citizens but rather since what Mannheim terms the 'new ruling class' of The Third Way will need to 'manipulate' the 'social techniques' of society in order to produce consensus: 'only one who can see the important ramifications of each single step can act with responsibility required by the complexity of the modern age', and it is the development of this vision which sociology can assist with (Mannheim 1951:xviii and ff). Indeed, for Mannheim, sociology has a central role to play in the first stage of education, where the goal is to teach 'basic conformity, cohesion, habit-making, emotional training, obedience' to shared social values which sociology has helped define and promote (Mannheim 1943:52).

It is also important to note that the object and function of critique has shifted. As has been outlined by Boltanski (2002), following the events of 1968 we increasingly move from a social critique (based upon the understanding of structural factors and often drawing upon political economy) to an artistic critique (based upon a concern with diverse identities and taking individual emancipation as its goal). While, of course, this is an ideal type split and it is possible to identify sociologists who draw on both forms of critique, this does change the normative ends of sociology. The focus on individual emancipation, pluralised identities and political formations makes the visionary role of alternatives much more challenging. It is hard, for example, to imagine a critical sociology based upon the artistic critique sharing Mannheim's claim that 'the vital needs of the community should everywhere and always override the privileges of individuals' (Mannheim 1943:9), or G.D.H. Cole's claim that the purpose of social theory is 'to tell people how to be socially good' (Cole 1950:10).

It is beyond the scope of this discussion to either condemn or praise this sociology of critique, so at this point I just note the trend. Importantly, however, this shift to critique has not been accompanied with the open proclamation of alternatives. This is despite a clear contradiction: to be critical and say something is negative implies the conception of an alternative good which should be sought out. Therefore, while it may be tempting to stop here and say that the shift to critique, and to a greater focus on the artistic critique, has caused the decline of work which develops sociological alternatives, this would be mistaken. After all, many of the sociological alternatives outlined above use an artistic critique, including Geddes and Branford, as well as Marcuse and Lefebvre. Therefore, let us now turn to possible reasons for the decline in the mapping out of sociological alternatives.

Reasons for the decline

In what follows I identify seven potential explanations for the decline in sociological alternatives. These partly draw upon trends noted in the discipline during recent years; however, below I relate these specifically to the discussion of sociological alternatives. All of the possible explanations have solid points to make, though no one explanation is entirely satisfactory.

The first picks up on the shift in the form of critique, and argues that a reason for this could be the decline in the power of intellectuals: we can say whatever we want; the powers that be are unlikely to take our advice. Moreover, we are even less likely to be the powers that be. This is a point made by Fredrick Cooper in his review of post-colonialism, where he argues that:

> the increased prominence of colonial studies comes at a time when intellectuals are profoundly disillusioned with their own possibilities for influencing social change. To locate racial and cultural hierarchy and exclusion in the heart of 'postenlightenment rationality' is to make such a sweeping point that one is justified in doing nothing about it. Such a move privileges one side of the intellectual's place in society, that of a critic.
> (Cooper 2002:48–9)

The awareness of such potential influence was indeed a central factor in earlier sociological alternatives; reading them now one is struck by the expectation on the part of the authors that they will be listened to, an expectation often realised. For example, Marcuse was considered so dangerous in his role as academic voice of the New Left that he was denounced publicly by Pope Paul VI as opening 'the way to licence cloaked as liberty', by *Pravda* as a 'false prophet' and by Ronald Reagan, then governor of California, as 'not qualified to teach' (Katz 1982:173–4). Indeed, things got so bad that at one point Marcuse's PhD students would guard his house at night in light of death threats addressed to 'Filthy Communist Anti-American Professor Herbert Marcuse' (Katz 1982:175–6).

This is an important point; however, it may also exaggerate the influence of intellectuals in the past. For example, Fournier's (2013) biography of Durkheim makes clear his subject's worries that he was not being listened to and that his project would die with him. Furthermore, such a role was not open to all academics. While Marcuse and others certainly had their audience some were not so lucky, a fact which partly inspired Du Bois' move into activism and his claim that 'one could not be a calm, cool, and detached scientist while Negroes were lynched, murdered and starved' (Du Bois 1984:67).

This then leads us to the second explanation, which focuses on the outcome of this sense of intellectual power. Perhaps what marks out the current generation of sociologists is that they lack the formal and informal links to power found in the membership of political parties, learned societies and other forms of social capital. This is especially true in Britain where, as Raymond Aron once put it, initially sociology was an attempt to 'solve the intellectual problems of the Labour Party' (Halsey 2004:110) and, as Maggie Studholme (1997) argues, Giddens's Third Way is partly an attempt to re-establish the links with New Liberal politics found in Hobhouse's work. Indeed, when the Sociological Society was formed in 1904 it demonstrated this link by counting among its members a future Liberal (Asquith) and Labour (Macdonald) Prime Minister, as well as a clutch of MPs (Scott and Bromley 2013:57). It is also true that many of those involved in developing sociological alternatives had close party and/or social movement links: Hobhouse with the Liberals; Addams with the Republican then Progressive parties; and Marxists with their respective parties. Meanwhile, feminists maintained their traditionally strong links to social movements, such as in Selma James's formation and leadership of the International Wages for Housework campaign.

Again, this has some truth, but it obscures the fact that some of those committed to constructing sociological alternatives specifically rejected a link to any party, such as in Durkheim's resistance to joining the Socialist Party and advocacy of corporations in contradiction to the party's Marxian position. Meanwhile, Lefebvre was thrown out of the French Communist party partly because his alternative was contrary to the Stalinist line at the time. Furthermore, Max Weber had as strong a party link, in his case to the German liberals, as any other sociologist but, as we know, eschewed the offering of normative claims. Therefore, while links to a political party and/or social movement certainly encourage thinking through alternatives – and provide an outlet for them – the decline in these relationships would not seem an entirely convincing explanation for the shift which I have identified.

A third explanation, linked to the previous two, is the change in expectation regarding the intentions of politicians and governments. Boardman's biography of Geddes notes that:

> With complete faith in the good intentions of the Allied nations thoroughly chastened by four years of war, [Geddes] believed that he had only to point out certain causes of the world conflict and to sketch the kind of material and spiritual reconstruction that Europe

would find imperative. Surely the people were this time for a genuine 'Making of the Future'.

(Boardman 1944:364)

Not only does this indicate a belief in the ability of intellectuals to be heard, but also in the good faith and noble intentions of governments. However, what we might call the disenchantment or alienation of publics from politicians has, as Hay (2007:162) notes, also been true of academics. This could be seen as problematic when so many sociological alternatives, such as Dworkin's campaign to ban pornography or Mannheim's Third Way, rely upon a powerful and willing governmental force. To use a phrase from Bauman, sociologists have given up their state-dependent role as legislators and instead become interpreters (Bauman 1987).

However, many sociological alternatives have not relied on state action. For example, Mead's moves towards creating a rational democracy were solely local and relied more often on voluntary action and the civil sphere than on regional or national government (Deegan and Berger 1978). Furthermore, Durkheim's alternative specifically sought to lessen the power of the state since, for him, 'government, instead of regulating economic life, has become its tool and servant' (Durkheim 1952:216). The fact that so many sociological alternatives did not rely upon the power of the nation-state suggests that reliance on state power is not necessary for alternatives.

Thus far we have considered factors external to the academic discipline of sociology, so now let us turn to questions of intellectual history: what has happened to the theories and tools used by sociologists which could account for this decline? An initial response is to ascribe the search for sociological alternatives in the past to the discipline's search for scientific recognition. After all, many linked their advocacy of alternatives to the scientific status of sociology, such as in Branford and Geddes' (1919:20) claim that sociology is 'a task for experimental solution'. However, some advocates of sociological alternatives found the quest for scientific recognition uncomfortable. As we saw, Du Bois rejected the role of 'detached' scientist for his own advocacy of alternatives and Mead claimed that 'the academic attitude of creating problems for Doctor's theses is not favourable to the just realisation of what problems are when they are genuine' (Mead 1938:326). Indeed, as Turner (2014) has shown in relation to American sociology, the quest for scientific legitimacy has led more often to a decline in the construction of sociological alternatives than the opposite.

A different angle is to claim that the decline of grand theory and emergence of postmodern and poststructuralist positions, with their attempts to reject universalising claims, are not conducive to the broad, societal-wide claims made by many sociological alternatives. An obvious victim here would be Marxist alternatives. It is also difficult to imagine many sociologists, postmodernist or not, now fully subscribing to Hobhouse's emphasis on progress and evolution in his sociological alternative (Hobhouse 1994). In turn, as a result of the emergence of the 'post' theories, we are left with critique without an alternative, or, as Bauman once put it in reference to Baudrillard, there is only the 'sweet scent of decomposition' (Bauman 1993).

This is an alluring explanation and one which would seem to find an echo in Giddens's vociferous attempts to distance himself from postmodernism (Giddens 1994:83). However, it would be short-sighted to entirely dismiss the potential for the visionary elements of alternatives within 'post' theories. As Sargisson has noted in her work on contemporary feminist utopianism, poststructuralism and postmodernist approaches have proven fruitful since 'deconstruction and utopianism destroy and create simultaneously...one cannot occur without the other' (Sargisson 1996:111). The rejection of binary formulations at the heart of the postmodern project expands the potential and reach of utopianism, of outlining alternatives, in contemporary feminism. Sargisson's argument seems to convincingly demonstrate that an adherence to a postmodernist approach does not necessarily exclude the possibility of outlining ideas for different worlds and, indeed, can expand their potential.

To this point we have considered the following reasons as to why sociological alternatives are less prominent today: the decline in ideas of intellectual's power and reach; the severing of the links between the academy and political parties/social movements; the lack of a clear agent to enact change in light of the decline of the nation-state; the early quest for scientific recognition; and the rise of the poststructuralist/postmodernist positions. I have suggested that while many of these explanations have some worthwhile points to make, none fully explain the decrease in sociological alternatives. There are two further explanations which, while also not perfect as explanations, seem particularly useful. These concern the political position of sociologists and whether we should be offering alternatives in the first place.

To start with political position, it could be argued that sociologists do not offer alternatives any more because there is an assumed consensus as to what we desire: a social democracy with a strong welfare state. This, it could be argued, is because of the decline of two groups prominent throughout sociology's history: a Marxist left and a conservative right. To start with the latter, the decline of the right is notable in sociology. While Peter Saunders (2011) has been most vociferous in bemoaning the leftward turn of British sociology, this shift was also indicated in the decline of the centre and moderate right in Halsey's survey of sociology professors (Halsey 2004:162). There are other examples. As I noted earlier, Jane Addams was for much of her life a member of the Republican Party and while a member of its progressive wing, later joining that party, she was part of the 35 per cent of early US sociologists who aligned themselves with the Republicans against 15 per cent Democrat and 3 per cent Socialist, indicating a significant political plurality which later disappeared (Carey 1975:49–55). Furthermore, Peter Berger's autobiography, which speaks proudly of his work spying on anti-smoking groups for tobacco companies (Berger 2011:169–75), also makes clear his alienation from sociology because of his belief that 'sociology is radical in its debunking analysis but conservative in its practical implications' (Berger 2011:176).

With the decline of this right wing, it is striking how much sociology has become associated with the left, both outside and within the discipline. For example, discussing her appointment as President of the Pontifical Academy of Social Sciences, Margaret Archer defends the sociological imagination of pontifical teaching on the basis of the *Rerum Novarum*, since 'it's a remarkably radical document – it's leftist and progressive rather than rightist and defensive. So it's not difficult to extend the sociological imagination – it's there already' (Archer, quoted in Trueman 2014:27). Here being left wing is taken as, *ipso facto*, being sociological.

However, this period has also seen the decline of a Marxist left, especially since 1989, in sociology. This has in turn meant a greater coalescing around other forms of socialism (always strong in Britain) or social democracy, thus creating the aforementioned political consensus around the welfare state. Such a consensus has also been encouraged by political factors; the attack on welfare provision by governments throughout the world and the historic link sociologists have had with the welfare state (Gouldner 1968) has helped forge a consensus in its defence.

Giddens is the greatest example of this shift within the sociological left. Reading his engagement with Marxism in his *Contemporary Critique of Historical Materialism* now, what is striking is not only Giddens's depth and appreciation for Marx's work, but also his identification with some of its precepts, most notably the value of praxis (Giddens 1993:2, ff). In Volume 1 of the *Critique*, he identifies himself as a 'libertarian socialist' (Giddens 1993:175) and elsewhere at this time spoke openly about the need to embrace the emancipatory potential of socialism (Giddens et al. 1982:64–5). However, post-1989, we find Giddens arguing that 'the very idea of socialism, as Marx conceived of it at any rate, has been shown to be something of a dead-end' (Giddens 1993:x), and explicitly presenting The Third Way as a social democratic, not socialist, project. As part of this move he castigates much of the contemporary left for becoming 'conservative' in their defence of the welfare state (Giddens 1994:2) and focusing on the 'bads' of capitalism at the expense of the 'goods' (Giddens 1994:100–1). Perhaps the best indicator of Giddens's shift is that the book which announced his new allegiance, *Beyond Left and Right* (1994), was originally intended to form the third volume in the critique; originally to be titled *Between Capitalism and Socialism*, it would have considered how we could move to socialism in conditions of advanced capitalism (Giddens 1993:1).

Therefore, the increased political homogeneity of sociology has lessened the impetus for the debating of alternatives, in so far as we all know what we want. Giddens becomes an exception to this rule by positioning himself in opposition to this 'defensive' and 'conservative' consensus. This is in contrast to the situation in which past sociological alternatives were developed, which were incredibly politically diverse. It is hard to reconcile the alternatives offered by Marcuse and Lefebvre, say, which share a Marxist base, let alone those of, for example, Du Bois and Hobhouse.

This brings us to our final possible explanation: perhaps we shouldn't have been offering alternatives in the first place. Eldridge's chapter concludes with a reminder that for Weber 'ethical neutrality is, of course, not the same as moral indifference' and that his advice for sociologists to 'keep a cool head in the face of the ideals prevailing at the time...just might be more invigorating than floating along in the slipstream of the Third Way' (Eldridge 2000:143). In this reading, a Weberian position may permit critique as an appropriate mode of sociological investigation; however, to take the next step and engage in the offering of alternatives is to bring values into scientific discussion. We might also, to justify this position, point that out when sociologists have been in positions of power and/or have offered alternatives they have not necessarily been commendable. Recent scholarship has increasingly spoken about the involvement of sociologists and social scientists in regimes such as Nazism (Ingrao 2013), apartheid South Africa (Connell 2007:99) and, especially in Britain, the empire (Steinmetz 2013). Indeed, when the LSE Calendar for 1904–05 announced its first sociology class it said this would be useful for, among others, 'civil servants destined for the tropical portions of the Empire' (Husbands 2014:167). Therefore, as Connell (2007:9) notes, 'sociology was formed within the culture of imperialism'. Furthermore, the stories of Peter Berger's spying for tobacco companies, Giddens's hailing of Gaddafi's Libya as a potential 'Norway of North Africa' (Giddens 2007), Daniel Moynihan's role in the US War on Poverty and the Nixon administration as well as the history of eugenics in British sociology may give us pause for thought. Indeed, the engagement of sociologists in offering alternatives can sometimes reach the level of the farcical, such as the time that Geddes, now appealing to colonial powers in India for help in implementing his ideas of conservative surgery, planned a parade featuring white elephants. Discovering there were not any white elephants in that part of the country, Geddes just painted some pink elephants white (Boardman 1944:388). Perhaps, as John Carey has pointed out, the relations between intellectuals and the 'masses' has not been as progressive as the former would like to suggest (Carey 1992).

Given these precedents, then, is it possible to say sociologists can or should avoid offering alternatives? To answer this I want to turn to the work of Ruth Levitas.

Levitas on sociology and Utopia

I am not the first to note the lack of sociological alternatives in the contemporary discipline; indeed this has been a key part of Levitas's recent work in which she has noted that the goal of contemporary sociology is 'critique, not utopia, for "utopian" remained a derogatory term' (Levitas 2013:95). I want to discuss Levitas's work not only since, for me, it provides a vital way of thinking about the craft of sociology, but also because it hinges on this question of whether sociologists should offer alternatives.

For Levitas, we must first define utopia as 'the expression of the desire for a better way of being or of living', a definition clouded in the rush to ascribe 'utopianism' to the fanciful or dangerous (Levitas 2013:xii). This makes utopianism an omnipresent part of human praxis; it is 'braided through human culture' (Levitas 2013:xii) as well as an appropriate topic for sociology. More importantly for our discussion, it delineates a clear ground for utopia as a 'method' of sociological analysis based within what Levitas calls the imaginary reconstruction of society.

This involves three elements: the archaeological (trawling through writings and proclamations to discover the desired end of such ideas), the architectural (constructing this ideal society) and the ontological (the conception of human nature drawn upon in this vision) (Levitas 2013). It is only when this utopian method is employed that a truly critical sociology is possible. Levitas has applied this method to the neo-liberalism of New Labour, which led her to conclude that:

> In Blair's fantasy land, the rich deserve their wealth and are not resented. The poor have presumably abolished themselves through the saving grace of working in McDonald's and call centres, ventures indirectly subsidised through tax credits. Children have stopped playing truant partly through fear of police sweeps, and partly because they understand the consequences of educational failure. Teenagers do not have unprotected sex. People accept their obligation to maintain their employability, so that they can exploit the changing opportunities provided by markets, make individual provision against risk, discharge their obligations as parents and active citizens when they have done earning a living. (They are too tired to protest on May Day, and know anyway that all demonstrators are anarchists, meaning mindless thugs, or anti-capitalists, meaning much the same.) Continuing growth ensures a rising tax take without increased tax rates. Public funds can thus be used to underwrite essential services, mainly contracted out to the private sector where successful businesses (or, increasingly, multi-national concerns) make profits subsidised out of taxation.
>
> (Levitas 2001:458–9)

However, for Levitas, sociologists themselves also engage in the imaginary reconstruction of society. Even when not openly offering alternatives, and indeed sometimes rejecting claims of utopianism, much 'critical' sociology is utopian since it relies upon an unspoken image of the good society with which to critique the current form, meaning:

> sociologists carry silent utopias in their work, both as inspiration and substance. Most sociologists who work in fields of social inequality – economic inequality, class, gender, ethnicity – are driven by a critical conviction that these inequalities are damaging and wrong. Somewhere underpinning this is an implicit idea of a good society in which such inequalities are absent.
>
> (Levitas 2010:538)

And this is where Levitas turns to a forgotten figure in British sociology: H.G. Wells (Levitas 2010). As she highlights, Wells was a frequent contributor to sociological circles in the first years of the twentieth century and was, for a while, considered a candidate – most notably by Wells himself – for the Martin White chair of Sociology at the LSE, the first sociology professorship in the UK (Levitas 2010:533–5). However, Wells's lasting contribution came in a paper given to the Sociological Society in 1906 titled 'The So-called Science of Sociology' (Wells 1907). In this piece Wells condemns the 'scientific pretension' of the subject since 'there is no such thing in sociology as dispassionately considering what *is*, without considering what is *intended to be*' (Wells 1907:364; 366–7). Therefore, Wells defends a sociology which engages in the 'exhaustive criticism' of utopias, as in Levitas's critique of New Labour, as well as in their construction (Wells 1907:367).

Therefore, following Wells, for Levitas utopianism is unavoidable in sociology. If sociology criticises and argues that something is negative or bad, it implies a world, most likely imaginary, in which such a thing doesn't exist: it engages in utopianism via the imaginary reconstruction of society. For Levitas, the fact Wells was not appointed to the Martin White chair and effectively 'gave up' on the discipline was an indicator of its search for scientific recognition and the attempt to suppress the utopian impulse present within sociology (Levitas 2010:538). However, to be silent on alternatives is not, despite the intent, to eschew utopianism since:

> While sociologists may legitimately claim particular competence in understanding systemic connections and mapping alternatives, they of course do not have any such claim to superior ethical competence. Wells referred also to the exhaustive criticism of utopias, and this is a matter both for professional expertise and for democratic public debate. If sociologists do not engage in this way, they cede the ground to others, chiefly engineers, global capitalists, and evolutionary psychologists. Our very silences shape utopias.
> (Levitas 2010:546)

As we have seen, for Levitas, utopianism is an inherent part of human existence, and for sociology to reject this is to allow others the ground; others who may lack a sociological imagination. Levitas doesn't pretend this work is easy, or claim that it will have an immediate impact; sociology and society more broadly remain suspicious of utopianism. However,

Sociology must reclaim utopia, those normative, prescriptive, future-oriented elements that have suffused the discipline from the beginning, but are too often a cause of embarrassment rather than celebration. It needs to be released from damaging self-censorship, and turn to the vision of a better world that is so often what draws people to the discipline in the first place... [Sociologists] should have something to contribute to understanding systemic connections and thus mapping alternatives. If sociology has nothing to offer here, I really don't know quite what it is for.

(Levitas 2013:217)

Conclusion

In a recent piece on sociology as a 'third culture' Eldridge argues that 'sociology is an untidy subject, with blurred boundaries, theoretical disputes, arguments about its purposes and disagreements over the role of value judgements' (Eldridge 2014:354). I have perhaps demonstrated the untidy nature of the discipline during this chapter. In particular, we have seen how the various justifications, forms and positioning of sociological alternatives reflect the intellectual diversity of, and disputes in, the discipline. However, I hope I have also shown that there is a large body of sociological literature which does, in varying ways, engage in the process of offering alternatives. Furthermore, as the work of Levitas has suggested, doing so has an intellectual justification. It is not my intention to claim as a result of this that every single article or book should list alternatives at the end, or even that this should become a majority occupation. Instead, I can probably indicate my intention best with a story.

In 1904, at the second meeting of the Sociological Society at the LSE, a paper written for the occasion by Durkheim and his collaborator Paul Fauconnet was read out by the philosopher Bernard Bosanquet (Renwick 2012:139). Entitled 'Sociology and the Social Sciences', it notes a worrying trend: sociologists tend to spend a large amount of time talking about what their discipline *should* look like when in fact

> Sociology exists; it has a history displaying its nature; there is, therefore, no place for efforts to imagine what it is. We can observe it. Though no good purpose is served in disputing *in abstrato* what the science ought to be, there is on the contrary a real interest in becoming acquainted with the course of its development, in giving

an account of the various elements whence it resulted, and of the parts they occupy respectively in the whole structure.

(Durkheim and Fauconnet 1905:259)

More than 100 years after Durkheim and Fauconnet wrote these words sociology is still spending much time debating what it is and should be. It may be, as Bauman has suggested (Bauman 1978:225–46), that such existential questions are integral to a discipline hoping to respond to the challenge of hermeneutics. However, even if this is the case, we should not forget their reminder that sociology has a history; it has been sociology for at least 150 years. As Eldridge's work argues, it has often been a discipline engaged in offering alternatives. This tradition has been lost in sociology, despite what Levitas highlights regarding our implicit utopianism, and it is up to us to decide if we want it back.

References

Abbott, A. (2007) 'Against Narrative: A Preface to Lyrical Sociology', *Sociological Theory*, 25 (1): 67–99.
Back, L. (2012) 'Live Sociology', *Sociological Review*, 60 (S1): 18–39.
Bauman, Z. (1978) *Hermeneutics and Social Science*. London: Routledge.
Bauman, Z. (1987) *Legislators and Interpreters: On Modernity, Post-Modernity and Intellectuals*. Cambridge: Polity Press.
Bauman, Z. (1993) 'The Sweet Scent of Decomposition', in C. Rojek and B.S. Turner (eds.) *Forget Baudrillard?*. London: Routledge, pp. 22–46.
Beer, D. (2014) *Punk Sociology*. Hampshire: Palgrave Macmillan.
Berger, P. (2011) *Adventures of an Accidental Sociologist: How to Explain the World without Becoming a Bore*. New York: Prometheus Books.
Boardman, P. (1944) *Patrick Geddes: Maker of the Future*. Chapel Hill: University of North Carolina Press.
Boltanski, L. (2002) 'The Left after May 1968 and the Longing for Total Revolution', *Thesis Eleven*, 69: 1–20.
Branford, V. (1919a) 'Towards the Third Alternative', *Sociological Review*, 11 (1): 62–5.
Branford, V. (1919b) 'The Third Alternative', *Sociological Review*, 11 (2): 142–51.
Branford, V. and Geddes, P. (1919) *The Coming Polity*. London: Williams and Norgate.
Burawoy, M. (2005) 'For Public Sociology', *American Sociological Review*, 70 (1): 4–28.
Carey, J. (1975) *Sociology and Public Affairs: The Chicago School*. Beverley Hills, CA: Sage.
Carey, J. (1992) *The Intellectuals and the Masses: Pride and Prejudice among the Literary Intelligentsia, 1880–1939*. London: Faber and Faber.
Cole, G.D.H. (1950) 'Scope and Method in Social and Political Theory', in G.D.H. Cole, *Essays in Social Theory*. London: Macmillan, pp. 1–16.

Connell, R. (2007) *Southern Theory: The Global Dynamics of Knowledge in Social Science*. Cambridge: Polity Press.
Cook, G. (1993) *George Herbert Mead: The Making of a Social Pragmatist*. Chicago: University of Illinois Press.
Cooper, F. (2002) 'Decolonising Situations: The Rise, Fall and Rise of Colonial Studies, 1951–2001', *French Politics, Culture and Society*, 20 (2): 47–76.
Dawson, M. (2012) 'Autonomous Functions of all Countries, Unite! You Have Nothing to Lose but Your Economic Anomie'. Émile Durkheim's Libertarian Socialist Critique', *Critical Sociology*, 39 (5): 689–704.
Deegan, M. (2013) 'Jane Addams, the Hull-House School of Sociology, and Social Justice, 1892–1935', *Humanity & Society*, 37 (3): 248–58.
Deegan, M. and Berger, J. (1978) 'George Herbert Mead and Social Reform: His Work and Writings', *Journal of the History of Behavioural Sciences*, 14 (4): 362–73.
Du Bois, W.E.B. (1984) *Dusk of Dawn: An Essay Toward an Autobiography of a Race Concept*. London: Transaction Publishers.
Du Bois, W.E.B. (1986) 'The Talented Tenth' in W.E.B. Du Bois, *W.E.B. Du Bois: Writings*. New York: The Library of America, pp. 815–26.
Durkheim, E. (1952) *Suicide*. London: Routledge.
Durkheim, E. and Fauconnet, P. (1905) 'Sociology and the Social Sciences', in Sociological Society (eds) *Sociological Society Sociological Papers 1904*. London: Macmillan, pp. 258–80.
Dworkin, A. (1989) *Pornography: Men Possessing Women*. London: Penguin.
Eldridge, J. (2000) 'Sociology and the Third Way', in J. Eldridge et al. (eds.) *For Sociology: Legacies and Prospects*. Durham: Sociology Press, pp. 131–44.
Eldridge, J. (2014) 'Between Science and Humanities: Sociology as a Third Culture?' in J. Holmwood and J. Scott (eds.) *The Palgrave Handbook of Sociology in Britain*. Hampshire: Palgrave Macmillan, pp. 338–59.
Fournier, M. (2013) *Émile Durkheim: A Biography*. Cambridge: Polity Press.
Fraser, M. (2009) 'Experiencing Sociology', *European Journal of Social Theory*, 12 (1): 63–81.
Geddes, P. (1888) 'Co-operation *versus* Socialism', *Co-operative Wholesales Societies Annual for 1888*, 285–308.
Geddes, P. (1904) 'Civics as Applied Sociology', in Sociological Society (eds.), *Sociological Papers 1904*. London: Macmillan, pp. 103–18.
Geddes, P. and Slater, G. (1917) *Ideas at War*. London: Williams and Norgate.
Giddens, A. (1993) *A Contemporary Critique of Historical Materialism: Power, Property and the State*. 2nd Ed., London: Macmillan.
Giddens, A. (1994) *Beyond Left and Right*. Cambridge: Polity Press.
Giddens, A. (2007) 'My Chat with the Colonel', *Guardian*, 9 March, http://www.theguardian.com/commentisfree/2007/mar/09/comment.libya, date accessed: 30 August 2014.
Giddens, A., Bleicher, J. and Featherstone, M. (1982) 'Historical Materialism Today: An Interview with Anthony Giddens', *Theory, Culture & Society*, 1 (2): 63–77.
Gouldner, A. (1968) 'The Sociologist as Partisan: Sociology and the Welfare State', *The American Sociologist*, 3 (2): 103–16.
Halsey, A.H. (2004) *A History of Sociology in Britain*. Oxford: Oxford University Press.

Hay, C. (2007) *Why We Hate Politics*. Cambridge: Polity Press.
Hobhouse, L.T. (1994) *Liberalism and Other Writings*. Cambridge: Cambridge University Press.
Husbands, C. (2014) 'The First Sociology "Departments"', in J. Holmwood and J. Scott (eds.) *The Palgrave Handbook of Sociology in Britain*. Hampshire: Palgrave Macmillan, pp. 155–88.
Ingrao, C. (2013) *Believe and Destroy: Intellectuals in the SS War Machine*. Cambridge: Polity Press.
James, S. (1975) 'Wageless of the World', in W. Edmond and S. Fleming (eds.) *All Work and No Pay: Women, Housework and the Wages Due*. London: Power of Women Collective and the Falling Wall Press, pp. 25–34.
Johnson, J. and Rosenberg, L. (2010) *Renewing Old Edinburgh: The Enduring Legacy of Patrick Geddes*. Argyll: Argyll Publishing.
Katz, B. (1982) *Herbert Marcuse and the Art of Liberation*. London: New Left Books.
Lefebvre, H. (1966) 'Theoretical Problems of *Autogestion*', in N. Brenner and S. Elden (eds.) (2009) *Henri Lefebvre: State, Space, World Selected Essays*. Minneapolis: University of Minnesota Press, pp. 138–52.
Levitas, R. (2001) 'Against Work: A Utopian Excursion into Social Policy', *Critical Social Policy*, 21 (4): 449–65.
Levitas, R. (2010) 'Back to the Future: Wells, Sociology, Utopia and Method', *Sociological Review*, 58 (4): 530–47.
Levitas, R. (2013) *Utopia as Method: The Imaginary Reconstruction of Society*. Hampshire: Palgrave Macmillan.
Mannheim, K. (1943) *Diagnosis of our Time: Wartime Essays of a Sociologist*. London: Routledge.
Mannheim, K. (1951) *Freedom, Power and Democratic Planning*. London: Routledge.
Marcuse, H. (1969) *An Essay on Liberation*. London: Allen Lane.
Marx, K. (1996) 'Afterword to the Second German Edition', in K. Marx and F. Engels, *Karl Marx and Frederick Engels Collected Works: Volume 35*. London: Lawrence & Wishart, pp. 12–22.
Mead, G.H. (1938) 'History and the Experimental Method', in G.H. Mead (1964) *On Social Psychology*. Chicago, IL: University of Chicago Press, pp. 319–27.
Renwick, C. (2012) *British Sociology's Lost Biological Roots: A History of Futures Past*. Hampshire: Palgrave Macmillan.
Rowbotham, S. (1973) *Woman's Consciousness, Man's World*. London: Penguin.
Sargisson, L. (1996) *Contemporary Feminist Utopianism*. London: Routledge.
Saunders, P. (2011) 'Academic Sociology and Social Policy Think Tanks in Britain and Australia: A Personal Reflection', *Sociological Research Online*, 16 (3): http://www.socresonline.org.uk/16/3/10.html, date accessed: 28 August 2014.
Scott, J. and Bromley, R. (2013) *Envisioning Sociology: Victor Branford, Patrick Geddes and the Quest for Social Reconstruction*. Albany: State University of New York Press.
Steinmetz, G. (2013) 'A Child of Empire: British Sociology and Colonialism', *Journal of the History of the Behavioural Sciences*, 49 (4): 353–78.
Studholme, M. (1997) 'From Leonard Hobhouse to Tony Blair: A Sociological Connection?', *Sociology*, 31 (3): 531–47.
Trueman, T. (2014) 'The Pope is Cleaning out the Stables from the Top-Down', *Network*, 117 (Summer): 26–8.

Turner, S. (2014) *American Sociology: From Pre-Disciplinary to Post-Normal*. Hampshire: Palgrave Macmillan.
Wells, H.G. (1907) 'The So-Called Science of Sociology', in Sociological Society, (eds) *Sociological Papers 1906*. London: Macmillan, pp. 357–69.
Zueblin, C. (1899) 'The World's First Sociological Laboratory', *American Journal of Sociology*, 4 (5): 577–92.

7
The Media and Collective Memory: The Obituaries of Academics

Bridget Fowler

My concern in this chapter is to start an exploratory analysis of the newspaper obituaries of academics. The ways of seeing such documents of life are many and varied. My own formative approach to this aspect of the media was indebted in part to John Eldridge, particularly for his sensitive understanding of the power-soaked nature of mass communications. But in dissecting obituaries I argue that we need other theoretical resources as well. Here I have drawn particularly on Halbwachs as the theorist of social memory and Bourdieu as the theorist of distinction and canon formation, reinforcing the approach taken in my earlier book on obituaries (Fowler 2007). Further, to address academics' obituaries I argue that we need to understand Bourdieu's *Homo Academicus* and *The State Nobility* as responses to Kant and Mannheim. This theoretical paving of the way is then followed by a content analysis of contemporary academics' obituaries, highlighting the unusual character of these obituaries as an unreciprocated gift exchange. Under Bourdieu's auspices, as it were, we note that these are fields whose actors have relatively privileged social origins but also troubles, springing either from the wider geopolitical clashes of power or from the field itself. I conclude by noting that many of these obituaries signal the dangers to intellectual autonomy within current university structures. Taking up Holmwood's striking words in his foreword to this volume, I also argue that it would be the worst form of sociological conformism or complicity not to draw attention to the undesirable side effects of managerialism, marketisation and league-table rationalisation to which these academic obituaries bear witness.

Obituaries: Theoretical approaches

When I first came to write on obituaries, many of my intellectual interests meshed closely with those of John Eldridge. We both deeply admired Raymond Williams, especially his analysis of how literary works may capture clashing structures of feeling at the maximum intensity (Eldridge 2014; Eldridge and Eldridge 1994; Williams 1977:128–35). John's work with the Media Group seems to me to tie into this element he admired so much in Williams, including his later distinctive essays detailing his own approaches to the media (Eldridge 1993, 1995a, 1995b). In particular, Eldridge, like Williams, had an enviable capacity to walk the knife-edge path between conspiracy theory on the one hand and an undiscriminating model of pluralism on the other: an outstanding example is Eldridge's *That Was the World that Was* (1995a; cf. Williams 1995).

But John adds other resources to these media studies, including the valuable insights gained from his studies of industrial conflict. He drew, for example, on symbolic interactionists to understand newsroom professional routines. Of these, his attention to Goffman, in particular, has been influential for my own ethnographic awareness of obituary editors' everyday procedures, including their framing assumptions (Beharrell et al. 1980; Eldridge 1995a). His reflections on Gouldner and Wright Mills are vital, especially their ways of addressing how power elites shape the 'contested terrain' of media as well as how conflicts within the public sphere often surface as private troubles (Eldridge 1983:58–60, 103–4, 75–7; 1993:15–24).

Perhaps the most striking evidence testifying to this appeared with the newspapers' reflections on Margaret Thatcher's death. These extremely long obituaries – *six pages* in *The Times* (9 April 2013), all, bar *The Independent*, highly positive – serve as an excellent example of how the media responds to political power. They reveal, in particular, how a figure from the elite is transferred via a commemorative cult from mere party prominence into the national pantheon. In Britain this occurs figuratively as a secular mark of honour to a distinguished individual; in France, physically: the deceased's body is transferred to the built monument of the Invalides or Panthéon (sometimes out again, as in the case of Marat) (Ben-Amos 2000:31). Yet a word of warning is also necessary here. Obituary editors have a complex relationship to power, refusing to serve as the mere amplifiers of economic orthodoxy or gatekeepers of vested political interests; this is particularly true of those newspapers with a tradition of dissent (such as *The Guardian* and *The Independent, Le Monde* in its first 30 years). For example, the Marxist historian, Christopher Hill, was *also* honoured with long obituaries despite having been a creative contributor to counter-hegemonic historical culture. Significantly, although Hill reinvigorated the Left, he also held a pivotal place within the British elite, having for long occupied that unusual space, the Mastership of Balliol, Oxford (*The Guardian* 26 February 2003; *Daily Telegraph* 27 February 2003) (Taylor and Steele 2011).

My intellectual and personal debts to John Eldridge have been too numerous to itemise here. But I was also led in a somewhat different direction, towards the sociology of Pierre Bourdieu. However, whereas many of those influenced by Bourdieu have stressed mainly his phenomenology (for example, Robbins 2006:528–35), his allegedly exclusive attention to language and other symbolic goods as resources of domination (Susen 2013), or his supposed lack of historical contextualisation (Calhoun 1993:68–9), I interpret him in a different way. In this chapter I want to draw on the Bourdieu *I* have read, who needs to be carefully separated from the many critiques attributing to him a neo-Michelsian 'iron law' of endless class or gender reproduction. Bourdieu does indeed show how profound inequality recurs and how such processes can even take on the guise of natural necessity, but he also has a theory of social transformation. In my own recent work I have tried to show how a less familiar Bourdieu can be mined for an understanding of historical points of crisis and change, a stance supported by Steinmetz (2011), Eyal et al. (1998) and Gorski (2013). Indeed, Gorski has gone so far as to say – rightly in my view – that '[t]o accuse Bourdieu of being a reproduction theorist is to confess that one has not read much of his work or that one has not read it very closely' (2013:11).

Bourdieu's theory of practice includes an unacknowledged debt to his French sociological predecessor, Maurice Halbwachs, who elaborated on the concept of 'collective memory'. Halbwachs had a pioneering understanding of social memory that has certain parallels with Durkheim's notion of collective representations. His inventive use leans heavily on the power of the group, including the social spaces and ceremonies linked to the group which together help individuals remember. It thus offers a powerful riposte to radical individualism and an outstanding gain to the sociological imagination. This is particularly true given that Halbwachs is remarkably free from the Romantic organicism with which he is sometimes charged (see Osiel 1997). For example, in referring to the significance of the 1871 Commune in the collective memory of the French, he carefully differentiates between dominant or official memory on the one hand and the memory of servants or the subordinate classes on the other. He thus paves the way for later thinkers, who also distinguish between dominant and counter-memory: Foucault, of course, but in a more empirically rooted historical analysis, Ben-Amos (2000), who leans on Halbwachs and Lukes.

Bourdieu himself uses the term 'collective memory' only once: in his Kabylean study, when he refers to the interdependence of the habitus and those linked activities of the agricultural calendar 'which are socially recognised as the most representative and successful, those worthiest of being preserved by the collective memory' (1977:98). Later, when he set out his general theory of practice, any explicit reference to the concept of 'collective memory' had disappeared (1990). Yet one vital constituent is still what he calls, following Durkheim, the 'collective unconscious' (1990:56). Here he stresses that although actors are preoccupied with the ongoing formation of their *new* selves, group experiences transmitted to each member from their earliest years live on:

> The habitus – *embodied history*, internalised as a second nature and so forgotten as history – is the active present of the whole past of which it is the product. As such it is what gives practices their relative autonomy with respect to external determinations of the immediate present.
>
> (Bourdieu 1990:56, my italics)

The habitus's 'embodied history' is surely identical here to 'collective memory' in its most famous use, that of Halbwachs (1997; see also Coser 1992).

Moreover, when we come to the Bourdieusian division of labour or 'fields' such as the sciences or visual arts, we note, as with Halbwachs, that their professionally most well-equipped members are also the most well-informed bearers of their fields' histories or collective memory (Bourdieu 2004). Indeed, symbolic or scientific revolutions, far from being *precluded* by knowledge of the field's tradition, may be actually *facilitated* by this.

Bourdieu was very alive to one aspect of this 'collective memory': what he calls the politics of 'eternal life', namely who acquires and who bestows it. In this sense he is a valuable founding figure for the sociology of obituaries, since these exist alongside memorial services, auto/biographies, statues, curricula and exhibitions as sources for remembering significant historical figures and their ideas. I have written elsewhere about clashes over the commemoration of politicians, writers and trade unionists (Fowler 2007). As we shall see, the newspaper obituaries of academics are more often highly positive.

In remembering academics, Bourdieu's two mid-career studies of higher education are valuable, *Homo Academicus* (1988) and *The State Nobility* (1996), which he later admitted to have been shockingly demystifying – *terrains brûlants* [incendiary areas][1] (Bourdieu and Chartier 2010:22–3). Here he goes beyond Marx in depicting the accumulation of *cultural capital* – 'Capital breeds capital', he remarks, its acquisition being marked through gaining and managing a reputation (1988:91). The accumulation of cultural capital occurs through academic strategies that appear formidable and yet curiously effortless. Indeed, so much in tune is this activity with the prevailing ethos that it seems simply the mark of an innate ability or 'natural' distinction (Bourdieu 1998a). But such strategies are inseparable from the use of academic power, often acquired in zero-sum competitive arenas, such as gaining favourable reviews. Crucially, they compel the successful academic to impose their own stance on the research problematic, requiring the protracted expenditure of time by doctoral students preparing theses under them (1988:88–9) and the measurement of their impact by the number and quality of their postgraduate students (1988:92–3, cf. Lamont 2010).

Bourdieu's sociology of the higher educational field breaks importantly with the more problematic elements of Karl Mannheim's sociology of knowledge (1936). Mannheim had emphasised the division in interests, ideas and values between the dominant class (typified by the Prussian/German military aristocracy) and the industrial working class (typified via the socialist culture of the Second International). Hence there could be, in his view, no dissemination of an absolute reason, universally recognised as valid; there was only perspectival thinking. Nevertheless, Mannheim privileged intellectuals as distinctively free-floating or socially unanchored and attributed to them a capacity for 'relationist' understanding (1936:70, 76, 137–48, 254); that is, objectivity as derived from a juxtaposition of perspectives or perspectivism (1936:266).

Mannheim's theories of deracinated, typically socially mobile intellectuals have certain well-known flaws. His model is based on more upward mobility of scientists and scholars than has been evident from historical records. Further, his hypothesised mingling of backgrounds linked to a free-floating intelligentsia has nowhere occurred for very long. Indeed, where there have been rootless intellectuals – especially autodidacts – they have been treated with extreme suspicion – see, for example, French late nineteenth- and early twentieth-century fears of an uprooted intelligentsia (Silverstein 2009). Indeed, the more usual pattern has been the routine production of a stratum of the bourgeoisie with distinctive cultural power, plus a subsidiary dialectic: the conversion of cultural capital into a comfortable level of economic capital. In Germany, for example, from the late eighteenth century on, these were the civil servants, Protestant ministers, gymnasium teachers and university professors (Ringer 1992). In other words, it is preferable to see the intellectual from the unskilled or factory working class as being a 'miraculous survivor' of the educational structures rather than created in equal numbers to those from other classes or class fractions (Bourdieu 1996; Ringer 1992). Moreover, Mannheim's 'totality of perspectives' should be viewed – I argue – as only feasible under certain conditions. Such conditions include not just the growth of an autonomous 'corporation' of intellectuals possessing an academic habitus, but an acquired disposition towards reflexivity or realist rationalism (see Bourdieu 1989; 2004; Bourdieu and Wacquant 1992).

The promise of Bourdieu's *Homo Academicus*, *The State Nobility* and *Science of Science* is, therefore, that he offers a sociology of intellectuals which is shorn of Mannheim's more idealist elements. With our particular objective of throwing light on the academics' obituaries, we must then turn to how this theory might provide a set of constructs and concepts for a preliminary mapping of the wealth of Nobel Prize-winning scientists, philosophers and literary critics that crowd these columns, as well as explaining editors' *rejection* of certain other academics whose proffered obituaries or offers of obituaries are politely dismissed as insufficiently distinguished.

It goes without saying that academic battles (including over the publication of obituaries) are organised around a classification of academic spaces. Such a classification is provoked by cherished conceptions of the ideal career, the promotion hierarchy and also the recent formal bureaucratic ranking of universities, in Britain via the Russell Group. But Bourdieu's *Homo Academicus* is also organised around an updated model of Kant's *The Conflict of the Faculties* (1992 [1798]). Kant viewed the university as structured around a profound division between the higher and lower faculties. Bourdieu claims that such a division now is between those faculties – such as law and medicine – that aid the Right Hand of the State in retaining secular power and those aiding the Left Hand of the State, which allow greater autonomy or critical freedom (1988:ch.2). Thus deep cleavages in academics' social origins and lived experience relate to these faculty destinies – the higher your social origin in France, the more likely you are to be situated in the higher faculties; conversely, the lower the faculty, the more likely you are to come from subordinate social origins, from Protestant and Jewish backgrounds rather than Catholic ones (in France) and from more fragile domestic units, with smaller families and more divorces (1988:49, 51–2).

Academic conflicts surface strikingly in Bourdieu's studies, in the form of bitter competition over money and protection – staff, buildings and the favour of the Vice-Chancellor or equivalent. Bourdieu is persuasive in seeing such acrimonious struggles as rooted ultimately in clashes of intellectual habitus, rather than purely idiosyncratic differences. His most famous illustration of this is the account of the conflict between a traditional literary critic, Raymonde Picard, and a 'new intellectual', Roland Barthes (1988:xxii–iii, 115–18). This battle stands, for Bourdieu, as part of the wider intellectual gulf between those who are members or supporters of the *Académie Francaise*, with its historic *closeness to political power*, and those who are secular *prophet* figures hostile to the Academy, Church and State, who point critically to the existence of contradictions and the need for change (1988:xviii–vi). This subsidiary polarisation is detectable beneath the higher/lower faculty division. It is with these persuasive arguments in mind that I turn to the further empirical study of intellectuals' obituaries.

Obituaries: Empirical analysis

Contrary to common perceptions, obituaries in general do not always encourage positive portrayals of their subjects. The obituary space is a clean slate on which can be imposed judgements of various types – typically, as I have argued, positive but also (secondly) harshly negative or critical, (thirdly) tragic, (fourthly) ironic and finally as profoundly marginal or heterodox figures (Fowler 2007:17–22). Surprisingly, in the case of academics, virtually no such negative, ironic or tragic genres appear. Figures viewed negatively abound amongst politicians but not amongst British professors. Certainly, 'heretics' or (in Bourdieu's terms) heterodox subjects emerge – erstwhile outsiders or radical dissenters, such as Edward Said or Eric Hobsbawm. These figures might attract the occasional bitterly critical obituary on the internet; but in newspaper obituaries, such dissidents have been recuperated or consecrated – to use Bourdieu's term – by the time they died. The mechanisms for this have yet to be fully understood, but it appears that their holding of earlier academic institutional positions confers on them certain rights to autonomy. Sadly, the price for this may sometimes be paid by a certain reduction in their danger to those with power.

Yet academics' obituaries, viewed widely, are also testaments to the extraordinary reproductive powers of the dominant classes (including higher professionals), as Bourdieu argues (1988:218–9). If I take the 90 academics from the systematic sample of British, French and American newspapers used in my 2007 study, we can see that the total from grammar or high schools was only 43 per cent whilst notably more (57 per cent) were from public (independent) schools. At the higher educational level, those who graduated either from Oxbridge, the Ivy League or French Grandes Écoles came to as many as 49 per cent (contrasting with only 18 per cent from other British universities and 32 per cent from non-British other universities). Even more strikingly, there is an extraordinary reproduction of the gender division of labour: only 11 per cent of these sampled academic obituary subjects were women.

This sample was taken from the obituaries selected at regulated bi-weekly intervals in 1900, 1948 and 2000–01. I recently took a new, supplementary sample of 75 contemporary academics' obituaries from 2000–13, all except one from British newspapers, although non-British subjects, such as Said, are occasionally included. This was a *convenience sample*, gathered irregularly, so it should be regarded as purely exploratory.

These later obituaries show a slight change. Excluding those academics whose education was unknown, the grammar school-educated were represented in the same proportion as before (43 per cent) – but this group was now very slightly *greater* than those who went to public schools (41 per cent). A further 12 per cent had been at American high schools and 4 per cent either at a seminary or with tutors. However, at the higher educational level, Oxbridge, the Ivy League and the Grandes Écoles (referred to in shorthand as 'Oxbridge') had slightly strengthened their predominance. 57 per cent of the 72 known were educated here as opposed to 38 per cent from other British, American or French universities. Taking the 45 *British* obituary subjects alone, as many as 30 (66 per cent) had been educated at Oxbridge.[2] Further, as many as 27 or 36 per cent of these British subjects had *worked* for a substantial part or the last part of their careers at Oxbridge.[3]

In brief, even in this period – well before the £9000 fees were mounted like a Berlin or Palestinian wall around English universities (Bauman 2012:51) – academics from working-class origins proved to be strikingly rare. Of the 63 academics' obituaries out of the 75 for whose parents we have some details, 65 per cent had broadly reproduced their parents' secure upper-middle-class or elite occupations, usually higher professional. Only 22 per cent had experienced major mobility from working-class origins: one such rare figure, for example, was Alan Bullock, whose father had been a gardener for many years, later a Unitarian minister (*The Independent* 3 March 2004). A further 13 per cent had undergone minor mobility, that is, from the ranks of the petty bourgeoisie[4] – shopkeepers or primary-school teachers.[5]

Further, masculine domination is still very apparent. Only 7 per cent of the academic obituaries in this contemporary sample were of women, and their authors frequently remark on the obstacles to jobs or promotion that their women subjects have experienced, especially if they had children. Whiteness also predominates: 85 per cent were from the dominant ethnic group, whilst only nine (12 per cent) were referred to explicitly as Jewish, together with one Palestinian and one African-American.[6]

This is the poor baseline from which social mobility has since declined (Piketty 2014:484–7). Important as this is, I want to turn to some more unexpected aspects.

A further remarkable characteristic of these academics' lives is how geographically mobile they were. Exiled or refugee groups may disproportionately gravitate to academic professions; they certainly enhanced British university life, as Charles Turner (2014) and Perry Anderson (1968) have both brilliantly shown. Nazism, notably, but also Stalinism, the collapse of Havel in Czechoslovakia in the face of neo-liberalism, apartheid, the Islamist subversion of the 1979 Iranian Revolution: these various regimes produced exiles, some of whom eventually made their way into British academia. But there is another independent phenomenon as well and this fits more with Boltanski and Chiapello's (2005) notion of 'connectionist man' (*sic*): the presence of a globally circulating elite, going from Cambridge to Caltech (Fred Hoyle is an example), or rotating between Harvard and Oxford, or Harvard and UCL (Ronald Dworkin). One of the longest obituaries, Alan Ryan's for Stuart Hampshire, satirises these circular movements between Oxford, Cambridge and University College, London as philosophers' 'musical chairs' – a round which in his subject's case had a further dynamic, since Hampshire's second wife had been formerly married to A.J. Ayer (*The Independent* 17 June 2004).

How, then, should we begin to conceptualise these university obituaries? I have suggested that we should start with Bourdieu; but his *Homo Academicus* should not be read as deriving from a Hobbesian form of disenchantment – implying a struggle of all against all (see, on this, Bourdieu 2004:46). Certainly, academic life for him is a paramount arena for the pursuit of strategic advantage and, with it, symbolic profits.

But it also reveals – though less often noticed – *solidarities across a field or sub-field*. This form of interdisciplinary solidarity may draw on earlier educational affinities: Bourdieu writes about how *normaliens* (academics from the Ecole Normale Supérieure) are linked together across different subject areas (1988:87). It is also to this solidarity around a common set of rules that academics appeal in their membership of a 'corporation of intellectuals' (Bourdieu 1989), especially in relation to one's own 'ideological family' (Bourdieu 1988:86). This crucially moderates the individualistic character of strategic action. For example:

> [S]cientists have things in common which in one respect unite them and in another respect separate them, divide them, set them against each other – ends, for example, even the most noble ones, such as finding the truth or combating error, and also everything that determines the competition and makes it possible, such as a common culture.
>
> (Bourdieu 2004:46)

Following his own rule of 'domesticating the exotic', Bourdieu has urged us to see interdependencies or *gift exchanges*, such as the familiar Trobriand Islands' kula ring, as also going on in academic life: A will review B's book favourably, but some time down the line B might agree to show goodwill to A, perhaps doing the favour of becoming the external examiner of a PhD student she supervises (see 1988:86; 1996:384–5). Such exchanges of services, escaping the public gaze, help individuals acquire symbolic profits. The more independent the actors appear, the greater the apparent legitimacy of the actions they perform.

Now, returning to the academics' obituaries, you might at first be led to think that they are all by junior journalists. Their authors appear simply as unadorned names. For example, the human geographer, Professor George Peters, receives an obituary written by a David Harvey (*The Independent* 15 November 2001). But if you act as a detective in the digital archives you can see that often the obituary is a gift exchange between academics who have great prominence in their shared field: in this example, the David Harvey who wrote the obituary, without any trumpeting of his own titles, is actually the internationally renowned David Harvey of Oxford and City University New York. He – and the other authors – appear momentarily stripped of the aura of their professorships, honours or even celebrated university locations. But *this* homage appears as a gift exchange without any possibility of counter-gift since in the nature of things the subject is dead (Mauss 2002). Thus writing an obituary without the self-advertisement of titles looks more like a case of disinterested or altruistic respect – these authors often say that they had an *obligation* to their colleague or friend to write an obituary. Of course, we could say that the academic contributor had an *interest* in this *disinterestedness* – if known by a small circle, they may bask in the reflected glory of their colleague's reputation; whilst even unknown (as in the anonymous obituaries), s/he stands to benefit from collective egoism in having his/her common field made temporarily more prominent, thus reviving the solidarity of the 'tribe' (theoretical physicists, geophysicists and so on). But on this latter score, the participant is acting more as a member of a *cooperative corporation* of intellectuals than as an actor aiming to appropriate symbolic capital as an individual (see Bourdieu 2002:6). The difference is telling.

In brief, the distinction of so many of the obituaries' *authors* is my first unexpected discovery. It makes the academic obituaries especially illuminating because their authors, not just their subjects, are often at the forefront of their fields. Omitting the fact that they may have had many obituaries, examples include the constitutional lawyer, William Wade, the author of whose obituary, David Williams, is actually Professor Sir David Williams, public lawyer, barrister and later Vice-Chancellor of Cambridge; Francis Crick's is by Mark Bretscher, who turns out to be an FRS and head of MRC Molecular Biology at Cambridge; Peter Laslett's is by Quentin Skinner, Professor of Queen Mary's, University of London and Fellow of Christ's and Caius College, Cambridge; Bernard Williams's by the philosopher, Richard Wollheim; the physicist and cosmologist Thomas Gold's by Herman Bondi, FRS, Professor of Maths, at King's College, London; Anne Warner's (Emeritus Professor of Physiology, UCL) by Jonathan Ashmore, FRS (Professor of Geophysics, UCL); the Nobel Prize-winner Edward Lewis's by Howard Lipshitz, Professor of Molecular Genetics at Toronto; and so on.

Further, close reading of these obituaries reveals their subjects' scholarly and intellectual achievements rather than their contributions to a conservative and exclusive Establishment. Indeed, not a few of these academics have produced what Bourdieu calls great *symbolic or scientific revolutions*. They are the authors of new paradigms (2004:64) – in this sample alone, one could cite Frances Crick (one of whose obituaries, by Bretscher, is adorned by DNA diagrams), Fred Hoyle, Bryan Pippard, Edward Said, Christopher Hill and Pierre Bourdieu himself.

The corollary: obituaries are no longer given to those who possess a capital of academic 'reproductive' power alone, except at the Vice-Chancellor level (Bourdieu 1988:40, 94–5). In other words, those who are only reliable administrators, locally illustrious Deans or worthy teachers no longer appear, as once was the case, particularly in the case of Oxbridge fellows. Academics may work on so-called 'peripheral areas' but they must now be notable for their own scientific or intellectual capital.

Secondly, these obituaries also touch on the social fissures that can have such devastating effects on personal lives. These academics' obituaries show not just their subjects' distinction but also their *sorrows*. These are the private troubles that Eldridge so powerfully recalls when writing on Wright Mills, often shaped by deeper social forces and conflicts at the macrostructural level (1983:103–4). More recently, Holloway (2010), amongst others, has written of the distorting effects of twentieth and twenty-first-century capitalism. Many current academic obituaries express regrets about such constrained choices.

In other words, if we approach these obituaries of academics as ethnographic documents, they open up certain rather surprising aspects. Academic conflicts over the 'value' of their capital regularly occur – even in 1989, Bourdieu's interviewees comment bitterly that what counts now are research grants alone, since they bring in money. Similar disputes over academic value appear as subterranean currents within these generally positive obituaries. Some such fractures take the form of theoretical challenges, splitting apart whole disciplines, such as the Barthes/Picard dispute over structuralist literary theory mentioned above (Bourdieu 1988:115–18). A similar dispute over deconstructionism is at stake in the Derrida obituary by Derek Attridge and Thomas Baldwin (*The Guardian* 11 October 2004). This laments both the mystifying '[r]esistance to his thinking' and the caricatures of their admired subject, whilst pointing to the fact that '(the French academic establishment never took him to its heart, and academic philosophers everywhere were generally uncomprehending)'. Other obituaries of Derrida were less appreciative: indeed, the *New York Times* and *The Economist* obituaries are exceptions to the rule that academics' obituaries are never hostile (ex-sample, *New York Times* 10 October 2004 (Jonathan Kandall) and *The Economist* 21 October 2004.).

Purely personal vendettas – at least on the surface – can occasionally surface as part of these clashes. One Professor X is dismissed in Bourdieu's *Homo Academicus* as the 'Barbara Cartland of Greek Studies' (1988: 84). Similarly, in the obituary recollections, it was 'academic back-stabbing' from American and German historians which distressed Wolfgang Mommsen after he had founded the German Historical Institute in London (*The Independent* 19 August 2004). Indeed, Fred Hoyle's angst about 'the Cambridge system... [in which] key decisions can be upset by ill-informed and politically-motivated committees' even pushed him to emigrate to the States (*The Guardian* 23 August 2001).

How can we *categorise* what the obituaries tell us about the subterranean necessities and conflicts within these celebrated lives? I divide these into, firstly, personal crises which derive directly from the *wider field of global class or political power*, such as enforced asylum-seeking or exile, and secondly, those which emerge from the field of the university itself.

Global political struggles

First, exile. Using my collection of 75 cases, we see immediately that this has figured as a major feature of the lives of many academics. To use Wright Mills's categories, the great macro-societal conflicts of Nazism, the Iranian revolution and anti-imperialism have left their marks on the biographical experiences of many thinkers. Take only two of the many academics in this period who became refugees from the Nazis and fascists, some of whom had extraordinary experiences. For example, we learn from the obituary of Jan Karski, a political scientist with a photographic memory, that as a wartime member of the Polish Resistance he persuaded a guard to admit him to Auschwitz; horrified, he made arduous journeys to report on the starvation and devastation he saw to Allied leaders – Churchill, Roosevelt and the Chief Rabbi of America – *none of whom believed him* (*The Times* 17 July 2000). Rita Levi-Montalcini's obituary (*The Times* 1 January 2013) sheds light on Italian Jews' vicissitudes: she herself lived literally underground during the war, managing to continue her research on the action of chick embryos in eggs, although twice forced to move to flee Nazis. Later, she became a highly regarded biologist and was honoured as an Italian senator.

Or there is the diaspora of Iranian academics, of which Hamid Ghodse (CBE) was a part, forced under the Shah, because of his 'passion for social justice', to leave his birthplace for exile in Britain. Subsequently, '[f]or more than forty years he had a monumental and inspirational, transformative influence on psychiatry in clinical service development [to patients suffering from substance addiction], teaching and training, research and policy' (*The Times* 7 February 2013). Another Iranian who survived against the odds through the theocracy is recalled in the memorable obituary for Amir Aryanpour. Deported from America after his Princeton PhD at the height of McCarthyism, he later became the 'most popular secular' lecturer at Tehran University and author of a seminal textbook on sociology. Well known as a 'thorn in the flesh' of both the Shah's and Khomeini's regimes, he only survived by moving from the social sciences to theology. Sacked from the University of Tehran in 1980, this forced trajectory produced, in the end, an effective silencing (*The Guardian* 3 August 2001).

Moreover, the liberal democracies – such as Britain and America – have inflicted their own priorities on these individuals too, as already noted in Aryanpour's deportation from the States. For example, two academics in the sample were prevented from doing the fieldwork they planned in Africa by MI5, Peter Worsley and Bill Epstein. As J.D.Y. Peel's obituary reveals, Peter Worsley, a member of the Communist Party who left after Hungary in 1956, had been blocked from East Africa as a consequence and forced into sociology:

> The course of Worsley's career was shaped by the interventions of MI5 on account of his communist associations. They snooped on his Swahili teaching in East Africa and spiked his plan to do fieldwork in Central Africa. [After his PhD thesis in Canberra, he had no] choice but to move sideways from anthropology to sociology.
>
> (J.D.Y. Peel, *The Guardian* 21 March 2013)

Similarly, Alan Rew explained in Epstein's case how he had been denied the chance of undertaking the urban research he had wanted to do:

> It was not Epstein as an individual who had challenged the system in colonial Africa but his strong advocacy, by example, of the craft of anthropology. To talk to Africans, to share their festivals...put Africans on a footing of equality and this, the authorities feared would demolish the delicate political balance. The subversion was to have dared to act as an anthropologist within towns rather than in a rural location.
>
> (*The Independent* 19 November 1999)

Western-approved South African Apartheid had the same consequence as many fascist European countries in the 1930s: it pushed many students and staff out of their home country into at least temporary exile. For many, this loss of their homeland became permanent. For examples written by sociologists alone, see John Rex (by another exile, this time from Salazar's Portuguese empire, Herminio Martins, *The Independent* 19 March 2012), Percy Cohen (Christopher Husbands *The Independent*) and Stanley Cohen (David Downes *The Independent* and Laurie Taylor *The Guardian* 23 January 2013).

We *do* now have celebrated cases of women academics, of whom we could mention Elizabeth Anscombe (*The Guardian* 11 January 2001), Gillian Rose (*The Independent* 13 December 1995) and Inga-Stina Ewbank (*The Independent* 14 June 2004). But we learn from many obituaries that refusals to take women's work as seriously as that of the men held women academics back. Charlotte Jolles (*The Independent* 2 February 2004), for example, was first of all a victim of academic marginalisation by the Nazis thanks both to her dissident approach to the novelist Theodor Fontane and to having a Jewish father: she was banned from attending the German award ceremony for her PhD. But in exile in Britain, she was also the victim of delayed recognition as a woman academic, despite being President of the Fontane Society. Even more spectacularly, Chrissie Miller (*The Guardian* 30 July 2001) never gained a professorship at all – despite having won the notable Keith Prize for her discoveries in inorganic chemistry and gaining an eminent DSc by the time she was 30.

The almost total absence of men and women of colour in these obituaries can be explained in part by their earlier exclusion from high-status institutions within the educational field and, in the case of the US (reported in British newspapers), their ghettoisation within their own African-American universities. This was a period in which Jewish men and women could gain entrance to universities, although even in the late 1930s American universities (such as Cornell) still maintained quotas for Jewish students (Gleik 1992). But the fact that there is only one Afro-Caribbean/African-American obituary in this sample, and that there is a total absence of staff of South Asian origins, indicates the extraordinary hurdles that had to be surmounted before these academics could begin to be acknowledged as shaping their respective fields. Stuart Hall later, against the odds, did break through and received long and favourable obituaries in *The Guardian*, *The Independent* and *The Daily Telegraph* for founding cultural studies, as well as for his political analysis and writings on black photographers. But his death in 2014 and his obituaries fell outside the scope of even my supplementary sample.

Field struggles[7]

It is difficult to tell exactly from many obituaries what form of capital or type of power the academic subjects possessed. As we have seen, only a tiny number of these obituary subjects have relied solely on the power of academic committees and autocratic patronage. It is precisely this form of patronage which Bourdieu's rebellious 'book for burning', *Homo Academicus*, could be read as obliquely attacking. However, personal troubles, great and small, can still be closely related to the clashing play of forces *within the academic field*. Howard Zinn, the historian, lost his job at an African-American women's college because he refused to teach the students how to be 'ladies' (*The Guardian* 30 January 2010). George Batchelor, the Cambridge mathematician, lamented the continued disproportion of money given at Cambridge to experimental physics at the cost of maths (*The Independent* 17 April 2000), whilst the organisation theorist, Michel Crozier commented bitterly that Bourdieu had 'colonised public opinion' in France (Anne Corbett *The Guardian* 19 June 2013).

It has not usually been noted that when Bourdieu describes the academic field he is describing vividly the great fault line between heresy and orthodoxy, or in his own words, countering 'prophets' – with their distinctive scientific, historical and interpretative techniques – to the academic 'priests' or university 'clergy'. These latter 'men of order' or routinised discipline stand for known 'good taste' or assumed 'common sense', and are characterised by their 'secret resistance to innovation and intellectual creativity' (1988:116–7, 95). In brief, he is reiterating in secular and contemporary terms that great division between sectarian movement and church that Marx, Weber, Hill and Thompson saw as so important in earlier periods.

In particular, from *State Nobility* onwards, Bourdieu writes compellingly of a great secular shift: the downgrading of the Ecole Normale Supérieure and l'Ecole des Hautes Etudes en Sciences Sociales with their philosophers and social theorists, often working in libraries and small scientific research groups, in favour of the more commercially useful and bureaucratised research produced in the Haute Ecole Commerciale and the well-known government elite school l'Ecole Normale d'Administration (1996:207–14). This he describes in *Acts of Resistance* as a crucial and telling part of the new 'conservative revolution' (1998b:53): it is, of course, familiar in Britain and other societies (McGettigan 2013:7, 122–3, 176).

Thus in Britain, recently, individual miseries not infrequently relate to the restructuring of universities, or what *The Times* obituary for Richard Wollheim (8 November 2003) refers to acerbically as 'the Thatcher revolution... in higher education'. We find many academic obituary subjects, with the highest reputations in their fields, who have been pushed into retiring or emigrating – Wollheim himself left UCL to become Head of Department in Berkeley. Indeed, since 2001, obituaries frequently reference the systems of accountability of the RAE and REF with their commercial language of 'outputs' and university 'brands', which have scarred academic lives. Wollheim had seen the whole of philosophy as under attack from neo-liberal instrumental rationality, whilst Bernard Williams was reported to have left England for the US for 'a variety of reasons, amongst which the Thatcherite attack on universities and on independent intellectual endeavour counted for much' (*The Independent* 17 June 2003). Michael Roper raises obliquely some related issues in his obituary on his colleague, Ian Craib, from his own vantage point as Professor of Sociology at Essex, introducing a question Craib posed only two days before he died: ' "How long does an academic book last?...Ten, fifteen years at the most".' What mattered more was the difference he hoped he had made to his students (*The Independent* 24 January 2003). Or again, here are Bechhofer and McCrone on Tom Burns:

> He would not have been happy working in the environment of the past decade with its emphasis on measurable outputs of 'product', he knew from his professional work [on organisations] that the impact of really innovative research is not easily tracked, especially in the short term, and would probably have expressed his opinion robustly.
> (*The Guardian* 21 June 2001)[8]

The dangers to intellectual and scientific autonomy within contemporary universities are raised vividly in one of Said's obituaries. Tariq Rahman, a Professor of Linguistics in Islamabad, stresses the role of Columbia University, New York, in allowing a Said to flourish:

> If we want to pay true homage to Edward Said we must have intellectual spaces [in Pakistan] like Columbia University – places where dissent and knowledge create that magic personality which comes once in a while. We must remember that moral courage, like cowardice, is not only innate; they are also constructed. Laws which ensure freedom from fear; spaces like universities which create courage. If we create such spaces the Edward Saids will live amongst us and become our conscience
> (*The International News*, Pakistan, 2 October 2003)

The implicit contrast is with Pakistan. But in the face of neo-liberalism we need to look to our own universities too.

Conclusion

Despite the relative diminution of inequality in the period in which they came to maturity (Piketty 2014), university academics can be shown from the later systematic and exploratory samples (2000–13) to be from predominantly privileged educational origins, with very few working-class representatives. In that respect, they amplify theories of social reproduction (Bourdieu 1988). Nevertheless, as I have shown, such obituaries can still be used to gain insights into certain struggles within the academic field, including the contemporary malaise provoked by marketisation (Martins 2005).

They are also highly illuminating in other respects. We consistently gain insights into the importance of academic autonomy and especially of autonomous working groups and labs, such as those to which John Eldridge has contributed so much. The academic obituary fleetingly unveils scholarly worlds apart that are usually fenced off because of the high qualifications necessary to gain access to them. These obituaries – gift exchanges by those expert in their fields – briefly reveal to us what were the issues at stake when their subject was engaged with them and the difference their subjects' skilled dedication has made. They offer a form of translation, not unlike that radical opening up of the foreign enacted by the expert translator, allowing access to a different perspective from one's own (Bielsa 2014:4). It might be one of the small achievements of the obituary to contribute to such 'genuine intellectual universalism' (Bourdieu 2002:5). For this reason and within the limits discussed, the academic obituary makes a contribution to the possible re-enchantment of the world.

Notes

1. Bourdieu writes that, unlike a historian's accepted recourse to the archives, his use of such archived obituaries had provoked outrage, a work of 'monstrous demolition' or desecration (Bourdieu and Chartier 2010:23 cf.; 1988:218–9; 1996:42–53, 398–9).
2. In 2012–13 Oxford and Cambridge combined had 39,825 (2.3 per cent) undergraduates and postgraduates studying in the UK (Higher Education Statistics 2014).
3. Compare this 36 per cent with the higher education statistics (Higher Education Statistics 2014), which reveal that in 2012–13 10,880 (5.8 per cent) staff were working at Oxbridge.
4. As with Fowler (2007), the measures of mobility used here relate to the classifications of occupations and classes used by Bourdieu (1984).

5. Bourdieu's *Homo Academicus* provides evidence for the highly plausible case that social class origins are strongly related to the choice of discipline and faculty, and not just the type of institution chosen by students (1988:48–9). I analysed both my samples of academics' obituaries to assess whether a similar trend is evident in these, using type of school attended as a proxy for social origins more broadly. No clear pattern emerged, perhaps partly because the samples contained so few medical and law faculty academics.
6. The 2011 census also reports 86 per cent who gave their ethnicity as white. But this includes Jews, whereas I have analysed Jewish academics separately where the obituary mentions them as such.
7. These field struggles are approached as though they were entirely separable from the wider political conflicts just discussed. But of course the field is often shaped by these, not least with respect to the neo-liberal university. Detailing them separately is an analytical device which leaves aside the issue of causal determinants.
8. Indeed, John Eldridge did stem some of these changes when, in 1981, as President of the British Sociological Association, he championed sociology as a 'third culture' (Eldridge, 2014, see Holmwood's foreword to this volume).

Bibliography

Anderson P. (1968) 'Components of the National Culture', *New Left Review*, I (50): 3–57.
Bauman, Z. (2012) *On Education*. Cambridge: Polity Press.
Beharrell, P. et al. (1980) *Bad News*. London: Routledge and Kegan Paul.
Ben-Amos, A. (2000) *Funerals, Politics and Memory in Modern France 1789–1996*. Oxford: Oxford University Press.
Bielsa, E. (2014) 'Cosmopolitanism as Translation', *Cultural Sociology*, 8 (4): 392–406.
Boltanski, L. and Chiapello, E. (2005) *The New Spirit of Capitalism*. London: Verso.
Bourdieu, P. (1977) *Outline of a Theory of Practice*. Cambridge: Polity Press.
Bourdieu, P. (1984) *Distinction*. Cambridge: Polity Press.
Bourdieu, P. (1988) *Homo Academicus*. Cambridge: Polity Press.
Bourdieu, P. (1989) 'The Corporatism of the Universal', *Telos*, Fall: 99–110.
Bourdieu, P. (1990) *The Logic of Practice*. Cambridge: Polity.
Bourdieu, P. (1996) *The State Nobility*. Cambridge: Polity Press.
Bourdieu, P. (1998a) *Practical Reason*. Cambridge: Polity Press.
Bourdieu, P. (1998b) *Acts of Resistance*. Cambridge: Polity Press.
Bourdieu, P. (2002) 'Les Conditions Sociales pour la Circulation Internationale des Idées', *Actes de la Recherche en Sciences Sociales*, 145 (Décembre): 3–8.
Bourdieu, P. (2004) *Science of Science and Reflexivity*. Cambridge: Polity Press.
Bourdieu, P. and Chartier, R. (2010) *Le Sociologue et l'Historien*. Marseille: Agone.
Bourdieu, P. and Wacquant, L. (1992) *An Invitation to Reflexive Sociology*, Cambridge: Polity.
Calhoun, C. (1993) 'Habitus, Field and Capital', in C. Calhoun, E. Lipuma and M. Postone (eds.) *Bourdieu: Critical Perspectives*. Cambridge: Polity, pp. 61–89.
Coser, L.A. (ed.) (1992) *Maurice Halbwachs On Collective Memory*. Chicago, IL: University of Chicago Press.

Eldridge, J. (1983) *C. Wright Mills*. Chichester: Tavistock.
Eldridge, J. (1993) 'News, Truth and Power', in J. Eldridge (ed.) *Getting the Message: News, Truth and Power*. London: Routledge, pp. 3–33.
Eldridge, J. (1995a) 'Introduction: That Was the World that Was', in J. Eldridge (ed.) *Glasgow Media Group Reader, Vol. 1: News Content, Language and Visuals*. London: Routledge, pp. 1–26.
Eldridge, J. (1995b) 'Ritual Tasks', in J. Eldridge (ed.) *Glasgow Media Group Reader, Vol.1: News Content, Language and Visuals*. London: Routledge, pp. 364–81.
Eldridge, J. (2014) 'Between Science and the Humanities: Sociology as a Third Culture', in J. Holmwood and J. Scott (eds.) *The Palgrave Handbook of Sociology in Britain*. Basingstoke: Palgrave Macmillan, pp. 338–59.
Eldridge, J. and Eldridge, L. (1994) *Raymond Williams: Making Connections*. London: Routledge.
Eyal, G., Szelenyi, I. and Townsley, E.R. (1998) *Making Capitalism Without Capitalists*. London: Verso.
Fowler, B. (2007) *The Obituary as Collective Memory*. London: Routledge.
Gleik, J. (1992) *Genius: Richard Feynman and Modern Physics*. London: Little Brown.
Gorski, P.S. (2013) 'Introduction: Bourdieu as a Theorist of Change', in P.S. Gorski (ed.) *Bourdieu and Historical Analysis*. Durham, NC: Duke University Press, pp. 1–18.
Halbwachs, M. (1997) *La Mémoire Collective*. Paris: Albin Michel.
Higher Education Statistics (2014) 'Students in Higher Education', www.hesa.ac.uk/index.php?option=com_pubs&Itemid=&task=show_year&pubId=1&versionId=25&yearId=297, date accessed: 29 October 2014.
Holloway, J. (2010) *Crack Capitalism*, London: Pluto.
Kant, I. (1992 [1978]) *The Conflict of the Faculties*. Nebraska: Nebraska University Press.
Lamont, M. (2010) 'Looking Back at Bourdieu', in E. Sylva and A. Warde (eds.) *Cultural Analysis and Bourdieu's Legacy*. London: Routledge, pp. 128–41.
Mannheim, K. (1936) *Ideology and Utopia*. London: Kegan Paul, Trench and Trubner.
Martins, H. (2005) 'The Marketisation of Universities and some Contradictions of Academic Capitalism', *Metacritica*, 4: http://revistas.ulusofona.pt/index.php/metacritica/article/view/2747/2099, date accessed: 3 May 2015.
Mauss, M. (2002) *The Gift*. London: Routledge.
McGettigan, A. (2013) *The Great University Gamble: Money, Markets and the Future of Higher Education*. London: Pluto.
Osiel, M. (1997) *Mass Atrocity, Collective Memory and the Law*. New Brunswick, NJ: Transaction.
Piketty, T. (2014) *Capital in the Twenty-First Century*. Cambridge, MA: Harvard University Press.
Ringer, F. (1992) *Fields of Knowledge*. Cambridge: Cambridge University Press.
Robbins, D. (2006) *On Bourdieu, Education and Society*. Oxford: Bardwell Press.
Sapiro, G. (2013) 'Structural History and Crisis Analysis: The Literary Field in France during the Second World War', in P.S. Gorski (ed.) *Bourdieu and Historical Analysis*. Durham, NC: Duke University Press, pp. 266–85.
Silverstein, P.A. (2009) 'Of Rooting and Uprooting', in J.E. Goodman and P.A. Silverstein (eds.) *Bourdieu in Algeria*. London: University of Nebraska Press, pp. 164–98.

Steinmetz, G. (2011) 'Bourdieu, Historicity and Historical Sociology', *Cultural Sociology*, 5 (1): 45–66.
Susen, S. (2013) 'Bourdieusian Reflections on Language: Unavoidable Conditions of the Real Speech Situation', *Social Epistemology*, 27 (3–4): 199–246.
Taylor, R. and Steele, T. (2011) *British Labour and Higher Education: 1945–2000*. London: Continuum.
Turner, C. (2014) 'Exiles in British Sociology' in J. Holmwood and J. Scott (eds.) *The Palgrave Handbook of Sociology in Britain*. Basingstoke: Palgrave, pp. 282–301.
Williams, R. (1977) *Marxism and Literature*. Oxford: Oxford University Press.
Williams, R. (1995) 'Coda: "Isn't the News Terrible?"', in J. Eldridge (ed.) *The Glasgow Media Group Reader, Vol. 1: News Content, Language and Visuals*. London: Routledge, pp. 382–8.

8
The Humanitarian Crisis in Sociology

John MacInnes

> God forbid that Truth should be Confined to Mathematical Demonstration
>
> (William Blake in Gleick 2003:186)
>
> Individual lives cannot be aggregated or equated or dealt with *quantitatively* in any way
>
> (Leavis 2013:66, my emphasis)
>
> It is the business of sociologists to conduct a critical debate with the public about its equipment of social institutions
>
> (Burns 1962:211)

Introduction

For me, John Eldridge's work has five elements: it has always been resolutely empirical and profoundly radical; it has been 'public' not only in its impact, but also in the sense of treating issues of public concern: industrial disputes, impartiality in television news, media health scares; it has often concerned itself, following the work of Raymond Williams, with 'culture'; and it has been consistently subversive, in the sense of challenging the established order, whether of other social institutions, such as broadcasting, or his own, the university. What follows is a sketch, rather than a fully worked out thesis, of what some of these terms – sociology, culture, public, empirical and radical – might have to do with each other, and also how they might relate to another term: science. My thesis is a simple one. Sociology has paid too much attention to stories and too little attention to science. It has emulated the humanities, rather than the natural sciences. My aim here is to subvert sociology by posing what might at first seem a preposterous question: why do the disciplines of English Literature and Sociology appear to have swapped places over the last half-century? In contrast to this development, I'll argue that sociology should recover its relationship with the natural sciences.

Sociology as literary criticism

Too much of contemporary sociology resembles the aesthetic critique of society treated as a legible 'text'. By this I mean that it offers value-based commentary on society, focusing on the use of language to explore the meaning of concepts, often under the banner of 'theory', using the tools of literature, rather than a more material and systematic analysis of it using 'scientific' methods. I am thinking here not just of explicitly 'postmodern' approaches but a wider shift within the discipline. For example, Mills (1959) entitled his influential survey of the discipline the sociological *imagination*. Goffman (1956) introduced the *dramaturgical* perspective of analysing social interaction in terms of on-stage and back-stage performance. Butler carried the metaphor farther with her elaboration of the concept of *performativity* within which it was asserted that discourse '*produces* the phenomena that it regulates and constrains' (Butler 1993:2, my emphasis; 1997). Sociology has been seen by some as about *narrative* and *storytelling* (Berger and Quinney 2004; Franzosi 1998; Stanley 2013). There has been a focus on language and words, often at the expense of attention to things, rather like the approach to philosophy of the later Wittgenstein criticised by Gellner (1964). Neither imagination nor the use of dramaturgical metaphors necessarily undermine a scientific sociology, but they both encourage a focus on interpretation of meaning, on stories and accounts, whether for actors at the micro level, or the macro 'critique' of institutions once their historical significance has been decoded. Too often they underestimate the power of material structures and constraints: the state, the labour market, resources, power.

It used to be novelists who explored *identity*. The essence of the story is usually the resolution of various conflicts between that identity and the world that it confronts. However, identity has now become a key theoretical concept for sociology: class, status, gender, sexuality, race, ethnicity, nationalism and nation-building are often treated within its terms (Brubaker and Cooper 2000; MacInnes 2004; 2006). At the 2013 conference of the British Sociological Association, 41 per cent of all the papers presented had identity as a focus.[1] Similarly, the invocation of 'reflexivity' has become ubiquitous enough to render the term banal. For example, Giddens (1991) uses the term to transform the social determination of individual biography into agency; insofar as a person's self-identity is their 'reflexive' understanding of their own biography, it becomes a 'project' of self-realisation.

This is not just good news for individual members of society, it is wonderful news for sociologists, whose reflexivity presumably undoes the Gordian knot of the relativism of knowledge and offers to turn mere prophecy into self-fulfilling prophecy. This is a powerful tool at the hands of a work of fiction: the ability to summon up a compelling life world in the imagination. However, even as lords of the realm, who would concede that either sociologists or individuals *create* the world they investigate or live within? Sociologists rarely aim for either prophecy or prediction, but what seems like good news has two stings in its tail. The promise of the escape from relativism – individuals can reflexively know the world – only delivers us deeper into its clutches: if they do so as *individuals*, what claims can they have over the way *other* individuals do so? Worse: if all individuals can gain knowledge of the world, what special role is left to the sociologist? Sociology, surely, needs some account of the way in which a comprehensive knowledge of society is systematically *unavailable* to its members, or encourages them to think of it in certain ways. This was certainly the view of Marx, Weber and Durkheim, although their accounts of the nature of this process differed. Worse still, one of the key insights of sociology and social anthropology has been the way in which the core concepts and ways of thinking about a society that are available to its members have typically been heavily self-referential. Priests, magicians, saints or other guardians of ideology have usually been able to keep the horizon of reflexivity well within the status quo. How might we know that our contemporary social order is any different in this respect? The only answer to this question, it seems to me, is that the contemporary world is one in which, for the first time, science is available and systematically applied, both to understanding the natural world and to the social. The touchstone of science is that knowledge claims are not tested 'reflexively'; instead they are tested against external referents: identity, no matter how internally coherent it might imagine itself to be, becomes superficial – something to be understood not in terms of its own narrative, but of the historical conditions that make it possible.

It would be wrong to conclude that *all* sociologists use the concepts of identity and reflexivity as loosely as Giddens. However, these concepts offer a way of exploring culture that brings sociology closer to literature and fiction. Thus Woodward's (2002) monograph on 'identity' centres on narrative and the link between public and private 'stories', so that the ability to tell one's own story becomes the root of agency and the potential to define an identity. This seems to me to be an excellent description of the nature and function of identity in 'closed' pre-modern agrarian societies with a relatively fixed material, ideological and moral structure, little social change and rigid ascription to the places within it. With historical hindsight, we'd surely hesitate to describe the stories about either themselves or their society that the members of such societies could tell as either sociological accounts of their society or proof of their agency within it. Can we be so sure that contemporary society is different? Of course we know it is different in at least one way: it is infinitely more mobile than its predecessors. But this merely returns us to our original difficulty: as a fluid society it produces neither a stable or universal culture (with the exception of language) nor any fixable range of identities, so that while all its members may lay claim to an 'identity' they would struggle to describe it, either to themselves or to a visiting sociologist, in empirical terms. Identity is indeed 'liquid' in contemporary affluent society, although many of its more material aspects are anything but. A hermeneutic sociology rooted in reflexive analysis of this liquid identity could surely produce only chaos. One aspect of this has been the proliferation of ever more obscure and specific concepts and terminology, together with the creative use of punctuation and scare quotes as it struggles to capture the dynamic florescence of identities and cultures in contemporary society in the 'network' age.

A good recent example of this is to be found in the sociology of masculinity over the last three decades. Regardless of which author one turns to, Connell, Hearn, Mac an Ghail, Kimmel, Messner and many others, one finds a preoccupation with the (changing) meaning and representation of 'masculinity', as an identity and the way in which it is held to constrain the behaviour of both men and women and reproduce men's power. Elaborate theories, with their own obscure language, are erected to invariably conclude that (a) masculinity is not determined by sex, (b) men exert power over women, (c) masculinity is in 'crisis', but (d) this 'crisis' doesn't seriously threaten men's 'hegemony'. 'Crisis' becomes a convenient term to describe hermeneutic chaos. Identities, including gender identities, multiply as mobile contemporary society produces an almost infinite range of potential cultures. Identity becomes, as Giddens recognises, an increasingly individual choice, but rather than an agency that then constructs the social order, isn't it better understood as a reflection of the far more powerful and material forces in that order which make it possible? One searches in vain in this literature for firm empirical evidence about the extent, nature and characteristics of men's power, how it relates to other dimensions of social inequality, or other core institutions of modern society (the economy, the labour market, income, wealth, education, politics). This is strange because, so far as I am aware, contemporary, secular, affluent Western societies are the first in recorded human history where ascription by sex is no longer the most basic and determining feature of the social order. How have capitalism, liberalism and the rule of bureaucracies progressively demolished the power of the father/husband and breadwinner in a couple of centuries? How has material patriarchy crumbled so fast? The *sociological* answer to this question does not lie in the liquid superstructure of identities and meanings; it lies in institutions, the market, the liberal state, the family and so on. Exploring the manifold meaning of 'hegemonic masculinity' tells us little about this process.

Stories

Literature is stories. Stories are as old as civilisation. Of course, that's a nonsensical statement since they are the same thing. Conceptual thinking, language and communication are the stuff of social as opposed to biological action. The dimensions of human experience and imagination are always and everywhere explored and communicated through stories. Probably as old as stories are attempts to distinguish tall from true ones, and in particular, to do this with reference only to the nature of the story or its teller. Such attempts have never got very far, and it is difficult to see how they could. Logicians can tell us about where we can take premises, but as for the truth of a premise itself, logic and philosophy offer no guarantees.

As such, stories hardly seem promising material for sociology. One important reason for this is that stories are rarely used, either to 'tell the truth' or even make reports. They have many other functions, which sociologists and others have explored. An important one for my purpose here is their contribution to what has been called 'ontological security': sufficient faith not only in the orderliness and predictability of the world around us, but also in the validity or our personal understanding and moral evaluation of it, to let us get on with our lives. 'Ontological smugness', were that not such an ugly expression, might be a better description. And of course such smugness applies just as much to visions of alternative possible worlds as it does to the 'natural' character of the one we inhabit.

Leavis and literary criticism

Literary criticism is essentially the investigation of stories. While sociology has become enchanted by narrative, some approaches to English Literature, in part via its detour through cultural studies, have taken on a veneer of sociology. A key figure is Leavis (Raymond Williams has sometimes been described as a 'Left Leavisite'), and it is worth considering his work, not only because of his original influence but also because the recent 50th anniversary of his spat with C.P. Snow has been the occasion for a surprisingly positive evaluation of his part in it (Snow 2013). For Leavis the critic's job was to nourish language to explore and understand 'vital intelligence', 'full humanity' and 'power for life'. Culture was rooted in the careful cultivation of language. Such an approach was irreducible to any theory, method or philosophy but developed in debate with a community or public that by using good language might create a genuine culture. This task had been made more urgent by the debasement of language and culture caused by modernisation and industrialisation. The study of English Literature, which he wished to see at the heart of every university, could nourish such a 'minority culture' in the face of the dehumanising impact of mass 'civilisation':

> Who will assert that the average member of a modern society is more fully human, or more alive, than a Bushman, an Indian peasant, or a member of one of those poignantly surviving primitive peoples, with their marvelous art and skills and vital intelligence? ... the advance of science and technology means a human future of change so rapid and of such kinds, of tests and challenges so unprecedented, of decisions and possible non-decisions so momentous and insidious in their consequences, that mankind – this is surely clear – will need to be in full intelligent possession of its full humanity.
>
> (Leavis 2013:72–3)

Leavis always insisted that criticism, no more than the writing it engaged with, could never be reduced to a philosophy or a method. What method might 'prove' that this or that author properly belonged to a canon? In place of method came 'close reading' and debate: the common exploration of what language, and all those who use it, might do or aspire to achieve. The context of such exploration was a culture, or what sociologists would recognise as *Gemeinschaft*. One might say that for Leavis the problem was to produce the right story, one that rather than reinforcing the ontological security of narrator or reader dramatically challenged them to recover their 'vital intelligence'.

Leavis's argument that 'Individual lives cannot be aggregated or equated or dealt with *quantitatively* in any way' might be taken as a manifesto for the turn to qualitative methods in sociology. Taken literally this argument is clearly wrong. Economics does this very successfully all the time. Could sociology say much about society without reference to official statistics? But there is also a kernel of truth to it. Measurement, categorisation and quantification, no matter how expertly done, cannot hope to capture any individual's 'full humanity' or 'vital intelligence' in all its subtlety and complexity. Too often what we can reliably measure seems only to scrape the surface of what we really want to get at. Qualitative methods offer to replace measurement by interpretation of meaning and understanding: to return, in effect, to the public debate and exploration of stories. This takes us back, once again, to the problem of how the sociologists establish the special nature of the story they tell, including any claims they might make for its scientific status.

Cultural studies developed in part as a response to Leavis's 'reactionary elitism'. It largely shared Leavis's views on language, of the link between cultural products and social change, the dehumanising impact of science and quantification, culture's radical social and political potential, and distrust of method, but saw radical cultural products emerging in mass civilisation itself rather than a narrow literary canon. Thus Leavis, although I doubt he would ever have seen it this way, poses a potential answer to the relativism of reflexivity. Rooted in the right culture, nurtured through public debate, modern atomised man or woman might regain the full humanity and vital intelligence of the 'Bushman', peasant or primitive. His reference to the 'Bushman', however, calls to mind Weber's comment that the 'savage knows incomparably more about his tools' (Weber 2009:139); but his argument was almost the inverse of Leavis's. The technical and moral 'knowledge' of the 'savage' was rooted in an enchanted society with a fixed and low division of labour and associated culture. Only confused romantics might aspire to return to it.

However, Leavis opened a bridge, via cultural studies, from literary criticism to sociology. His approach not only disavowed science, it was consistently romantic in seeking a return, if not to a thoroughly premodern social order, at least to pre-modern forms of knowledge. Given a stable community, given a stable culture, given a set of values that define what it is to be 'fully human', then the study of the 'facts' can reveal not only how that society functions but also how it *ought* to function. A 'value-free' analysis would be impossible, since any fact could be understood only in relation to the wider moral cosmos of which it formed a part. Science, in a sense, was the *problem*: the origin of a rationalist world view that insisted on the rigorous separation of fact from value. What Leavis offered, and his followers accepted, was a *moral* order: a journey back to enchantment from the iron cage of enlightenment rationalism on the one hand and its liquid moral soup on the other.

But this bucolic, enchanted view of *Gemeinschaft* is surely something sociology originally set out to confront, for it also inevitably implied a closed, status-ridden, wretched social order quite incapable of self-critical knowledge, well summed up by Marx as 'rural idiocy'. This may have been the world of most of human history, and its legacy has been slow to wither, but it is also a world we have lost. Disenchanted society is one without a collective moral compass, values, standards or culture: at least in principle, in modern society these are freely chosen and chaotically diverse. Sociology's task, as Weber recognised, was one of understanding this new moral multiverse in which truth or the facts could no longer to be defined by moral or any other authority.

One legacy of Leavis on literary studies was to sociologise it, as it were, by foregrounding both the society from which an author and their work emerged, and social commentary within that work, as well as the more traditional study of the technical and artistic means by which the author achieved their aims. Any review of the syllabus or textbook content of courses in English Literature today shows just how much attention is paid to the analysis of the social relations of production and consumption of authors and the texts that they produce. For example, 'post-colonial' studies claim to examine ways of imagining and understanding the world made possible by the era of imperialism and its aftermath. From a very different perspective, the transformation of literary criticism into social science has reached its logical conclusion with calls for the application of statistics and 'scientific methods' in the analysis of the mass of data now accessible through digitised and machine-searchable corpora to 'generate firmer and surer knowledge about the things we study' (Gottschall 2008).

Debates and the public

For Leavis, debate between critic or author and their audience or public about the value or significance of a piece of literature was a substitute for method. Such debate gives the public new ways of understanding and appreciating literature, while forcing critics to reconsider and revalue their views. There can be no final resolution of such debate, no 'correct' answer: *the debate itself is the point*. Indeed, were this not the case, it is very difficult to see what the point of literary criticism could be. The public addressed in the debate was the entire society, since it was essentially a debate about how the whole moral order. Sociology has tended to embrace this model, most recently as 'Public Sociology' (Burawoy 2005).

The term public is a powerful but dangerous one, because its meaning and usage is so slippery. It is at once singular and plural, empirical and, as Benedict Anderson has encouraged us to think, 'imagined'. Burawoy's lecture on public sociology starts by quoting Walter Benjamin's famous passage about the Angel of History fighting against the wreckage that progress hurls at mankind. Burawoy claims the job of public sociology is to defend 'the interests of humanity'. However, what strikes me about this claim (aside from its grandiosity, as if sociology was not only the guardian of some deeper wisdom about what comprises the human condition, meaning of life or 'interests of humanity' but also an expert mechanic of the motor of history) is its profoundly unsociological character. Publics, plural, are creatures of the societies that create them and make them possible. The fundamental feature of modern societies is that morality, values and interests are left, at least in principle, to the individual, not *the* 'public'. The term 'public' as used by Burawoy is little more than a rhetorical device. But what a device! It allows the lone academic to warrant the value of what they do, and what value it turns out to be. The academic as Angel, saving the world. The parallel between Leavis and Burawoy, not only in the way they perceive their role, but the way in which they imagine the public and their relation they have with it, is striking. They both appeal to an imaginary public complete with a conception of what its moral order should be, proceeding from which the defects and discontents of society can be securely analysed 'in the interests of humanity'. The debate is essentially about values and perspectives, about ways of seeing the world.

Such public sociology risks being sectarian. Sects always imagine themselves to be the guardians of the truth and visualise emancipation as the public coming to share its vision. Sectarian hysteria is functional. The virulence of the language and imagery sustains members' faith in the face of the profane world's indifference. 'Debate' is strictly one way, from the guardians of belief to those wallowing in false consciousness. The purpose of the debate is to invite the members of contemporary society's plethora of cultures and identities and the moral commitments they involve to explore new and different ways of making sense of the world they live in and their part in it. For Leavis this meant their coming to embrace the Great Tradition. For Burawoy it presumably means their coming to realise what 'the interests of humanity' comprise. Both beg the question of how such interests or tradition might be defined or identified. Moreover, for a sociology concerned to explore that plethora of cultures and identities the purpose of such debate is far less clear. At best it might comprise the confrontation of diverse perspectives and values: making the exotic mundane and the familiar strange.

Debate requires the use of stories, but to be critical rather than a shouting match, it needs evidence, which is where it connects back to science. Debate between competing hypotheses, theories or interpretations rests neither on the quality or elegance of the stories told, nor the biography or aims of the authors, but on whether it is consistent with a wider range of, or stricter test by, *empirical evidence*. Science doesn't tell people how to live, but it can try to tell them how their institutions currently operate, what might be changed with what sort of results, anticipated or not, and so on: in short the kind of critical debate that Tom Burns proposed and which much of Eldridge's work comprised.

Thus in Eldridge's work I think we can see a rather different kind of debate at work. The purpose of debate is less to swap perspectives, nor reveal what values, cultures or identities might be recognised, tolerated or embraced. Rather it is to use empirical evidence to challenge assumptions about how different institutions work, or whose interests they appear to serve. What are the causes, nature and consequences of industrial disputes? How do the constraints and opportunities faced by a public-owned media institution impact on how it reports on them? Are there unintended consequences of journalistic procedures that turn attempts to report 'the facts' into particular kinds of presentation or interpretation of them? What leads its audience to see these reports as 'fair' or biased? What measurements might be made to assess this? Is some 'objective' standard obtainable, or are other alternative ways of evaluating the evidence possible? This requires no grand perspective about the interests of humanity, let alone that of the audience for news bulletins or of those who produce them. But it does challenge both, with empirical evidence, to consider whether this particular institution works in the way they may assume that it does or want it to do. Rather than a debate addressed to society as such, it identifies who some of its actual participants might be.

Orwell

We have been here before and, paradoxically perhaps, the best short expression of our predicament comes not from a sociologist but a literary figure. Almost 70 years ago, in his essays 'Politics and the

English Language' and 'In Front of Your Nose', Orwell (1946a; 1946b) noted the barbarism committed against plain words through needlessly abstract, complex or vague formulations, stale hackneyed imagery and pretentious diction:

> prose consists less and less of words chosen for the sake of their meaning, and more and more of phrases tacked together like the sections of a prefabricated henhouse... In certain kinds of writing, particularly in art criticism and literary criticism, it is normal to come across long passages which are almost completely lacking in meaning.
> (Orwell 1946b:127–8)

Orwell was wise enough to avoid the conclusion that how we write or speak about something can *change* that thing, but he did argue forcefully that barbarous language usually had its origins either in sloppy thinking or logic on the part of the author, or a desire to camouflage the author's real meaning with a cloak of euphemism or confusion. Used in this way, language lost contact with the facts. Indeed, this was its purpose. He argued that this frequently allowed authors to advance mutually contradictory arguments with aplomb:

> The point is that we are all capable of believing things which we *know* to be untrue, and then, when we are finally proved wrong, impudently twisting the facts so as to show that we were right. Intellectually, it is possible to carry on this process for an indefinite time: the only check on it is that sooner or later a false belief bumps up against solid reality, usually on a battlefield.
> (Orwell 1946a:124)

Key themes of his satire *1984* were the language Newspeak, in which the Party aspired to make subversive thoughts impossible to express; its partner doublethink, or the ability to simultaneously hold and accept mutually contradictory views; the memory hole, in which the past was continually reconstructed to be consistent with the present; and numbers used to bamboozle and confuse. *1984* was about spin, not only about the Party's spin rooted in the total relativism of all knowledge, but also that of the opposition, rooted in the fantasy that 'If there is hope... it lies in the proles'. It is important to remember that *1984 was satire*. Orwell's argument was that history, no matter how well rewritten, does constrain its own interpretation. Battlefields *do* exist. Thought and language, no matter how carefully constructed, cannot prevent the expression of subversion. His argument (that might have come straight from Descartes) was the need for clear thinking, empirical evidence and alertness to what methodology refers to as 'confirmation' bias: our unremitting ability to make new evidence fit our existing values and prejudices, to maintain our personal ontological security until the struggle becomes just too much. Whether Orwell lived up to his own ideal (Ingle 2008 and Barnes 2012 doubt it, Crick 1982 is more positive) his core arguments have value: 'complex' language may be a cover for dissimulation, even to its author; *evidence* is all.

Science

Although Orwell would never have characterised it this way, one might summarise his argument as 'stories and science are fundamentally different'. Language can achieve almost anything. We typically use it either to console or confound others and ourselves. However, the 'battlefield' of empirical experience limits this process. 'Hard reality' can expose false beliefs. *Anyone* can construct beliefs, stories, accounts, theories, concepts, discourses or ideologies. Freedom of thought is always, to some extent, possible. Newspeak is a logical impossibility.

The Enlightenment was precisely about exploring ways in which thought might aspire to liberate itself entirely from 'custom and example', and escape the domination of either authority or revelation. One consequence of this was a kind of democratisation both of cognition and of nature, including human 'nature'. There could be neither any privileged standpoint from which the world might be understood, nor any aspects of nature granted 'special' status in order to avoid problems of logical order or smuggle in accounts of its 'purpose' that might replace accounts of divine purpose. Questions about why there might be any order in nature were consigned to metaphysics, while science examined how it worked. Facts were to be ruthlessly separated from values. Science was to be amoral. What is done with scientific knowledge, how it goes about its work, may be genuinely ethical and moral questions, but the knowledge of gravity, light or quantum mechanics itself is neither 'good' nor 'evil'.

Not for nothing is the motto of the Royal Society 'Nothing on another's word'. If *any* belief was, in principle, possible, and the standpoint, credentials or authority of its holder no longer any warrant of its value, then testing against 'hard reality' was fundamental. Experience, marshalled as experiments, was to be the battlefield where belief confronted nature. Moreover, the results of any such test were only provisional. Knowledge was cumulative, but paradoxically this process was to proceed via the progressive destruction of existing knowledge by ever more refined tests. Insofar as this spills over from science itself to technology and production, we have the 'constant revolutionising' of existing society that Marx and Weber described so well. Replication of results was essential. One might have said 'the history of all hitherto existing societies has been the history of confirmation bias'. Comfortable, plausible, powerful or obvious knowledge, including that of the scientist, could be recognised as such only if it could pass some external test.

Of course, guaranteeing the validity of such tests, agreeing the interpretation of their results, dealing with inconsistency and uncertainty in the results were all more complex than the simple idea of confronting ideas with 'hard reality' allowed. The sociology of science has shown how far its actual practice might depart from its theory. 'Experience' can never be ultimately validated, except by other experience. However, we do know three things. Science works. There is no other explanation of the meteoric rise in the resources and power of the societies that incubated and then harnessed it. Second, the Faustian pact of such progress was the acceptance of disenchantment in all its forms. Like Humpty Dumpty, facts and values once separated cannot be put back together again. Finally, as soon as God was expelled from the natural world, it begged the question of whether the methods of natural science might also be applied to the study of society. The *possibility* of sociology was born.

However, just as the natural sciences emerged from pre-scientific modes of enquiry such as alchemy or astrology, or imagined themselves to be examining *how* nature revealed God's purpose, so too did the idea of the scientific study of society emerge from pre-scientific modes of understanding. Again this is far too large an issue for this brief sketch, but let me make four observations. The first is that, with the partial exception of Weber, all the founding fathers of sociology were as much philosophers as social scientists. They all drew on a much longer tradition of thinking about society or 'human nature', and it was their relationship to this tradition, rather than any commitment to scientific method, that established their reputation. To use the language I've used in this sketch, they dealt in stories more than science.

The second is that none of them, with the partial exception of Durkheim, made much contribution to method. Even more surprising, they barely discussed or drew upon or the work of the myriad of nineteenth-century investigators who set out to apply empirical scientific methods to the study of society. As Hacking (1990), Porter

(1986) and others have shown, the early nineteenth-century produced 'an avalanche of numbers' as attempts were made, for the first time, to describe it in quantitative rather than moral terms, to measure it, discover its 'laws of motion' and in manifold ways to subject it to 'reason'. Quetelet tried to apply the methods of astronomy to social processes. The discovery that pathological or irrational behaviour exhibited stable regularities – the favourite was suicide well before Durkheim's interest – not only raised the prospect of discovering hitherto invisible social 'laws' but also unleashed a debate about how law-determined behaviour could be reconciled with individual will and moral responsibility. I doubt that contemporary formulations of the structure/agency contradiction have improved much on it.

Third, such were the methodological achievements of this social science in the treatment of probability and uncertainty that natural scientists turned to it to resolve the accumulating difficulties of Newtonian mechanics in dealing with matter at the atomic level. Statistics is now the common logic of interpretation of all the experimental natural sciences. Yet its origins lay in what its practitioners thought of as social science. It was Galton who first developed and applied the technique of regression and correlation, in the course of his studies of inheritance of ability. Pearson generalised and developed it. Modern statistics was born. Moreover, statistics offered fundamentally new answers to the problems of the relativism of knowledge and ontological security. Individual insight, no matter how expert or incisive, could now be measured against the evidence of the regularities of and dependencies between what had hitherto appeared as discrete or chaotic events. The focus could shift from *why* things might be so to *how* things tended to operate in practice, perhaps quite independently of the firm convictions of those involved.

Finally, I doubt that anyone has suggested that Quetelet, Galton or Pearson ought to be given 'founder' status. This is not because social science has discarded their insights. On the contrary, there is no quantitative description of contemporary society of any worth that does not rest upon them. It is because they told the wrong stories. The theories and ideas which inspired the proto-statisticians of the nineteenth century were typically those of the older social orders they were emerging from. They set out to measure the 'natural' differences between races, peoples, sexes and classes, or between the insane and criminal and the 'normal'. They embraced or flirted with phrenology, eugenics or racism. The crucial missing ingredient in their methods was, precisely, a 'sociological imagination'.

At the BSA 2000 conference *For Sociology*, I was struck by how participants often quoted (approvingly) the following passage from Gouldner's book of that name:

> It would seem that social science's affinity for modeling itself after physical science might lead to instruction in matters other than research alone. Before Hiroshima, physicists also talked of value-free science; they, too, vowed to make no value judgments. Today many of them are not so sure. If we today concern ourselves exclusively with the technical proficiency of our students and reject all responsibility for their moral sense, or lack of it, then we may some day be compelled to accept responsibility for having trained a generation willing to serve in a future Auschwitz.
>
> (Gouldner 1973:25)

The grandiosity is a clear antecedent of Burawoy's 'interests of humanity'. Are we seriously to believe that sociology professors are the only source of students' 'moral sense'? Were scientists moral innocents before August 1945? However, most startling of all is the argument that technical proficiency (presented as a zero-sum alternative to morality) leads to the Holocaust. Where does this suspicion of technical rationalism come from? One, perhaps decisive, component is the unsavoury political and moral outlook of so many of its nineteenth-century pioneers of a statistical approach to the social sciences.

Science as a vocation

This takes us to Weber and 'Science as a Vocation' (2013). Although he made few contributions to method as such, he alone amongst the founding figures developed an explicit account of the relationship between sociology and science (leaving aside Marx's claim that science comprised the discovery of the laws of historical development). As far as I know, Leavis never read Weber. Weber's arguments about value freedom were very widely criticised in the methods wars as implying at best moral relativism and at worst an unwitting enslavement to the existing social and political order. A commitment to stories seemed a more radical option. However, Weber's argument about value freedom and value relevance surely rescues Leavis, and us, from the predicament of how to make thinking about the human condition or society radical, relevant and systematic without having to define what the essence of the human condition, vital intelligence or fine living might be, nor have some grand sense of the true 'interests of humanity'. Like Leavis, Weber neither believed that all values were equal nor that there was any method or philosophy that might demonstrate the superiority of one value to another. Like Leavis he believed that there could only be 'debate'; but unlike Leavis he no longer believed in the possibility of reversing disenchantment. He argued strongly that there were 'scientific' methods that could demonstrate (i) the compatibility of different values in a given social context and (ii) given a value and a given social context, what alternative means might be available to pursue it and what unanticipated implications for other ends might such means imply. This gives us a much sharper sense of the context and participants in any debate. In his approach 'facts' become separable from the theory alleged to 'saturate' them. His distinction between value relevance and value freedom opened up the possibility of the application of scientific methods to the analysis of social institutions, behaviour and belief, while at the same time making clear that there could never be a science of the final purposes of such action itself. Far from rendering sociology apolitical, this handed sociologists their most powerful weapon in social and political debate: scientific methods using evidence. Like all weapons this one had its price: it could be used to argue 'given the ends, these may be useful means', but it could never be used to demonstrate the value of the ends themselves. Holistic philosophies of history, whether Marxist, Hegelian or Platonic, lie beyond its proper reach. What sociologists could do is analyse institutions, debate with the relevant publics about whether they in practice operate in the ways they might assume, or make clearer the kinds of unacknowledged value assumptions and compromises their operation requires.

Science is piecemeal. It offers disjointed, falsifiable, partial, provisional insights. It has no control over their application once discovered. The general public is likely to learn about it, if at all, in a simplified and bowdlerised form that distorts its original insights. In a few decades or years the work will come to appear quaint, riddled with the fleeting preoccupations of the time when it was produced. But it will be progress. It will be progress, paradoxically, precisely because it is *not* addressed to any imagined public but has been won from the 'battlefield' of empirical research. Not all facts are socially constructed, at least in the way this term is usually employed. Many useful ones lie there, 'in front of our noses', if we only have the will and wit to gather and use them intelligently. Surely one of the greatest motors of social progress over the last half millennium has been the slow, incremental, halting, piecemeal application of science not only to relations between people and nature but to relations between people themselves. The true sociological imagination requires some commitment to scientific methods. It is not some vision of the general good that turns out to be a product of the particular imagined public that the sociologist happens to cherish.

Whether Weber was correct lies beyond the scope of this chapter, but his solution is certainly radical, and *more* subversive of the existing social order than approaches rooted in stories and claims that all 'facts' and evidence are ultimately theory saturated and socially constructed. Using the battlefield of empirical evidence and its logical interpretation, sociologists can slay the false beliefs that lie in front of our noses, doing so in the name of science.

How did we get here?

The argument I've sketched out here is that two rather contradictory intellectual traditions co-habit in sociology. One is a sociological version of Leavis's 'Great Tradition'. It produces radical critiques of contemporary society, rooted in a definite value or moral perspective, or explores the perspectives of the plethora of identities and cultures that contemporary society throws up in order to confront the exotic and mundane. It pursues 'vital intelligence'. However, like Leavis, it either struggles to account for how it might claim scientific status, or rejects that as an ideal. The other is the scientific tradition, resting its knowledge claims on tests against empirical evidence. However, unlike its natural science counterparts it has largely failed to build any cumulative knowledge. It often struggles to operationalise empirically the grander issues with which sociology is concerned, so that it is routinely accused of analysing only that which is capable of *measurement*. Reliant upon observation rather than experiment for its evidence, it can always be claimed that some unobserved, or even unobservable, factor renders its findings incomplete. Finally it labours under the prejudice that its commitment to technical proficiency renders it suspicious. I think there can be no doubt that the first of these two traditions has been dominant. It is no surprise that the majority of sociology undergraduates see the discipline presented to them in their degrees as one that belongs to the humanities rather than to the sciences (Williams et al. 2008).

There are also perhaps material reasons for the dominance of the first of the two traditions. Three arguments strike me as worth exploring. First, British higher education expanded rapidly after the Robbins Report. Good measurement is fiendishly difficult and therefore expensive, especially before the explosion of information technology in the 1980s. It was much cheaper to model the social sciences on the humanities. Universities rushed to recruit a cohort of academic staff and employed many with little or no methods training. One does not need to be a materialist determinist Marxist to see how the explicit denial of method in English Literature might prove an attractive model, not only to this generation of staff, but to the university vice-chancellors who needed only to afford desk space and lecture rooms, rather than the whole paraphernalia of labs, computers, survey fieldwork and the like. Second, measurement and the robust analysis of surveys or official statistics require a reasonable command of maths. Arguably, British maths education has been poor at producing pupils well qualified in maths and excellent at giving many more a lifelong antipathy to the subject. If it followed a humanities model, sociology did not need to compete for scarce maths talent with the natural sciences. Third, the supply of students who are expert in debate, discussion and 'comparison and contrast', and who can choose their words with care, skills honed through countless undergraduate essays, perhaps meets the ever-increasing demand for authors of social comment or 'spin' (MacInnes 2004). Unfortunately, the skilled cultivation of language, facility in debate and the ability to connect given values to the available facts can be used not only to imaginatively explore human experience and its potential, but also to legitimate squeezing it into the boxes provided by the latest policy or plan. Cleaners become 'members' of the 'train presentation team'. Plodding bureaucracy is brightened up with leaders, champions or tsars. Every tawdry policy document is littered with references to 'excitement'. Conservative governments bent on reducing the real public state talk about 'Big Society'. The relativism of knowledge meets its most forceful application here. Here is the obverse of Gouldner's nightmare: not technocratic but rather cultural skills deployed in the service of ends over which it has no control.

Conclusion

This takes me back to my starting point. I think John Eldridge's work has shown how sociology can be public, radical, relevant and subversive. I've argued here that for sociology to continue to be like that in the future, it needs to revisit its relationship to science and the humanities. It is often because of its *failure* to embrace scientific methods that it is no longer the radical discipline it imagines itself to be. Its over-reliance on the humanities tradition has too often produced arguments mired in relativism or irrelevance. Its emphasis on critical perspective rather than empirical evidence has undermined the kind of the debate a radical sociology might have with publics, plural, and too often left it as a sect addressing a public it only imagines. Its critical debate with the public should be about their institutions and how they work, about yawning gaps between publicly proclaimed and privately pursued intentions, and between intentions and results. It would do well to think about many of the features of John's work, in particular the way in which he has used empirical evidence, carefully assembled, to confront some prevailing cherished and conservative ideas in a radical way (that TV news, especially as broadcast by the BBC was impartial; that industrial disputes were about union bloody-mindedness; that industrial democracy was a straightforward panacea for poor industrial organisation). It could preoccupy itself less with the alternative perspectives available that people might use to make sense of their lives and their purposes. By leaving that job to others it could become a radical and subversive discipline by becoming a more scientific one.

Note

1. Based on a content analysis of 508 abstracts in the conference documentation. Papers were allocated to as many of the following categories as applied: Class/status; Culture; Families/relationships/intimacy; Education; Gender; Identity; Lifecourse; Material inequality; Nation/state; Power; Race/ethnicity; Sexuality; Space/mobility/migration.

References

Barnes, J. (2012) 'George Orwell and the Fucking Elephant', in J. Barnes, *Through the Window*. London: Vintage, pp. 26–40.
Berger, R. and Quinney, R. (2004) 'The Narrative Turn in Social Inquiry: Toward a Storytelling Sociology', Paper presented at the annual meeting of the American Sociological Association, San Francisco, CA, 14 August.
Brubaker, R. and Cooper, F. (2000) 'Beyond "identity"', *Theory and Society*, 29 (1): 1–47.
Burawoy, M. (2005) 'For Public Sociology', *American Sociological Review*, 70 (1): 4–28.
Burns, T. (1962) 'The Sociology of Industry', in A.T Welford, M. Argyle, D.V. Glass and J.N. Morris (eds.) *Society: Problems and Methods of Study*. Routledge and Kegan Paul, pp. 185–215.
Butler, J. (1993) *Bodies That Matter. On the Discursive Limits of Sex*. London and New York: Routledge.
Butler, J. (1997) *Excitable Speech: A Politics of the Performative*. London and New York: Routledge.
Crick, B. (1982) *George Orwell: A Life*. London: Penguin.

Franzosi, R. (1998) 'Narrative Analysis – Or Why (and How) Sociologists Should Be Interested In Narrative', *Annual Review of Sociology*, 24: 517–54.

Gellner, E. (1964) *Words and Things*. Harmondsworth: Penguin.

Giddens, A. (1991) *Modernity and Self-Identity*. Cambridge: Polity Press.

Gleick, J. (2003) *Isaac Newton*. New York, NY: Random House.

Goffman, E. (1956) *The Presentation of Self in Everyday Life*. University of Edinburgh: Social Sciences Research Centre.

Gouldner, A. (1973) *For Sociology: Renewal and Critique in Sociology Today*. Harmondsworth: Penguin.

Gottschall, J. (2008) 'Measure for Measure', *The Boston Globe*, 11 May.

Hacking, I. (1990) *The Taming of Chance*. Cambridge: Cambridge University Press.

Ingle, S. (2008) *The Social and Political Thought of George Orwell: A Reassessment*. London: Routledge.

Leavis, F.R. (2013) *Two Cultures? The Significance of C. P. Snow*. Cambridge: Cambridge University Press.

MacInnes, J. (2004) 'The Sociology of Identity: Social Science or Social Comment?', *British Journal of Sociology*, 55 (4): 531–43.

MacInnes, J. (2006) 'Castells' Catalan Routes: Nationalism and the Sociology of Identity', *British Journal of Sociology*, 57 (4): 677–98.

Mills, C.W. (1959) *The Sociological Imagination*. Oxford: Oxford University Press.

Orwell, G. (1946a) 'In Front of our Nose', in S. Orwell and I. Angus (eds.) *The Collected Essays Journalism and Letters of George Orwell, Vol 4. In Front of Your Nose 1945–1950*. London: Secker and Warburg, pp. 122–5.

Orwell, G. (1946b) 'Politics and the English Language', in S. Orwell and I. Angus (eds.) *The Collected Essays Journalism and Letters of George Orwell, Vol 4. In Front of Your Nose 1945–1950*. London: Secker and Warburg, pp. 127–39.

Porter, T. (1986) *The Rise of Statistical Thinking*. Princeton, NJ: Princeton University Press.

Snow, C.P. (2013) *The Two Cultures*. Cambridge: Cambridge University Press.

Stanley, L. (ed.) (2013) *Documents of Life Revisited: Narrative and Biographical Methodology for a 21st Century Critical Humanism*. Farnham: Ashgate.

Weber, M. (2009) 'Science as a Vocation', in H.H. Gerth and C.W. Mills (ed.) *From Max Weber*. London: Routledge, pp. 129–58.

Williams, M., Payne, G., Hodgkinson, L. and Poade, D. (2008) 'Does British Sociology Count? Sociology Students' Attitudes toward Quantitative Methods', *Sociology*, 42 (5): 987–1005.

Woodward, K. (2002) *Understanding Identity*. London: Bloomsbury Academic.

Part III
Sociology of the Media

9
Sociology, Propaganda and Psychological Operations

David Miller

Sociology has less to say about propaganda than it should and much less than it used to. Why is this? Can anything be done about it? Answering the first question is tricky but I will review some of the evidence. Amongst this is the fact that sociological attention has been diverted from propaganda in part by a successful (propaganda?) campaign to create alternatives to the term propaganda.

On the second question, only time will tell. I want, however, to make an argument by example. I want to try and suggest that propaganda – or whatever we decide to call it – can and should be an important topic for sociologists to examine. There is no need to leave it to the historians, the political scientists or to media studies, and certainly not to the subject specialists of 'public relations'!

My approach to propaganda and psychological operations (psyops) springs directly from my appreciation of the wider problems of media power that were inculcated in me after I found the Media Group in the summer of 1985.

I fell eagerly on the material in *War and Peace News* (Broadbent et al. 1985), which described the way in which TV news reproduced and amplified government misinformation – on the bombing of Port Stanley, for example, and the way in which protest movements like the women at Greenham Common were traduced by 'objectivity' and 'balance'. My first opportunity to contribute to the work of the Media Group was in the analysis of state and private attacks on broadcasters via Norman Tebbit and the Media Monitoring Unit, which had a weak empirical, yet strong ideological, grasp on how the media actually performed in the context of such controversies as the 1986 US attack on Libya.

John Eldridge was always clear that there was more to media studies than simply analysing news 'discourse', a word I am not sure I ever heard him use. So it came to pass that my own PhD research started with the media coverage of the SAS killings of three unarmed IRA volunteers in Gibraltar in March 1988 (Miller 1994). It was obvious in that case that the deluge of misinformation and falsehoods relayed by the press and TV were not just the product of pressures from within the media system. There was also pressure from without in the form of, firstly, intimidation, bullying and the strategic use of the law by the state and, secondly, (mis)information supplied by governmental institutions of organized persuasive communication. No-one at Glasgow warned me not to investigate government misdeeds directly. No-one said watch out, keep your investigations focused on media institutions, do not look at the government, the military, the police or the intelligence agencies. I didn't know that the encouragement I got in Glasgow was then, and remains now, a rare and very valuable commodity. Since then I have experienced discouragement and attempted discouragement on numerous occasions from colleagues, university bureaucracies and indeed from those who make their living managing public debate and decision-making in what Raymond Williams (1985:268) called the institutions of 'disinformation and distraction'.

The approach that is needed to understand the information strategies of government (and indeed of any organised actor) should not be mediacentric (Miller 1993; Schlesinger 1990) – that is, such an approach must see communications from the points of view of all those involved in the process not just the media (as much media studies continues to do) or indeed from the point of view only of the creators and authors of communicative strategies in government as seen via public records. It must be seen in terms of the wider set of interactions between different actors and audiences which comprise the 'circuit of mass communications' (Philo et al. 2015), itself a key part of the social totality. In other words, 'means of communication are themselves means of production' (Williams 1980:50). It is salutary to remember that no act of communication, from the utterance of an individual or its amplification via a megaphone, to leaflets, newspapers, books, films and indeed the internet and social media, leaps magically into existence from the force of our imaginations, but all such acts have social and material conditions of existence. As it is with communications media, so it is with 'propaganda'; with publicity, persuasion, advertising and marketing. It is very well known that the term propaganda originates from the creation in 1622 by Pope Gregory XV of Sacra Congregatio de Propaganda

Fide (The Sacred Society for the Propagation of the Faith). It is less often observed that the word applied to an organisation: 'One established a Propaganda', notes the British political scientist Terence Qualter (1985:108), 'to undertake certain activities'. As Qualter himself notes, but does not pursue, 'that usage has declined and is rarely met with today'. The Vatican's 'Propaganda Fide' changed its name in 1988, dropping the word propaganda and substituting 'evangelization'. Its official headquarters, however, remains in the Palazzo di Propaganda Fide, in Rome, and its mission to convert unbelievers, to 'propagate' the faith, is unchanged (Vatican 2015). The sense of propagating certain states of affairs makes the term propaganda superior to many of the alternative terms that were proffered after the term fell into disrepute in the twentieth century.

Propaganda and the symbolic

When we look back at the history of writing on propaganda from the 1920s on, what we find are mostly discussions only of the 'symbolic' dimensions of propaganda. According to Harold Lasswell in his classic 1927 study, 'Propaganda is the management of collective attitudes by the manipulation of significant symbols.' Similarly Paul Lazarsfeld and Robert Merton (1943:58) stated 'We understand by propaganda any and all sets of symbols which influence opinion, belief or action on issues regarded by the community as controversial. These symbols may be written, printed, spoken, pictorial or musical.' This definition has been long lasting – forming also the basis of Qualter's (1985:124) classic study some half a century later; the 'deliberate attempt by the few to influence the attitudes and behaviour of the many by the manipulation of symbolic communication.'

On the other hand, the classic accounts are worth re-reading, as John Eldridge (2007) shows in his short review of the work of Merton and Lazarsfeld. This is because they remind us both that several aspects of received wisdom on 'propaganda' are incorrect and because they help us to trace the process by which 'propaganda' was airbrushed from sociology (and social science) and from discussion in polite company more generally.

For example, the fact that 'propaganda' can be true was noted by Lazarsfeld and Merton. 'An authentic account of the sinking of American merchant ships in the time of war ... may prove to be effective propaganda inducing citizens to accept deprivations which they would not otherwise accept in good spirits' (Lazarsfeld and Merton 1943:58).

Propaganda, in other words, is not only about lies or about the deceptive use of communications. It is important to remember this given later attempts, which we will review below, to pretend that 'our' activities are truthful and thus not like 'their' propaganda or 'psyops'.

The dispute over propaganda

The dispute over the term propaganda emerged strongly in the US after the First World War and was not as simple as is often remembered. It is true that there was a dispute about how appropriate the term was, but also about how desirable the practice of propaganda was. There were thus four positions: in the first, the term was good but the activity, deceptive and manipulative, was to be deprecated (for example, Lee 1951; Lynd 1939). The second agreed the term was good and while the activity could be bad, it was not irredeemably so. Position two is today associated strongly with the work of many of those writers who undertake studies of 'propaganda'. British historian Philip Taylor (1999:260) is a prominent example. He concluded his historical overview of British propaganda with the *cri de coeur*: 'democracies may delude themselves' into thinking their activities 'not propaganda' but 'information'. However, he noted, 'their propaganda is in the right tradition... Democracies should not be ashamed of selling democracy.' The third position was that the term was bad, as it delegitimised the activity that was, if not noble, at least unavoidable (as for Lasswell, Lazarsfeld and Merton). The fourth position was that the term was bad and the activity it described was not acceptable in a democracy. Sometimes this position was principled, but it could equally be used to suggest that by definition or in practice democracies did not engage in propaganda. This latter is most closely associated with apologists for the public relations industry today (Dinan and Miller 2007).

The debate was a serious matter. In their 1935 annotated bibliography, Harold Lasswell and his colleagues (1969 [1935]) listed more than 3000 published items on propaganda and promotional activities. Timothy Glander (2000:2) describes the debate as raising 'fundamental questions about the very nature of society and the individual, and the proper relationship of the new mass media to both'. Glander (2000:16) goes on to note that by the late 1930s there were several organisations, 'including the Institute for Propaganda Analysis... that were actively involved in developing anti-propaganda... materials'.

With the approach of the Second World War, 'the institute faced mounting pressure to discontinue its operations'. The Rockefeller

Foundation refused to fund it, although they were content then and afterwards to fund Lasswell and Lazarsfeld amongst many other now prominent sociologists (Simpson 1994). Board resignations followed after the Institute became perceived as too critical of government defence policy. Then several board members became 'central figures in the organization and dissemination' of US propaganda during the war (Glander 2000:25). In 1941 it emerged that the House Un-American Activities Committee had been investigating the Institute for two years. The Institute never recovered, and the effective undermining of the anti-propaganda case left the field clear to those who saw propaganda as legitimate and necessary.

Propaganda was understood by its chief chronicler, Harold D. Lasswell, as a 'concession' to the 'wilfulness of the age'. 'The bonds of personal loyalty and affection which bound a man to his chief', wrote Lasswell (1927:198–9), 'have long since dissolved. Monarchy and class privilege have gone the way of all flesh, and the idolatry of the individual passes for the official religion of democracy.' In such a situation, the 'new antidote to willfulness is propaganda. If the mass will be free of chains of iron, it must accept its chains of silver. If it will not love, honor and obey, it must not expect to escape seduction' (Lasswell 1927: 199).

Although Lasswell sometimes appeared ambivalent about the term propaganda, he was a firm proponent of its continuation as a practice. According to Glander (2000:xi):

> Those individuals interested in utilizing propaganda in the conduct of the war orchestrated a semantic shift away from the term propaganda... By the onset of World War II, then, mass communications research was the new term to describe what were previously regarded as attempts to develop effective propaganda techniques.

So one of the key reasons that sociologists stopped talking about propaganda was that those who were critical of lies and manipulation lost out to those who favoured them. The latter decided not to call these processes propaganda at all, thus making it harder to focus discussion on the question of elite social power and communications. As one of the critics of propaganda, Alfred McClung Lee, put it in 1949:

> If managerial problems for industry and the military are to continue to dominate the research of leading social psychologists and sociologists, the value orientation of the managerial technician rather than the value orientation of the social science educator will dominate

what evolves and is called social science. The emphasis can thus shift from service to citizens in a democracy to service for those who temporarily control and who wish to continue to control segments of our society.

(cited in Glander 2000:38)

McClung Lee had been associated with the Institute for Propaganda Analysis and – so argue his biographers – this was related to the marginalisation he and Elizabeth Briant Lee (to whom he was married – she was also a sociologist) experienced in American sociological circles in the post-war period (Galliher and Galliher 1995).

From that point on Western liberal democracies, in particular the US and UK, invested much more in propaganda than they had before. This was the case not least in the funding of research on propaganda and psychological warfare as demonstrated in Christopher Simpson's path-breaking book *Science of Coercion*. He shows (1994:79) that 'projects secretly funded by the CIA played a prominent role in U.S. mass communication studies during the middle and late 1950s'. CIA funding was often given indirectly – laundered through a wide range of foundations, including the Rockefeller Foundation, which channelled '$1 million in 1956 to gather intelligence on popular attitudes in countries of interest' to communications research pioneer Hadley Cantril (Simpson 1994: 81).

As Glander puts it:

The construction of propaganda organizations during the war provided an important training ground for mass communications researchers; and through these organizations, mass communications researchers made important personal contacts that facilitated the establishment of the field in the postwar period.

(Glander 2000:40)

Simpson (1994:4) states that his research shows that:

At least six of the most important U.S. centers of postwar communication studies grew up as de facto adjuncts of government psychological warfare programs. For years, government money – frequently with no public acknowledgment – made up more than 75 per cent of the annual budgets of Paul Lazarsfeld's Bureau of Applied Social Research (BASR) at Columbia University, Hadley Cantril's Institute for International Social Research (IISR) at Princeton, Ithiel de Sola Pool's Center for International Studies (CENIS) program at the Massachusetts Institute of Technology, and similar institutions.

Lest we imagine that this at worst involved social scientists in message-testing for the state, we should note the direct involvement in coercion and torture which this work involved. In a case exhibiting all-too-familiar parallels with today, the CIA 'clandestinely underwrote the Bureau of Social Science Research's (BSSR) studies of torture – there is no other word for it – of prisoners of war, reasoning that interrogation of captives could be understood as simply another application of the social-psychological principles articulated in communication studies' (Simpson 1994:4). Clandestine funding was complemented by research access that would possibly test the limits of today's ethics policies. In 1952, for example, RAND Corporation social scientists, including Alexander L George (later of Stanford University), completed 'approximately 1000 interrogations of North Korean and Chinese POW's' (cited in Bowers 1968:244).

The case of the British military and 'Psyops'

So, although the term propaganda fell out of favour amongst sociologists, the practice only got more central in political life. But in sociology, though the practice was often endorsed, much scholarly effort was expended on finding more palatable alternative terms. The problem was that replacement terms also began to accumulate the taint of the old. Thus the replacement term 'public relations' has itself accumulated negative connotations (Dinan and Miller 2009). In the military, terms such as psychological warfare were replaced by psychological operations or psyops, before these became suspect too. But finding information on the internal deliberations of the security establishment is not easy. The British state, especially, likes its secrets.

Ian Cobain tells the tale of British official complicity in and perpetration of torture. Indeed, he shows how early British experiments in torture led to significant innovations in the tool box of techniques used by the British military and intelligence services and their ministerial masters today. I use the term 'tool box' advisedly. Cobain reviewed the experiments with 'brainwashing' carried out by the CIA, with direct involvement from both British scientists and intelligence agencies in the 1950s to the 1970s. He is probably correct in concluding that the outcome of all the various experiments was that brainwashing was not a viable approach. As a result more sophisticated kinds of psychological torture were the main focus of research and practice by British officials from the 1970s until today.

Most of this involvement was kept secret. Where small details leaked out, officials dissembled and misled the House of Commons, the press and the public. One of the rare leaks involved the *Daily Mail*, which in 1960 splashed the front page with 'Brainwash shocks' and reported on the activities of the 'Psychological Warfare Unit' based at the Intelligence Corps HQ at Maresfield in Sussex (Cobain 2012:125).

The MoD confirmed to the paper that military personnel undergoing what was called 'resistance to interrogation' training were

> locked in stocks for long periods, forced to sit for long periods on a small one legged stool, and locked in narrow boxes and doused in water. It was not true, the MoD insisted, that they were also stripped naked and forced to stand for long periods while chained to nearby objects.
>
> (Cobain 2012:125)

This was a classic 'non-denial denial'. The MoD went on to admit that some personnel were actually stripped naked: 'Men are made to stand and sometimes chained...but usually with underclothes on.' Questions were asked in the House, and the Prime Minister replied that 'the techniques to which these questions refer have never been used by any organisations responsible to Her Majesty's Government'. This was false. The British had been using torture in Cairo and in Cyprus as well as in Kenya and numerous other 'operations of the counter-revolutionary type', as the British Army manual on counterinsurgency called them (Ministry of Defence 1970). It also notes that 53 of these had taken place between 1945 and 1968. How many of us today can recall the names or locations of more than a handful of these operations?

The British developed a method of torture that involved the, subsequently famous, 'five techniques': isolation, sensory deprivation, seemingly self inflicted pain, exhaustion and humiliation. The 'self inflicted' pain included forcing suspects to stand in stress positions for long periods of time. However, as Cobain (2012) rightly points out, invariably accompanying the five techniques was 'a sixth, unspoken, technique': the threat and practice of severe violence for lack of compliance.

Labour MP Noel-Baker, who had personally witnessed, while in the military, the torture in Cairo, was told that the British only trained people how to resist brainwashing and were not taught to inflict such techniques. Then as now, this was a lie (Cobain 2012). British personnel are still taught R2I (Resistance to Interrogation) at the HQ of the successor to the Intelligence Corps. Today, as back in the 1960s, the

UK's 'psychological warfare' unit is also based there. Today it is called psychological operations.

In 1960 further enquiries by the *Mail* were headed off by the time-honoured British state technique of having a quiet word: the *Mail*'s editor Bill Hardcastle was approached by a senior MoD official and the story was abandoned (Cobain 2012).

Psyops in Ireland 1971–2

A beam of light can be thrown on the internal workings of the secret state by public inquiries such as the 12-year Bloody Sunday Inquiry. This revealed unprecedented detail regarding the events in Derry in January 1972, including significant new material on the operation of military and government propaganda. The account that follows is drawn from the documents, witness statements and cross-examination undertaken by the inquiry. But it also draws on other evidence from the Public Records Office that was not submitted to the Bloody Sunday Inquiry but throws a new light on some of the testimony there (Figure 9.1).

By the 1960s the term psychological operations (psyops for short) had been adopted by the British military, replacing 'psychological warfare'.

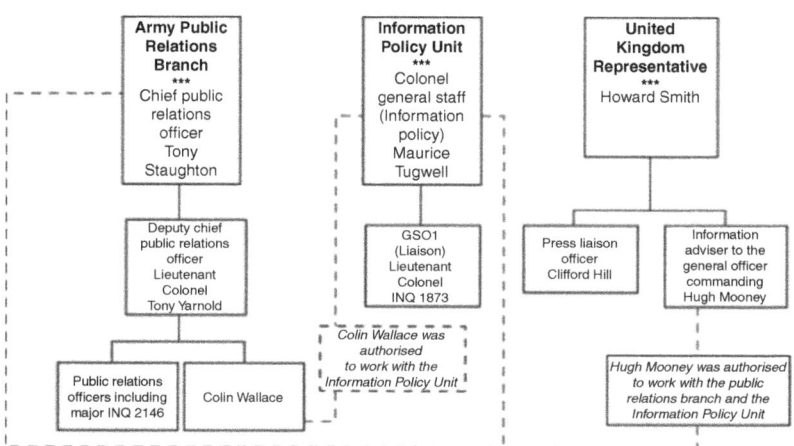

Figure 9.1 Northern Ireland information organisations in January 1972
Source: Report of the The Bloody Sunday Inquiry, Volume IX – Chapter 178 Psyops and military information activity. http://webarchive.nationalarchives.gov.uk/20101103103930/http://report.bloody-sunday-inquiry.org/volume09/chapter178/.

But it was not long before it began to suffer reputational damage. Thus in the terms of reference set for 'psychological operations staff' in July 1971, released to the inquiry, it was noted:

> Security
>
> 7 The term 'psyops' is always to be avoided. The staff will be referred to as the G (Liaison) Staff and some work is to be overtly connected with Community Relations.
>
> (INQ 1873; 1971)

In a later document Colonel Maurice Tugwell (1972), who was in charge of 'Information Policy' at British Army HQ in Northern Ireland from September 1971, had written: 'it is recommended that the term "psyops"' should not be used 'in view of its somewhat sinister connotations'. In general throughout the inquiry the idea that psyops was actually employed was downplayed by the official witnesses, with the exception of the whistleblower Colin Wallace. For example, in his initial statement to the inquiry, an anonymous witness known as INQ 1873 denied any involvement in psyops in Ireland:

> I am aware that the term Psychological Operations (Psyops) was sometimes used loosely in a general context but it is an emotive term and misunderstood. There is a principle that psychological operations may not be conducted against one's own people. That principle was adhered to in the Army's operations and activities in Northern Ireland, certainly during the time I was there – I left in June 1972. The IRA was not considered an enemy in the context of a war and the Republican Movement generally was not the subject of any psychological operations because, as I say, it was expressly forbidden – the citizens of Northern Ireland were 'our own people' and that included the IRA.

A more senior operative sent to join the team was Hugh Mooney, a former journalist from the Information Research Department (IRD), the covert anti-communist propaganda agency of the Foreign Office, subsequently closed down by David Owen when he was Foreign Secretary in 1977 (Lashmar and Oliver 1998; Smith 1980; Wilford 1998). He was given a cover title and said to be from the Home Office. He claimed that it was only junior staff that engaged in 'low level' psyops. Thus, under cross-examination he stated that witness INQ 1873 'was conducting PsyOps against and within the population of Northern Ireland, of course'. INQ 1873 then backtracked, saying: 'Depending on definition, that statement [that psyops was not used] should be amended, after a year of thinking' (INQ 1873; 2002:3).

Questioned as to whether Information Policy, the unit that was set up in late 1971, might in fact have been the realisation of a proposed psyops committee, witness INQ1873 gave the following, somewhat ambiguous, response:

> Q. You know that it appears from this document that the term 'PsyOps' was never to be used, or should not be used, because of its similar [damaging] implications. Could it be that the committee that was set up was called the Military Information Policy Committee?
>
> A. It may have devolved from that...

The general line pursued by the official witnesses was that they had not been involved in psyops and that such work was not regarded seriously by London. Mooney, for example, referred to his own role as 'counter-propaganda', a discipline he distinguished sharply from psyops, which he described as 'low level', 'ill conceived' and 'ineffectual' (Mooney KM6.32). Reading the background evidence to the inquiry, however, it transpires that INQ 1873, far from being rather junior and ineffective, was none other than the British Army's leading expert on psyops, responsible for running the pysops training course at the Joint Warfare Establishment at Old Sarum, Wiltshire, before being posted to Ireland (Powerbase 2015a).

Still, Tugwell told the inquiry:

> it [psyops] reflects to me the much greater obsession amongst civilian organisations, Foreign Office and the IRD [Information Research Department], very much inclined towards secrecy and psychological this and that. I was just not interested in that... [I]t did not affect my policy, which was to back off from PsyOps.

The disagreement was summarised in the Saville Inquiry Report:

> Colin Wallace's evidence was that psyops remained one of the duties of the Information Policy Unit after it replaced the Information Liaison Department. He said that the Unit had three roles, namely to liaise between the Army press room and the Army operations network; to act as a counter-propaganda organisation dealing in white information; and to act in a deniable role, using black operations ('dirty tricks').

Colonel Tugwell, Colonel INQ 1873 and Hugh Mooney denied that the Information Policy Unit had any involvement in psyops. Their disagreement with Colin Wallace's evidence was based to a significant extent on their definition of psyops. Colin Wallace regarded all three of the above activities as psyops. Colonel Tugwell agreed that the first two were duties of the Information Policy Unit but maintained that of these only the third, dirty tricks, should be classed as psyops. The evidence of Colonel Tugwell, Colonel INQ 1873 and Hugh Mooney was that the Information Policy Unit did not engage in this sort of activity. They said that the Information Policy Unit did not disseminate dishonest or misleading information.

In other words, the official line was that psyops had been ended with the creation of the Information Policy Unit. This was a difficult position to accept given that INQ 1873 had indicated that the plans for a psyops committee may have 'devolved' from the discussion they had. Furthermore, it was not at all clear from the evidence given that they really were denying that dishonest or misleading information was circulated. Their denials, were, in the manner observed above in the 1960 case, non-denial denials.

For example, INQ 1873 discussed psyops in Northern Ireland as involving 'anonymous letters to newspapers... occasionally a change in documents or forging documents; by that I mean copying documents and making them appear to be otherwise than what they are'. When asked whether inaccurate information was ever used, he said: 'Not as a general – not as a general distribution, no.' Then a couple of lines later, asked if the information contained in forged documents was 'generally, to your knowledge, be true?', he said, 'Depending on circumstances, ma'am.' Asked if material disseminated by the Information Policy Unit contained untrue information, the closest he got to a denial was: 'Not as a general rule, no' (INQ 1873; 2002).

Tugwell himself struggled to state clearly that deception and dishonesty were ruled out. Firstly, he drew a distinction between the two terms: 'it is not dishonest to carry... out small deception operations. There is nothing dishonest about that.' In cross-examination he was confronted with his own words from 1972: ' "black" activities are unlikely to benefit us except in rare, carefully controlled instances' (Tugwell 1972). He was asked if 'Your requirement was that black activities should be carefully controlled... by the Military Information Policy Committee; is that a fair inference?' to which Tugwell responded 'I think so, yes' (Tugwell

2002). This seems a clear admission that 'black' ops were not themselves ruled out.

A situation of great political delicacy

Downplaying of the role of psyops reflects the great sensitivity of the use of this kind of manipulative technique especially within the borders of the UK. This is further emphasised by a 1973 Ministry of Defence document on psyops that was not disclosed to the Bloody Sunday Inquiry. 'A situation calling for the use of troops in aid of the civil power in the United Kingdom would', it said, 'clearly be one of great political delicacy.'

The document confirms the evidence at the Bloody Sunday Inquiry that the term psyops was considered sensitive. It referred to a psyops teams in Hong Kong and one in Oman (since September 1971) which 'are referred to publicly as Army Information Teams (AIT) for reasons of local expediency' (Stanbridge 1973:A-4).

Contrary to the impression given by official witnesses at the Saville Inquiry, that psyops was a marginal activity which had been phased out, the document says explicitly that 'Strategic psyops' are 'a continuing activity with a high political content'. Formulation of policy and overall strategy in this area was said to involve 'several departments' through a committee (The Defence and Overseas Policy (Official) Committee (Ancillary Measures)) on which the MoD was represented along with Foreign Office departments including, unsurprisingly, the Information Research Department, Mooney's employer. Strategic psyops 'are not wholly or even mainly a military function and are not necessarily linked with actual military operations', though 'military forces may be involved in implementing' (A-2) them. As the document notes, 'Policy is laid down through the Northern Ireland Department', not being, therefore, a matter for relatively junior Army officers.

The document goes on to note that since the Second World War British forces have employed psyops on a number of occasions. In Malaya, they 'were used to isolate the terrorists from the civil population, create apathy, discord and defeatism within the terrorists' organisation, and eventually to conduct an effective surrender campaign'. In Borneo, psyops were 'used successfully'. In Oman, psyops 'have played a valuable part in encouraging the surrender of over 500 rebels, most of whom are now fighting as members of the Government Firquats' (Stanbridge 1973). The Firquats were a paramilitary force trained by the Special Air Service (SAS).

Government policy 'required at the time that "the Services... annotate certain posts to be psyops trained (five day course) by JWE [Joint Warfare Establishment]". In addition other posts were 'annotated' to be 'psyops briefed' (A-4). These posts were listed over six pages in an appendix to the document.

In short, the document gives a markedly different account of the role of psyops to that given by Tugwell and Mooney at the Bloody Sunday Inquiry. It says specifically that psyops is defined as 'planned psychological activities in peace and war directed towards enemy, friendly and neutral audiences to create attitudes and behaviours favourable to the achievement of political and military objectives' (Stanbridge 1973:A-1). This undermines the claim that only dirty tricks or 'black' operations are to be described as psyops. The document also describes UK psyops units in Hong Kong and one in Northern Ireland, which was said to include 'one Colonel and one Lieutenant Colonel at HQNI and one Major at HQ 8 Infantry Brigade all of whom are employed in information policy matters'. This was the unit headed by Tugwell. All the staff were, therefore, employed in psyops posts, a point at variance with his claim that psyops had been stopped. Mooney, of the IRD, had tried to maintain that his job of counter-propaganda was something separate from psyops, but the document unambiguously refers to 'counter propaganda and other aspects of psyops'.

The document also refers to psyops as 'improving relationships with allies, undermining the enemy's will to fight, promoting suspicion and distrust and exploiting disagreements among the enemy' to 'lower morale, promote defeatism, discord, and perhaps panic, and to encourage desertion, defection and surrender' (A-2). 'Deception' is thus referred to as a 'specialised form of psyops' (A-3) and is distinguished from 'public relations', which is 'concerned solely with the dissemination of factual information' (A-2). Much of the document, therefore, undermines the official testimony at the Bloody Sunday Inquiry.

Psyops today

Today psyops continues to be practised by the UK state, including by a secretive military unit called the 15 (UK) Psychological Operations Group, which is the successor to the psyops units deployed in Ireland and other arenas of counter-insurgency warfare.

As in the past the issue of what to call the activity is contentious. Those given the job of managing the communications of the military try to give an impression of openness and transparency. However, the same agencies are sometimes very sensitive to criticism, which can subvert their professed policies of openness.

The Ministry of Defence appointed a 'lead' for 'strategic communication', which was their preferred new term to replace propaganda and psyops (Powerbase 2015b). The Ministry's man in 2010 was Steve Tatham, a Naval officer who says he is the UK's 'longest continuously serving Officer in Information Activities'. He writes that 'Strategic Communication is widely misunderstood. At best it is seen by the military as a developing term for media and information operations. At worst it is seen as spin and propaganda' (Tatham 2008:24). The term 'spin', he notes,

> has gained increasing popularity, often used with reference to the distortion, perhaps even manipulation (perceived or otherwise) of information... In the UK military environment we are confident with terms such as Information and Media Operations, whilst in military staff colleges Influence and Persuasion are debated. Civilian academics may speak of Soft Power and Public Diplomacy and cynics might prefer the use of Propaganda. There is a real danger that Strategic Communication is associated negatively with emotive and often inaccurate terms.
>
> (Tatham 2008:9)

Tatham (2010:1) has claimed that 'I am absolutely required by military doctrine to provide only "factual" information to the media – a requirement I have championed and reinforced through various published academic papers in which I have promoted honesty, accuracy and openness in the military's dealings with the world's media'.

In 2010 Tatham took up the post of commanding officer of the 15 UK Psyops Group, though this was not announced publicly. The BBC reported in 2012 that Tatham 'remains keen to stress that British military psychological operations are not propaganda' (Wyatt 2012):

> 'I absolutely hate that word,' he sighs. 'The term propaganda is applied to untruthful past dictatorial regimes, which used media for their own devious ends. That's not the genesis of psyops. I know a lot of people on the web link propaganda and psyops together, but everything we do is perfectly truthful and perfectly attributable. That's cast in gold. A lie will always catch you out.'

As the BBC reported, 'they say that what they produce must be both attributable and truthful, in stark contrast to the traditional reputation of psyops in the US and on the internet, where conspiracy theories abound' (Wyatt 2012).

The trouble with such reassuring sentiments is that they appear to bear only an ambiguous relation to the truth. Let's take each in turn: the link between psyops and propaganda; 'attribution' and lying; and secrecy and openness.

Propaganda and psyops

Psyops is linked umbilically to propaganda. The accepted account of the genesis of the term is that it entered the English language from the German Nazi phrase *Weltanschauungskrieg* ('world view warfare') (Simpson 1994:11). The British version of the phrase was 'political warfare', as reflected in the name of the Second World War organisation responsible: the Political Warfare Executive. Both the British and German concepts for what later became known as psychological warfare 'links mass communication with selective application of violence (murder, sabotage, assassination, insurrection, counterinsurrection and so on) as a means of achieving ideological, political, or military goals' (Simpson 1994:11).

US military and intelligence organisations 'stretched the definition during World War II to cover a broader range of applications of psychology and social psychology to wartime problems, including battlefront propaganda, ideological training of friendly forces, and ensuring morale and discipline on the home front' (Simpson 1994:11).

Propaganda by Western democratic regimes is very much the origins of psychological warfare. Psychological operations is simply a term used in peacetime as a more palatable alternative to 'warfare'.

Attribution and truth

Claims of truthfulness and attribution can be examined in a number of ways. One is to examine the revised doctrine on 'Information operations' published by the Ministry of Defence published in 2009. It does not seem to substantiate the claim of honesty and accuracy.

> Information operations will on occasion require an aggressive and manipulative approach to delivering messages (usually through the PSYOPS tool). This is essential in order to attack, undermine and defeat the will, understanding and capability of insurgents
>
> (Ministry of Defence 2009:6–5)

Perhaps one can aggressively and manipulatively deliver honest and open messages? The question of attribution goes to the heart of whether psyops engages in 'black' operations. These are operations often thought of as 'dirty tricks', but can be more narrowly defined as activities where the source of the message is disguised or faked, perhaps through forged documents or through radio or TV broadcasts which claim to be from one's opponent. We saw examples above of discussion of this in Northern Ireland in the early 1970s. Colonel Bob Stewart, who commanded the British peacekeeping forces in Bosnia, reportedly 'made use of psyops techniques when he served as an intelligence officer in Northern Ireland during the Troubles' (Kelly 2008). He distinguishes between white and black propaganda: 'White is when you tell things as they are, while black is putting more devious stuff about.' 'The value of psyops can be immense,' he says, 'but whatever you say must be believable, and preferably the truth.' Note: 'preferably' the truth.

Secrecy and openness

Psyops and other official propaganda activities are also chronically secretive and lacking in openness. For example, in 2010 the MoD refused to name the new head of UK psyops even after a Freedom of Information (FoI) request. It was only via other sources that this was confirmed to be Steve Tatham. During the same period Tatham's hitherto open approach as a military spin doctor was reversed. His website had all content removed from it (see Powerbase 2015b). Subsequently, in 2012, Commander Tatham featured in an MoD press release as recipient of an award as commanding officer of 15 Psyops Group. This was the first time it had been acknowledged in public that he had that role. A further FoI request invited the MoD to confirm that he was indeed the commanding officer and the dates of his appointment. The MoD rejected the request on the grounds that it was 'vexatious', but relented on review. The subsequent disclosure included internal MoD correspondence debating whether to release the information in relation to the first (2010) request. In an email to Tatham, released under the FOI Act, an MoD official wrote:

> We are still battling with the FOI request. The latest question is can you confirm that your name as CO of 15 POG is not already in the public domain
> (2 November 2010; 18:44 hrs cited in Tranham 2013)

One of Tatham's subordinates replied in an email dated 3 November 2010 (09.11 hrs): 'just got hold of the boss, re below – absolutely not. He has been meticulous in ensuring that, in the public domain, his name has not been associated with 15POG.'

The Orwellian-sounding 'sword of peace' award was given to Tatham's unit for work to 'inform, reassure, educate and through the promotion of free and unbiased discussion persuade Afghans that their futures are best served not with the Taliban, nor with ISAF, but with themselves and their elected government' (MoD 2012).

The possibility that an occupying power might be able to promote 'free and unbiased' discussion seems, perhaps, a little unlikely in itself. We can note that in the UK (as elsewhere) psyops is part of military intelligence. The 15POG is a component of 1 Military Intelligence Brigade, based at Chicksands in Wiltshire. The base is a key hub for military and defence intelligence. Figure 9.2 (obtained under the Freedom of Information Act) shows the units housed at Chicksands in 2008. These include the Defence Intelligence and Security Centre, which itself houses the Defence School of Intelligence and several intelligence training units including the Human Intelligence Training Wing. Also

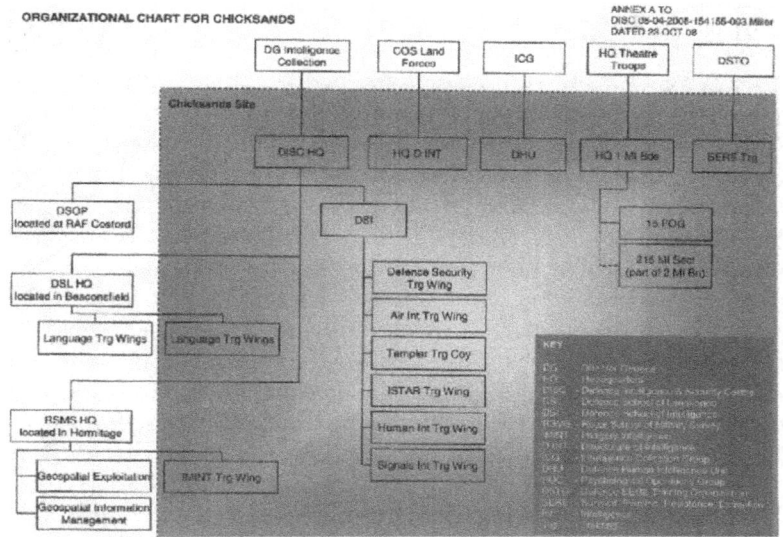

Figure 9.2 Organisational chart for Chicksands, 23 October 2008
Source: Released under FoI. Scan taken by author.

based there is 'SERE Trg', which is part of the Defence SERE Training Organisation. SERE is Survival, Evasion, Resistance, Extraction, and is where military and intelligence personnel are trained to 'resist' interrogation. Then known as the Joint Services Intelligence Organisation, the 'resistance to interrogation training' unit moved to Chicksands in the mid-1990s. There, as Ian Cobain (2012:283) shows in his coruscating book on British involvement in torture, the JSIO 'not only practised interrogation techniques that were cruel and illegal, but also taught others to do likewise'. The Heath government publicly banned torture in 1972 after the outcry about the use of the 'five techniques' used against internees in Northern Ireland. But privately they continued to condone the techniques. 'The use of hoods', notes Cobain (2012:283–4),

> had never been abandoned by the Intelligence Corps. Trainees were also told that prisoners should be kept awake before interrogation, that prisoners should be stripped naked and kept naked until they obeyed orders, and that trainees were permitted to use a technique known as 'harshing': threatening and screaming abuse at high volume as a distance of around six inches from the prisoners' faces.

Cobain notes that the 'R2I' (Resistance to Interrogation) and 'CAC' (Conduct After Capture) training was 'very similar' to the training that 'Guantanamo interrogators had studied at Fort Bragg in North Carolina'; so similar in fact that in the US it was called Survival, Evasion, Resistance and Escape while latterly in the UK it was renamed Survival, Evasion, Resistance, Extraction. Other similarities include the fact that as well as training in torture, Fort Bragg is the main base for psyops in the US, and houses the 4th Military Information Support Group (formerly the 4th Psychological Operations Group (Airborne)) and the 8th Military Information Support Group (Airborne). The Americans are a little more open than the British, having a psyops Facebook presence (see: https://www.facebook.com/8MISG).

In accepting the award on behalf of the 15POG, Steve Tatham (2012) said it was 'a real joy' to accept the award 'on behalf of the Unit which has until now not only been under-recognised for its work in Afghanistan but quite often deliberately misrepresented by conspiracy theorists, pseudo-academics and Hollywood producers'.

'It's easy', he went on, 'for armchair commentators who have never had to place themselves in harm's way to write utter guff...but it does a terrible dis-service to the men and women of the UK's Armed Forces who give so very much.' The 'utter guff' to which Tatham refers is the material on Powerbase, a website edited by the present author (see Powerbase 2015c). Suggesting that critics are 'deliberately misrepresenting' UK psyops is a hard charge to prove. In reality, the conduct and impact of psyops can only be properly analysed in relation to empirical evidence, as opposed to claiming knowledge of the intentions of critics. It is, of course, difficult for officials who are paid to engage in psychological operations, which can, according to the MoD, involve an 'aggressive and manipulative' approach, to step outside that position so as to credibly claim that any particular statement they make is *actually* true.

Psyops and coercion

It is not as if as Tatham, the MoD's 'intellectual lead' on strategic communications during this period, is somehow adrift of official doctrine. In 2008 he acknowledged that the official view does not see strategic communication as simply a matter of communication in itself. Any definition of the concept of strategic communications must 'recognise' he wrote, 'that the success of non-kinetic effect is amplified by threats of kinetic activity... Influence does not mean the exclusion of hard power' (Tatham 2008:15). To be clear: the term 'kinetic' in military doctrine refers to killing (Noah 2002). Major Harry Taylor, head of 42 Commando Royal Marines' psyops, described the approach taken in 2003:

> We use tactical and strategic methods. Tactically, on the first stage, we target the military by dropping leaflets stating the inevitability of their defeat, telling them they will not be destroyed if they play our game and exactly how they can surrender. On the second wave we show them pictures of Iraqi officers who complied. On the third wave we show them pictures of those people who did not.

Translation: co-operate or we will kill you. This approach can be seen in many of the psyops leaflets produced during the Iraq War, which emphasise that, for example, 'Coalition Air Power can strike at will. Any time, Any place' (US Central Command 2002) (Figure 9.3 and 9.4).

Another indication of how 'kinetic effects' or 'hard power' interact with psyops can be seen in the Abu Ghraib torture photos scandal. Some thought that the images of the degradation of Iraqi prisoners showed torture and were 'trophy photos' (Zimbardo 2005). They may have been. But there is evidence not only that the 'enhanced interrogation techniques' were authorised by the Bush administration up to and including the Vice-President and President (BBC News 2014), but also that the images were part of the torture as opposed to merely a record of it.

English Version	Arabic Version
Front: Coalition air power enforces the No-Fly Zones to protect the Iraqi people. Threatening these Coalition aircraft has a consequence. The attacks may destroy you or any location of Coalition choosing. Will it be you or your brother? You decide.	تقوم قوات التحالف الجوية بفرض مناطق الحظر لحماية الشعب العراقي. اي تعرض لطائرات التحالف سيؤدي الى عواقب وخيمة. وقد تدمركم الهجومات او تدمر اي موقع يختاره التحالف. ماذا سيحل بك او باخيك ؟ لك الخيار.
Back: Coalition Air Power can strike at will. Any time, Any place.	بامكان قوات التحالف الجوية القصف في اي وقت و في اي مكان.

Figure 9.3 Coalition air strike leaflets
Source: This image is in the public domain having been released to the media by Centcom.

Figure 9.4 Private Lynndie England with Iraqi prisoner on a leash
Source: This image is in the public domain: http://en.wikipedia.org/wiki/Abu_Ghraib_torture_and_prisoner_abuse#/media/File:Abu-ghraib-leash.jpg.

Seymour Hersh (2004) revealed that this operation ran by the name of Copper Green. According to one of his sources,

> the purpose of the photographs was to create an army of informants, people you could insert back in the population... It was thought that some prisoners would do anything – including spying on their associates – to avoid dissemination of the shameful photos to family and friends.

According to Lynndie England, the poster girl for the Abu Ghraib scandal:

> I was instructed by persons in higher rank to 'stand there, hold this leash and look at the camera.' The pictures were for Psyops reasons... They'd come back and they'd look at the pictures and they'd state, 'Oh, that's a good tactic... This is working. Keep doing it, it's getting what we need'.
>
> (cited in Ronson 2005:166–7)

The Abu Ghraib photos are not, therefore, just a record of torture, but an active part in the process of torture – an illustration of the coercive nature of this kind of psyops and of its continuing and close relationship with intelligence and torture.

Sociology and propaganda

Some conclusions: it is important to go back to examine the work of early sociologists as they have much to teach, not least on the importance of propaganda. Of course it might be that we don't learn the same lessons as they did, but at least we will understand more about how we got where we are now.

Propaganda is not simply a matter of the symbolic, but of concrete action (involving the symbolic) backed up by variably credible threats of force (or economic or other incentives) and sometimes involving actual 'kinetic effects', known more widely as violence and killing. In other words, propaganda is neither simply a matter of ideas and communication (the 'symbolic' or 'discursive'), rather it is a concrete practice involving both ideas and their expression in communication. But communication, being itself part of the material world, combines with the rest of the material (including economic and coercive power) to form social reality. No propaganda strategy takes place outside that. Furthermore, building on this, we can say that propaganda is situated not simply on the consent side of the consent/coercion distinction.

In the examples given above, we can see how the coercive power of the military is integrated into psyops strategies. It is better, I contend, to see propaganda as 'propagating' particular views and interests as a matter of organised persuasive communication.

The question of what we call propaganda is not going away. While the attempt to replace the term with less honest terms such as public relations has had some notable success, particularly in terms of scholarly production, propaganda has not been excised from common usage. The difficulty is that successive replacements for propaganda end up being tainted by association with manipulation and deception. This will continue to happen, as we saw in the example of psychological warfare and its replacement with psyops.

The attempts by state operatives to airbrush their communication strategies, by calling them something sweeter smelling, absorbs significant human and ideological resources. Question their work and you may find that government officials write to your employer to complain, suggest that material about them is 'removed' from the web, denounce 'conspiracy theorists' and 'pseudo-academics' who write 'utter guff' which 'deliberately misrepresent[s]' psyops.

Propaganda and psychological operations have historically been secret and are still not fully and openly acknowledged by the British state or its operatives and disciples. Secrecy is one reason why we have not properly appreciated how propaganda works. But, as we have seen, the willing subordination of sociologists to the interests and values of great power is another.

References

BBC News (2014) 'President George W Bush "knew everything" about CIA interrogation'. 11 December, http://www.bbc.co.uk/news/world-us-canada-30427211, date accessed: 8 May 2015.

Bowers, R. (1968) 'The Military Establishment', in P. Lazarsfeld, W. Sewell and H. Wilensky (eds.) *The Uses of Sociology*. London: Weidenfeld and Nicolson, pp. 234–74.

Broadbent, L., Eldridge, J., Kimmett, G., Philo, P., Spaven, M. and Williams, K. (1985) *War And Peace News*. Milton Keynes: Open University Press.

Cobain, I. (2012) *Cruel Britannia: A Secret History of Torture*. London: Portobello Books.

Dinan, W. and Miller, D. (eds.) (2007) *Thinker, Faker, Spinner, Spy: Corporate PR and the Assault on Democracy*. London: Pluto Press.

Dinan, W. and Miller, D. (2009) 'Journalism, Public Relations and Spin', in K. Wahl-Jorgensen and T. Hanitzsch (eds.) *Handbook of Journalism Studies*. New York: Routledge, pp. 250–64.

Eldridge, J. (2007) 'Merton and Lazarsfeld's Studies in Radio and Film Propaganda: an Exposition and Commentary', Unpublished paper.

Galliher, J. F. and Galliher, J. H. (1995) *Marginality and Dissent in Twentieth Century American Sociology: The Case of Elizabeth Briant Lee and Alfred McClung Lee*. Albany: State University of New York Press.

Glander, T. (2000) *Origins of Mass Communications Research During the American Cold War*. Mahwah, NJ: Lawrence Erlbaum Associates.

Hersh, S. (2004) 'The Gray Zone: How a Secret Pentagon Program Came to Abu Ghraib', *New Yorker*, 24 May. http://www.newyorker.com/magazine/2004/05/24/the-gray-zone, date accessed: 8 May 2015.

INQ 1873 (1971) Headquarters Northern Ireland Psychological Operations Staff Terms of Reference, ISEC 13/9 Copy 3 or 11, Secret, Locsen. KM6.108. http://webarchive.nationalarchives.gov.uk/20101103103930/http://report.bloody-sunday-inquiry.org/evidence/K/KM_0006.pdf, date accessed: 8 May 2015.

INQ 1873 (2002) 'Cross examination of INQ 1873', *Bloody Sunday Inquiry*, Day 242 Wednesday, 2 October. http://webarchive.nationalarchives.gov.uk/20101103103930/http://report.bloody-sunday-inquiry.org/transcripts/Archive/Ts242.htm, date accessed: 29 March 2015.

Kelly, J. (2008) 'The Secret World of "Psy-ops"' *BBC News*. 20 June. http://news.bbc.co.uk/1/hi/uk/7464430.stm, date accessed: 8 May 2015.

Lashmar, P. and Oliver, J. (1998) *Britain's Secret Propaganda War 1948–77*. Stroud: Sutton Publishing.

Lasswell, H. (1927) *Propaganda Technique in World War I*. New York: Alfred A. Knopf.

Lasswell, H., Casey, R. and Lannes Smith, B. (eds.) (1969 [1935]) *Propaganda and Promotional Activities: An Annotated Bibliography*. Chicago, IL: University of Chicago Press.

Lazarsfeld, P and Merton, R. (1943) 'Studies in Radio and Film Propaganda', *Transactions of the New York Academy of Sciences*, 6 (2) Series II: 58–74.

Lee, A. M. (1951) *How to Understand Propaganda*. New York: Rinehart and Co.

Lynd, R. S. (1939) *Knowledge for What? The Place of Social Science In American Culture*. Princeton, NJ: Princeton University Press.

Miller, D. (1993) 'Official Sources and Primary Definition: The Case of Northern Ireland', *Media, Culture and Society*, 15 (3): 385–406.

Miller, D. (1994) *Don't Mention the War: Northern Ireland, Propaganda and the Media*. London: Pluto.

Ministry of Defence (1970) *Land Operations Volume III – Counter Revolutionary Operation Part 3 – Counter Insurgency*. Army Code No 70516 (Part 3), 5 January.

Ministry of Defence (2009) 'British Army Field Manual–Volume 1–Part 10 Countering Insurgency', Army Code 71876, October, http://news.bbc.co.uk/1/shared/bsp/hi/pdfs/16_11_09_army_manual.pdf, date accessed: 8 May 2015.

Mooney, H. (2002) 'In the Matter of the Bloody Sunday Inquiry: Hugh Mooney States by Way of Supplementary Statement' 11 September. KM6.32. http://webarchive.nationalarchives.gov.uk/20101103103930/http://report.bloody-sunday-inquiry.org/evidence/K/KM_0006.pdf, date accessed: 8 May 2015.

Noah, T. (2002) 'Birth of a Washington Word: When Warfare gets "kinetic"', *Slate*, 20 November. http://www.slate.com/articles/news_and_politics/chatterbox/2002/11/birth_of_a_washington_word.html, date accessed: 8 May 2015.
Philo, G., Miller, D. and Happer, C. (2015) 'Circuits of Communication and Structure of Power: the Sociology of the Mass Media', in M. Holborn (ed.) *Contemporary Sociology*. Cambridge: Polity, pp. 444–71.
Powerbase (2015a) 'Bernard Renouf "Johnny" Johnston' http://powerbase.info/index.php/Bernard_Renouf_%22Johnny%22_Johnston, date accessed: 8 May 2015.
Powerbase (2015b) 'Steve Tatham', http://powerbase.info/index.php/Steve_Tatham, date accessed: 8 May 2015.
Powerbase (2015c) '15 (UK) Psychological Operations Group' http://powerbase.info/index.php/15_(UK)_Psychological_Operations_Group, date accessed: 8 May 2015.
Qualter, T. (1985) *Opinion Control in the Democracies*. London: Macmillan.
Ronson, J. (2005) *The Men Who Stare at Goats*. London: Picador.
Saville, M., Hoyt, W. and Toohey J. (2010) 'Psyops and Military Information Activity' *Report of The Bloody Sunday Inquiry*, Volume IX – Chapter 178, http://webarchive.nationalarchives.gov.uk/20101103103930/http://report.bloody-sunday-inquiry.org/volume09/chapter178/, date accessed: 8 May 2015.
Schlesinger, P. (1990) 'Rethinking the Sociology of Journalism: Source Strategies and the Limits of Media-Centrism', in M. Ferguson (ed.), *Public Communication: The New Imperatives*. London: Sage, pp. 61–83.
Simpson, C. (1994) *Science of Coercion: Communication Research and Psychological Warfare, 1945–1960*. New York: Oxford University Press.
Smith, L. (1980) 'Covert British Propaganda: The Information Research Department, 1947–77.' *Millennium: Journal of International Studies*, 9 (1): 67–83.
Stanbridge, B.G.T. (1973) 'Psychological Operations – Note by the Secretary', Chiefs of Staff Committee, Ministry of Defence. COS 17/73 No 104 of 108 copies. 6 April.
Tatham, S. (2008) *Strategic Communication: A Primer*. Advanced Research and Assessment Group, Defence Academy of the United Kingdom, Special Series, 8 (2), http://www.aco.nato.int/resources/9/Conference%202011/08%2828%29ST%5B1%5D.pdf, date accessed: 21 March 2015.
Tatham, S. (2010) 'Letter to Jim Macdonald', Principal, University of Strathclyde, 6 February. [Copy in the authors' possession]
Tatham, S. (2012) 15 (UK) 'PsyOps Group win Sword of Peace', *Behavioural Conflict*, 28 October. http://behavioural-conflict.tumblr.com/post/34357877060/15-uk-psyops-group-win-sword-of-peace, date accessed: 8 May 2015.
Taylor, P.M (1999) *British Propaganda in the Twentieth Century: Selling Democracy*. Edinburgh: Edinburgh University Press.
Tranham, A. (2013) Freedom of Information Act 2000 – Internal Review. Ministry of Defence. CIO/3/18/1/768 (AIT reference: 23-01-2013-124610-006). 2 August.
Tugwell, M. (1972) Military Information Policy Committee, Military Information Policy for January – Jun 1972 – A note by the Chairman Military Information Working Party, NISEC 13/5/2, 24 January 1972. http://webarchive.nationalarchives.gov.uk/20101103103930/http://report.bloody-sunday-inquiry.org/evidence/G/G70C.pdf, date accessed: 8 May 2015.

Tugwell, M. (2002) Under cross examination. Bloody Sunday Inquiry, 1 October 2002. http://webarchive.nationalarchives.gov.uk/20101103103930/http://report.bloody-sunday-inquiry.org/transcripts/Archive/Ts241.htm.

Vatican (2015) 'Congregation for the Evangelization of Peoples' http://www.vatican.va/roman_curia/congregations/cevang/index.htm, date accessed: 8 May 2015.

Wilford, H. (1998) 'The Information Research Department: Britain's Secret Cold War Weapon Revealed', *Review of International Studies*, 24 (3): 353–69.

Williams, R. (1980) 'Means of Communication and Means of Production' in R. Williams, *Problems in materialism and Culture*. London: Verso, pp. 50–63.

Williams, R. (1985) *Towards 2000*. London: Penguin.

Wyatt, C. (2012) 'Psy-ops: Tuning the Afghans into Radio', *BBC News*. 27 October, http://www.bbc.co.uk/news/world-south-asia-20096416, date accessed: 8 May 2015.

Zimbardo, P. (2005) 'The "Trophy Photos": Abu Ghraib's Horrors and Worse' *Zimbardo.com*. 25 October, http://www.zimbardo.com/downloads/Trophy%20Photos%20OP%20ED%20.pdf, date accessed: 8 May 2015.

10
Sociology of the Media: Towards an Ideal Journalistic Practice

Giuliana Tiripelli

Introduction

This chapter discusses the ways in which the concept of the *sociological imagination* can inform media studies and strengthen their emancipatory potential, and it does so by focusing on research about the Israeli-Palestinian conflict. It advocates a critical sociological approach in media studies, which can raise journalistic awareness about the practice of journalism as a social product and journalists as influential social actors. Drawing on recent literature and innovative approaches, which argue for a transformative yet responsible journalism, the chapter shows how critical sociological approaches to media can support journalism in redefining its practices and ideals and stimulating the development of a progressive journalistic field. Reflecting upon the concept of the *sociological imagination* in this light, it expands on the debate about engaged sociology in the field of media studies. It proposes ways ahead for the emancipatory project for media studies, which entails engaging with viable alternatives and transformation, alongside diagnoses and critique of problems (Wright 2010). Reflexivity about the discipline lies at the base of this project. What motivated C. Wright Mills to conceptualise the *sociological imagination* was his profound worry about the discipline of sociology, which in his view had become either a form of abstracted empiricism or a grand theory (cf. Du Bois 2000). The purpose of social science was, for Mills, to draw attention to and expose contemporary social problems, offering a lens through which the social structures affecting and shaping individual experience within history can be investigated. As Brewer declared in his reassertion of Mills's *sociological imagination*, sociology should 'hold individual biography, the social structure, history and political power in balance in the one framework' (Brewer 2003:33). For Mills this was not, however, the sole aim of the discipline, but rather an intermediate one and a part of the wider orientation of the sociological enterprise. Discussing the interest of social scientists in the history of social structures, Mills stated that:

> we study the structural limits of human decision in an attempt to find points of effective intervention, in order to know what can and what must be structurally changed if the role of explicit decision in history-making is to be enlarged.
>
> (Mills 2000:174)

In other words, the *sociological imagination* was also the product of an underlying aspiration for the discipline to contribute to fairer societies. This chapter aims to explore this idea further. Such an endeavour is based on a renewed interest in the individuals who develop sociology, namely the social scientists, who 'locate themselves within the intellectual life and the social-historical structure of their times' (Mills 2000:179). Initially, this reflexive prerequisite can be understood as a call for sociological awareness on the part of social scientists, and a reflection on their relation to the phenomena they research and the methods and categories they apply in their investigations. Secondly, such reflexivity can be understood as entailing critical awareness about the knowledge produced by the sociological enterprise. In the first case, situating the social scientist within the field of their own discipline is a way to avoid unexamined assumptions in the process of knowledge production. In the second case, it is a way to assess the validity of existing knowledge, acknowledge its historical production and hence accept that what is considered valid knowledge may change in time or space. On the one hand, developing the project of *sociological imagination* by incorporating the concept of change in the sociological enterprise entails the deployment of both aspects of reflexivity, in order to recognise knowledge construction as a social product, that 'also help(s) to constitute that social world' (Law et al. 2011:4). On the other hand, it also entails avoiding the risks that reflexivity may carry and which may hinder the sociological pursuit for improved forms of society when all forms of knowledge are taken to be equally valid. In this light, the present chapter discusses approaches in research about the role of media in the Israeli-Palestinian conflict, focusing in particular on the work of the Glasgow University Media Group (GUMG). It takes the latter as an example in order to reflect on how media studies have contributed to the production of knowledge about journalism in conflicts, and what the implications have been for the improvement of journalistic practices in the presence of social tensions, in order to highlight ways to strengthen the contribution of media sociology to social change.

The contribution of media studies to the sociological imagination

The Israeli-Palestinian conflict has been in the spotlight of mainstream media for many years. Research on, and political debate about, conflicts and the role of media have been especially attracted to this situation (see for example Ackerman 2001; Deprez and Raeymaeckers 2010; Lowstedt and Madhoun 2003; Noakes and Gwinn Wilkins 2002; Rinnawi 2007; Ruigrok et al. 2009; Wolfsfeld 2004; Zelizer et al. 2002) This research has highlighted many limitations in the coverage of this conflict. Here, the work of the GUMG has made a significant contribution, revealing the extent to which certain narratives dominate and remain dominant in the media, whilst others are marginalised (Philo and Berry 2011). Among the reasons for this, Philo and Berry list, first of all, the limiting factors originating from the ways in which the mainstream media sector works, such as time and space constraints (Philo and Berry 2011:319), which make it difficult for journalists to present a different coverage of the conflict. They also refer to the efficacy of the pro-Israeli PR machine, which operates to strengthen specific frames of coverage among professionals (Philo and Berry 2011:320). The GUMG argue that these factors are then incorporated and activated through the agency of journalists, who usually choose to rely on those established practices, narratives and frames which are also widely supported by the sector. In this way, they circumvent the complaints and pressures arising when alternative narratives are produced (Philo and Berry 2011:322). Such research is grounded in new methodologies, forged by the GUMG to analyse the communication process comprehensively. Based on a clear understanding of the limits of a discourse-focused analysis of news (Philo 2007), the GUMG have expanded their approach through analysis of the production and consumption processes of media outputs. Further, interviews with a variety of journalists working in the field have allowed for an in-depth examination of the factors that shape news content, revealing the reasons why certain explanations recur in mainstream media content. Similarly, interviewing audiences has exposed the narratives most commonly employed by the public and their links to mainstream media content. Philo and Berry, for example, discovered that 'in 2009, two thirds of our sample still did not know who was occupying the occupied territories' (2011:398). This reveals how a comprehensive analysis of the communication process is crucial for a measurement of the actual power of the media in shaping beliefs and attitudes about the Israeli-Palestinian conflict.

Through their work, the GUMG have continued the general tendency of media studies to contribute to the identification of current social problems in the way that Mills advocated. These studies can thus be understood as contributions to the 'truth', but also as contributing to the values of freedom and reason (Mills 2000:178–9). To powerful subjects, such as governments and politicians, researchers have imputed 'varying measures of responsibility for such structural consequences' (Mills 2000:185). In *More Bad News from Israel*, for instance, Philo and Berry have compared politicians' statements with those of the witnesses to the Mavi Marmara assault in 2010. In this way, they have showed how politicians reframed and shifted responsibility for the killing of nine activists, and how mainstream media, although critical of Israeli behaviour in that case, never clearly presented the Palestinian side of the story (Philo and Berry 2011:381–93). Media studies have also spoken to 'those whose actions have such consequences, but who do not seem to be aware of them' (Mills 2000:185), namely the journalists. They have done so by highlighting the social nature of what practitioners usually consider to be standard practice and the 'natural' bricks of free and professional behaviour. This is the case, for example, with requirements such as objectivity and balance in reporting, which have been critically discussed, and defined by scholars as social and historical constructs (for example, Schudson 2001). Finally, 'to those who are regularly without such power and whose awareness is confined to their everyday milieux', that is audiences and individuals living under forms of oppression, media research has revealed 'the meaning of structural trends' and 'the ways in which personal troubles are connected with public issues' and with 'the actions of the more powerful' (Mills 2000:185).

In these ways, this area of research has applied the *sociological imagination* to the Israeli-Palestinian conflict. Speaking to those with power, to unaware agents and powerless subjects, media research has highlighted the 'real' dimension of this conflict, showing the limits imposed to social discourse about it. Media sociology has also provided the tools to recognise who has responsibility in supporting and nourishing these limits, and it has shown that the media are important in maintaining beliefs that support particular interpretations of this conflict and prevent change.

Limits to the sociological imagination in media studies

However, there is still one issue that has remained largely unaddressed by research on media and journalism. Focusing solely on the circuits of existing coverage, media studies of conflicts have often let the burden of finding a solution to the agents in the field who, at the same time, they have depicted as constrained by structural factors. In other words, media research has done less to identify what Mills called 'the objective chances available... to become free and rational as individuals' (Mills 2000:184). Therefore, the following questions should be posed: are there ways in which media sociology could promote a different journalism while remaining a scientific endeavour; and can this different journalism support the transformation of this conflict while remaining an informative service? This section reviews the factors that prevent this development in the discipline of media sociology. It discusses how the underlying, unresolved tension between media studies and the subjects and phenomena under investigation subtly detracts from a contribution to a wider social understanding of the conflict and the possibility of arriving at solutions.

This tension is, first of all, a consequence of the focus of media studies on the role of the media in maintaining the status quo. On the one hand, this focus is justified by the fact that mainstream media operate conservatively, and that usually research investigates phenomena as they are in their current forms. On the other hand, this focus entails researching issues and developments as dictated and framed by the media themselves. In the case of the Israeli-Palestinian conflict, this translates into adopting a dichotomy, the Israeli versus Palestinian one, which also dominates accounts in the mainstream media. However, the means to understand how the conflict is maintained and how the media play this conservative role also lie in events, factors and discourses that are not part of the mainstream frames that are usually analysed. These factors and discourses are the more fluid and unexplored social aspects of life and action in the field. For example, they are embedded in the complex relations among different social groups within Israel, or within the Palestinian community, and the different kinds of relations between Israelis, Palestinians and foreign subjects (journalists, activists, NGOs); these factors even lie in the work of Israeli and Palestinian individuals who pursue the transformation of the conflict on the ground, who have relations with journalists and who participate, stage and even manage the events for the media. Lastly these factors and discourses are embedded in the power relations between foreign and local journalists (Bishara 2013), relations which shape media discourse in unbalanced ways without appearing in it. In other words, by avoiding what does exist in the field and on the ground outside media circuits and mainstream narratives, media analysis can constrain itself to a mediacentric understanding of social processes. It can thus contribute to concealing further those narratives and factors which the media already hides from their audiences, but which still operate in shaping the Israeli-Palestinian conflict and its coverage. A media focus of this kind, then, also has the effect of further silencing those narratives which could transform the conflict should they have been more visible.

Secondly, the tension between media studies and social phenomena is the product of the tendency to evaluate the media for their capacity to represent the conflict as it is defined in material terms (land, boundaries, victims and so on), all of which belong to the history of this conflict. The historical focus, however, can contract the space available for definitions of change and for a discussion of options that could facilitate such change. To highlight this point, it is useful to briefly reflect on the term 'occupation', and the subtle tension between its ability to represent vis-à-vis its ability to transform. Occupation is the legal term used to define Israeli management of Palestinians land. The term is a valid instrument to highlight the degree of oppression under which Palestinians live, and it is the outcome of the symbolic and pragmatic success of some part of their struggle to reveal the lack of justice and the need for change. At the same time, however, it can also reproduce a conflict dynamic, pushing the debate about the conflict and its transformation in a specific direction. This is because the term occupation is linked to material and historical terms of the conflict – the land occupied – and carries within it specific assumptions about its solution. It often implies that the land occupied in 1967 should be freed from Israeli presence in order for a Palestinian state to emerge alongside the state of the Israelis. This interpretation of change can limit alternative and potentially more transformative discussions such as, for example, the one-state solution. This option focuses on democratic principles and political rights instead of land and ethnicity. As clarified by former Israeli Prime Minister Ehud Olmert to *Haaretz* (Ravid et al. 2007), it is much more feared as a solution by Israel than a land swap for a two-state settlement because: 'If the day comes when the two-state solution collapses, and we face a South African-style struggle for equal voting rights (also for the Palestinians in the territories), then, as soon as that happens, the State of Israel is finished.'

The one-state option threatens and unveils the deeper causes of the conflict, the discrimination against the Palestinians and the lack of fully democratic political practices in Israel, which manifest themselves today in the politics of separation and closure, internal discrimination against Israeli Palestinians, the suspension of law (Gordon 2009:256–7), alongside occupation. Rebalancing the focus between occupation of land and political rights would allow the causes and solutions of the conflict to emerge innovatively in the public debate, adding transformative power to narratives of justice. Research has already demonstrated the ability of the media to reinforce a dominant understanding of the terms of the conflict. This example is useful in reflecting about approaches that can also explain how discourses and debates about the past and present of the conflict hide future options of 'peace', and how they prepare the ground for other scenarios.

Thirdly, despite their critical approach media studies have often adopted categories of analysis from the media sector, directly or indirectly relying on professional concepts as tools to evaluate the media.[1] This can create tensions, which journalist Loris Luyendijk highlights in his claim that 'while social scientists recognize that knowledge is never neutral, they do seem to expect from their media organizations objectivity and neutrality' (Luyendjik 2007:8). In reality, the ideal, positive journalism that media studies often seem to assume as best practice, namely that which gives equal space to Israeli and Palestinian explanations, stems from the widely supported legal expectation of balance. But a journalism that fulfils this ideal expectation would still produce a limited representation of reality for sociology, one which is based on a dichotomy dictated by journalism. Such implied ideal journalism is also in tension with the analysis that sociology has applied to representation. Representations are grounded, contextual readings of the real originating from multiple, specific social positions, arising from a continuous struggle over meaning, which is particularly intense in the case of this conflict. This struggle makes it difficult to select information in the absence of values and visions additional to the professional ones. This is clarified by Luyendijk, who speaks of his difficulty of covering the Israeli-Palestinian conflict:

> If you wanted to be objective, there were no neutral terms. And you couldn't just list all the terms: 'Today in Ramallah, on the occupied or disputed or liberated West Bank of the Jordan River or Samaria, two Palestinians or Muslims or Arab newcomers or terrorists or freedom

fighters were killed or slaughtered by Israeli soldiers or Israeli defence forces or Zionist occupying troops...'.

(Luyendijk 2009:141)

As a practice, journalism relies on its ability to make choices. The ideology of journalism makes practitioners think that choices which are congruent with the professional principles of journalism do not have intrinsic political aims. Media studies have already shown how a journalism which uncritically applies neutrality and balance in an unbalanced conflict risks conservatism, because it tends to draw on discourses that powerful subjects make available in society. In sociology, however, representing always entails positioning oneself and producing effects. This highlights the problematic nature of the norms of journalism as analytical categories in media studies. Although they allow scientists to measure whether the media do what they claim to do in the way that they claim to do it, these categories also shape the boundaries of knowledge production. They make it less sociological and they inhibit the engagement of research with alternative ideals for the profession, which arise from sociological normative approaches instead from the ideology of the sector, and which the journalists could use as alternative to make their choices. In sum, what has allowed media studies to contribute to the knowledge about this conflict and its coverage, its focus on the media, their peculiarities, language and ideas, can also be seen as a factor constraining the transformative potential in the discipline. It has limited space for an empirical analysis of those aspects that remain outside the media sphere of production, content and reception, but still shape the conflict and the debate about it, or which, more importantly, could promote its transformation. This focus has also prevented the full development of reflections on what could be the scientific contribution of media sociology to social change and the promotion of a renewed journalism that could give more space to hidden transformative factors. The next part of the chapter aims to reflect on this possibility, offering some insights into how this could be done.

Old and mew transformative constituents for media studies

In this second part of the chapter, I discuss how the relation between media sociology and the phenomena it studies allows for a scientific exploration of possible ways which can improve journalism and strengthen its progressive force. This section expands upon the concept of *sociological imagination* to discuss the theoretical basis for such exploration in media studies. The final section reviews current literature and provides examples in order to highlight paths ahead for a transformative sociology and journalism.

Mills contends that imagination constitutes a tool for the study of human variety (2000:225), the study of the present, instead of something which does not exist yet. However, he also spoke of the passion to solve problems as a largely lost value in social sciences (Mills 2000:122, 141). He believed that 'we study historical social structures, in brief, in order to find within them the ways in which they are and can be controlled' (Mills 2000:174). In his work, he called not only reason, but also freedom, fundamental values that guide sociological research. He defined the latter as 'first of all, the chance to formulate the available choices, to argue over them – and then, the opportunity to choose' (Mills 2000:174), and further argued that:

> Beyond this, the problem of freedom is the problem of how decisions about the future of human affairs are to be made and who is to make them. Organizationally, it is the problem of a just machinery of decision. Morally, it is the problem of political responsibility. Intellectually, it is the problem of what are now the possible futures of human affairs.
>
> (Mills 2000:174)

Therefore, the *sociological imagination* should also highlight 'under what conditions do men come to want to be free' (Mills 2000:175).

It is possible to expand upon the definitions originally provided by Mills to reflect upon how a static understanding of the multiple levels of social experience can transform into active knowledge about the Israeli-Palestinian conflict and the media. The transformative constituents of sociological inquiry can be coherently developed in approaches which promote a multi-dimensional understanding of change. In media studies particularly, the first of these transformative approaches entails the strengthening of an understanding of the changes already achieved, which can be measured. This can be linked to research that highlights, for example, the factors that allow for the formation of narratives that are alternatives to those dominating the media, both in relation to this conflict and beyond. Moreover, research which shows how media narratives of conflicts interact with other factors (such as smaller developments in the field, professional relations and so on – see Bishara 2013; or national narratives – see Ashuri 2010) to shape individual beliefs over time as well as how subjects, in turn, behave in their society as a consequence of this, can be included. The aim of this first transformative approach is not that of distorting the real space that minor narratives occupy and the power they exert. It is instead a way to reveal the out-of-sight conditions and spaces through which change can be negotiated and achieved, and to contribute to an appreciation of how social change can be arrived at. The second approach towards a transformative media studies can be developed through a more explicit discussion in research of ways in which to challenge and improve practices. This can be done by expanding the analysis of journalistic constraints beyond their identification as problems and approaching them instead as problems to be solved; thus framing a preliminary discussion for ways ahead and early steps for change, following the example of research such as that produced by Philo and Happer (2013). Reflecting upon and discussing potential or real alternatives to the specific conservative practices that the analysis has highlighted is a way to promote intersectoral dialogue about these practices and about potential alternatives.

However, opening a discussion about alternative narratives and ways of action may not be sufficient to stimulate change in the presence of established ideologies. As a consequence, a third necessary constituent of a transformative approach in media studies can consist of expanding the ethnographic element in media investigations of production, content and reception, in order to explain how micro-level practices concur in shaping dominant narratives, and how they could contribute to the transformation of this conflict, through a more anthropological lens. As will be discussed in the final part of the chapter, this lens could help the discipline to clarify for journalists the link between their individual choices and structural factors at play, revealing in new ways how, for example, their seemingly autonomous choices about what stories to cover and sources to use are practically determined by factors such as lobbying and political agents (Philo and Berry 2011:319–31). At the same time, a wider ethnographic approach to journalism can enrich current conceptualisations of journalism cultures (see for example Hanitzsch 2007) as has recently been done by Bourdon (2015), and can strengthen their alternative forms, as for example Peace Journalism (Lynch and McGoldrick 2005a). Finally, this expansion in research responds to the call for a renewal of ethnographic media studies (Cottle 2007; Zelizer 2004b:67–8). Ethnography can be particularly helpful to unveil the links between practices and the different virtual and physical spaces beyond the classic newsroom that journalists work and live in today.

Stretching the *sociological imagination* in this way, media studies can fulfil the mission that Mills envisioned for the discipline, namely the use of science to see what usually remains invisible in our lives and contexts. In addition, the transformative constituents might allow media studies to more easily move beyond critique and make a more direct contribution to positive social change. Firstly, reflecting on the possibility of change and formulating visions of social transformation allows researchers to think about whether measurements of distortions, constraints and other factors among those we label as media problems are fully consistent with the assumed 'good', unproblematic forms of journalism and society at the basis of research, and to evaluate these forms more openly. Secondly, a transformative focus can help in recovering and bringing to light the possibility of alternative social arrangements, and making clear the conditions by which choices about the future might be made possible. Reflecting on change in these terms then becomes a way in which to help journalism find a new balance between professional and social normative values, and redefine its role. In other words, it becomes a way to foster the ability of journalism to challenge attitudes rather than trigger reactions, an ability that belongs to those representations which are 'imbued with the sociological imagination' (McLaughlin 2002:4).

Transformative media sociology for a transformative journalism

There is a composite variety of literature and approaches which can be brought together and exploited in order to help journalism redefine its norms, and raise awareness about the social role of news in the sector. The first component of this literature is that which considers Peace Journalism. Peace Journalism engages with ideal forms of journalism (setting Peace Journalism as the professional ideal) and society (setting peace as the social ideal). It marries media and change within a progressive and normative vision of journalism, and it constitutes a development of the transformative approach in media studies. Galtung's model of Peace Journalism (reproposed in Galtung 2002; 2006, revisited by Lynch and McGoldrick 2005a) is being applied in the field.[2] This application can serve as a means to evaluate how media content can support change in such specific situations, and it focuses on the subjects directly affected by conflicts. According to the supporters of Peace Journalism, a journalism which chooses to play a transformative role instead of a conservative one in society also aims to remain an informative service for all. The problem of making social transformation a key aim of journalism and maintaining commitment to the truth has been at the centre of the debate about Peace Journalism. The responses of the advocates of this model rightly point to the fact that any story is a representation, and the news is always the result of choices made by the journalists. However, those representations provided by classic conflict-focused journalism, or 'war journalism', are less truthful. These contain 'a hidden bias in favour of violence' and they render 'conflict opaque, obscuring the structural factors driving the cycle of violence and occluding the political steps necessary to interrupt and divert it' (Lynch and McGoldrick 2005b:12). They are also biased in favour of official sources, events (over processes) and dualism (Lynch and McGoldrick 2005a:203–12), and can incite further conflict in comparison to Peace Journalism (Lynch and McGoldrick 2005a:6–31). The supporters of Peace Journalism thus do not advocate the fabrication of stories in order to produce certain effects, but they acknowledge the fact that there are alternative ways to truthfully represent, for example, Israel-Palestine relations and their tension, which are usually under-represented in the media, but which can also play a transformative role. The issue, therefore, is partly about the choice of alternative stories and language, for example: a focus on individual stories and humanisation of all sides; a focus on conflict formation instead of the conflict arena; giving voice to more groups involved instead of just the two sides (Lynch and McGoldrick 2005a:6). This choice is based on an awareness of the unavoidable social role and effects of all media. However, the original supporters of Peace Journalism are careful in distinguishing their model from peace activism, and to do this they reaffirm the importance of balance (Lynch and Galtung 2010:53–5, 61), and they state that 'the criteria of objectivity are at least as valid for peace as for war journalism' (2010:61). In this model balance consists of coverage that includes all the elements required by Peace Journalism (attention to all goals and all parties, people and elites, all phases of conflict),[3] instead of the partial ones (the conflict arena, goals of visible parties, elites, violent phase) required by classic war journalism (Lynch and Galtung 2010:54–5, 12–14). It is this coherent application of the model which prevents a partisan coverage. The way in which peace journalists have covered certain events shows that it is possible for journalism to engage with the idea of social normative aims for journalism, without betraying the need to provide accurate information, and commit to the professional normative aims of truthfulness and fairness of the news.[4] Lynch and McGoldrick also provide ideas for a Peace Journalism coverage of the Israeli-Palestinian conflict (2005a).

This coverage focuses, for example, on the experience of Israelis who supported Palestinians, and the support for peaceful solutions among both, in order to weaken the conflict-focused media dichotomy of Israelis versus Palestinians; or it focuses on the experiences of refuseniks and the militarism of Israeli society (2005a:168–77),[5] in order to shift 'some of the blame from the individuals on either side to the system of relations' (2005a:177). Following this model, journalism could further focus on the complexity and fragmentation in Israeli society, and how the conflict advantages only some Israelis, instead of representing Israel as a united entity standing behind the conflict, in order to promote future joint transformative action between some Israelis and some Palestinians; or it could focus on the more secular and modern aspects of daily life which Palestinians and Israelis share. This last focus could help an Israeli audience recognise Palestinians outside the frame of alien aggressors, but also outside the frame of victims living in poor conditions, or as belonging to an underdeveloped and archaic community. A journalist who decides to endorse this model will have to walk through alternative paths and directly experience the life of the people living the conflict. This is the opposite of detachment. This journalist will also have to decide what is the target of this transformative approach; and this is about choice, not balance. In other words, a journalism which is fully aware of its social nature takes charge of the social effects it produces, and can critically redefine its professional ideals in relation to the contribution that information makes to society whilst still adhering to an idea of truthfulness. Producing truthful information, peace journalists try to promote new understandings that can facilitate change, without providing the fuel for antagonistic and defensive arguments which can obscure the complexity of social life in the public debate.

However, Peace Journalism has delayed its engagement with questions of formation of audience beliefs. In other words, it has not comprehensively measured its impact on the people it wanted to affect. This gap in the literature has left an uncertainty about the possibility that the practice of Peace Journalism could effectively promote change, at least until very recently. A new contribution in this direction displays promising results and innovative methodologies (Lynch 2012, McGoldrick and Lynch 2014), and it lays the foundations for an approach in Peace Journalism which considers the wider and dynamic processes shaping audiences' reception and reaction to media texts. As highlighted by Philo and Happer, beliefs and behaviours are shaped through recurring dominant (and alternative) narratives in a variety of media outlets and forms, alongside changing flows of experience (2013:42). This enhanced vision of belief formation is the outcome of a comprehensive approach that has always marked the work of the GUMG. In addition, the group has recently contributed to our understanding of the transformation of beliefs with innovative and pioneering work in measuring audience reaction to media texts and discussing how change of beliefs and behaviours could be achieved (Philo and Happer 2013). Combined with a focus on the people living the conflict (discussed below), this comprehensive analysis of belief formation is the element that can enrich normative models such as Peace Journalism, fully developing the transformative potential within media studies.

In order for the models and findings of media sociology to have a wider transformative effect on journalism, there is also a need for an enhanced dialogue between sociologists and journalists at large. The work of GUMG has provided a basis from which to develop an intersectoral debate about ways in which to practically promote change in the provision of media information. In the conclusions to *Communicating Climate Change and Energy Security*, Philo and Happer call on climate scientists to engage with the media to provide contextualised information and clearly express commitment to 'take ownership of the debates' (2013:145), and to work with journalists (2013:146). In this way, they suggest paths ahead for the resolution of the problems they discussed, fulfilling the need to engage with the challenges they identify. Unlike climate change, however, conflicts are not problems that hard science can solve; they are, rather, the objects of analysis for social scientists, who have already shown strong commitment to this kind of social problem. At the same time, their collaboration with the wider journalist population is similarly weak, but much needed. In this case, it is the journalists who usually keep a distance from research findings. In order for media studies to benefit the journalists who still operate along the classic lines of journalism in this conflict, it can be necessary to expand upon a scientific discussion of solutions, one which allows scientists and practitioners to negotiate how change could be achieved and to propose ideal forms of journalism. Widening the space for this debate would help in legitimating the very idea of a need for alternative practices, those which traditional journalism labels as naïve and unprofessional, especially in the coverage of the Israeli-Palestinian conflict. Introducing options for a solution of problems alongside research results is also a way to reframe media problems as opportunities for those journalists who feel their professional identity is threatened by media studies, and who therefore do not engage with its findings.

A wider focus on journalists' perspectives and experiences as they understand them can also facilitate this dialogue. In order to challenge the ideals which journalists hold and through which they justify their current practices, and strengthen support for change within the sector, media studies can further show that journalists' beliefs are carefully taken into account before their products are evaluated; namely that researchers take not only the conditions of their work, but also the difficulties involved in choosing to act differently, into full consideration. Media studies have already offered a path to develop this transformative approach through the emergence of a new research focus on journalists' perspectives (Hanitzsch 2011; Hanitzsch and Mellado 2011). This focus can stretch our understanding of how journalists think, and how they come to agree with the ideology of their profession. More importantly, it allows for the translation of research findings into a discourse which places the journalists first as narrators of their world, as has been done by Bishara (2013), instead of objects of analysis in a highly contested debate. In other words, promoting transformative research means developing further the ethnographic leg of media studies in order to deal more widely with the experiences of those involved in the coverage of this conflict. If they build on the critical and comprehensive analyses of the media circuits provided by past research, micro-level explorations can enrich the understanding of wider social dynamics, providing new and fundamental knowledge for research which reorients its approaches and aims towards change.

Finally, media studies as a subject area can strengthen its contribution to social change by encouraging further ethnographic investigations about those subjects affected by the media. The GUMG has shown that, in general, direct experience is a determinant factor in shaping and changing the beliefs of foreign audiences (for example, Philo and Happer 2013:41). However, for the people living the conflict directly, the non-mediated experience of the other may have less power to challenge pre-existent beliefs. Bar-Tal and Teichman maintained that even change in the relationship between Israelis and Palestinians may not be enough to challenge existing ideological repertoires (2005:383). Among the bricks of ideological support for Israeli policies towards the Palestinians, there are elements which philosopher and psychoanalyst Carlo Strenger has defined as universal psychological mechanisms: the fear of loss, the difficulty in acknowledging wrong-doing, and the need to give meaning and protect a history and narrative on which identities depend (Strenger 2014). Factors such as these are essential in shaping dominant discourses about this conflict, but they need not be exclusively discussed as evidence of dominance. They are existing aspects of social life, which can be debunked once their peculiarities, dynamics and contradictions are completely and successfully revealed to the individual by sociological and journalistic accounts. In this light, media studies can also include a diversified set of individuals, their behaviours and beliefs, and investigate what emotive or non-informative elements trigger changes of perspective, both in the field and elsewhere. Finally, ethnographic audience research can give voice to narratives and elements that populate the experiences of the communities in conflict but are not covered by the media. In general, this focus on the individual can help to understand better the elements that can support dialogue between Israelis and Palestinians and avoid essentialist views that discourage it. Focusing further on people and their beliefs, media studies can help to create the conditions for the formation of alternative perspectives that individuals undergoing change can adopt to reshape their 'understanding of their biographical experiences... in order to transcend the past and the burden of history, and develop new sets of political interests that impact on the political process' (Brewer 2003:173).

Conclusions

Media sociology has a lot to offer towards a more progressive model of journalism. Past research has shown that new models can combine truthful information with new and progressive social aims. It has offered the tools to comprehensively understand how audience beliefs are actually shaped by the media, which can also be used to measure the effectiveness of normative models of journalism, and improve them. Media research has also discussed early steps for change, introducing the idea that social scientists and journalists can work together for this purpose. This research provides the basis for developing intersectoral reflection and debate between media sociology and journalism about their respective roles for finding solutions to social problems, and a fruitful collaboration for social change as they both commit to impacting on their respective audiences: media sociology on journalism and journalism on the world. Sociologists can support this dialogue with wider ethnographic investigations of the beliefs and practices of the journalists, as well as those of the people involved in the Israeli-Palestinian conflict. This reflexive engagement of media sociology can liberate ideas and visions, and bring together the energies to gradually challenge the factors that prevent a more progressive and transformative role for journalism in relation to social conflicts.

Notes

1. Barbie Zelizer (2004a:111) criticised the tendency in cultural approaches to adopt 'journalism's own self-presentation as indicative of what journalism is or could be'.
2. Among these, the project 'Consolidating Peace Journalism in Uganda' of the Uganda Media Development Foundation in collaboration with Bread for the World, the Mindanao News and Information Cooperative Center (MNICC) in the Philippines, or the more recent Media Association for Peace – MAP – based in Lebanon.
3. Other scholars advocate a similar multi-dimensional perspective: Starkey for example criticised balance built around the idea of two sides as reducing the complexities of the existent political positions (2007:38).
4. See, for example, Mindanews.com, or Mapmena.org. In addition, the Center for Global Peace Journalism at Park University in Missouri publishes *The Peace Journalist*, a semi-annual publication about Peace Journalism and related courses, research, projects and coverage, available at park.edu/center-for-peace-journalism.
5. Refuseniks are Israelis who refuse to serve in the army or to carry out specific military duties.

References

Ackerman, S. (2001) 'Al-Aqsa Intifada and the US Media', *Journal of Palestine Studies*, 30 (2): 61–74.

Ashuri, T. (2010) *The Arab-Israeli Conflict in the Media. Producing Shared Memory and National Identity in the Global Television Era*. London and New York: Tauris Academic Studies.

Bar-Tal, D. and Teichman, Y. (2005) *Stereotypes and Prejudice in Conflict. Representations of Arabs in Israeli Society*. New York: Cambridge University Press.

Bishara, A. (2013) *Back Stories. U.S. News Production and Palestinian Politics*. Stanford, CA: Stanford University Press.

Bourdon, J. (2015) 'Strange Strangers: The Jerusalem Correspondents in the Network of Nations', *Journalism*. Published online first, 21 April doi: 10.1177/1464884915579333.

Brewer, J.D. (2003) *C. Wright Mills and the Ending of Violence*. Basingstoke: Palgrave Macmillan.

Cottle, S. (2007) 'Ethnography and News Production: New(s) Developments in the Field', *Sociology Compass*, 1 (1): 1–16.

Deprez, A. and Raeymaeckers, K. (2010) 'Bias in the News? The Representation of Palestinians and Israelis in the Coverage of the First and Second Intifada', *International Communication Gazette*, 72 (1): 91–109.

Du Bois W.E.B. (2000) 'Sociology Hesitant', *Boundary*, 27 (3): 37–44.

Galtung, J. (2002) 'Peace Journalism. A Challenge', in W. Kempf and H. Luostarinen (eds.) *Journalism and the New World Order vol. II: Studying War and the Media*. Göteborg: NORDICOM, pp. 259–72.

Galtung, J. (2006) 'Peace Journalism as an Ethical Challenge', *Global Media Journal: Mediterranean Edition*, 1 (2): 1–5.

Gordon, N. (2009) 'From Colonization to Separation: Exploring the Structure of Israel's Occupation', in A. Ophir, M. Givoni and S. Hanafi (eds.) *The Power of Inclusive Exclusion: Anatomy of Israeli Rule in the Occupied Palestinian Territories*. New York: Zone Books, pp. 239–68.

Hanitzsch, T. (2007) 'Deconstructing Journalism Culture: Towards a Universal Theory', *Communication Theory*, 17 (4): 367–85.

Hanitzsch, T. (2011) 'Populist Disseminators, Detached Watchdogs, Critical Change Agents and Opportunist Facilitators: Professional Milieus, the Journalistic Field and Autonomy in 18 Countries', *International Communication Gazette*, 73 (6): 477–94.

Hanitzsch, T. and Mellado, C. (2011) 'What Shapes the News around the World? How Journalists in 18 Countries Perceive Influences on Their Work', *International Journal of Press/Politics*, 16 (3): 404–26.

Law, J., Ruppert, E. and Savage, M. (2011) *The Double Social Life of Methods*. CRESC: Goldsmiths Research Online. http://research.gold.ac.uk/7987/, date accessed: 17 November 2014.

Lowstedt, A. and Madhoun, H. (2003) 'The Intifada, Hasbara and the Media', *Palestine-Israel Journal*, 10 (2): 47–56.

Luyendjik, J. (2007) 'The Weaponization of News Media in the Middle East', *Arab Media & Society*, 1 (Spring): http://www.arabmediasociety.com/?article=29, date accessed: 27 March 2015.

Luyendijk, J. (2009) *People Like Us: Misrepresenting the Middle. East* New York: Soft Skull Press.

Lynch, J. (2012) 'Peace Journalism Works', *The Peace Journalist*, 1 (2): http://www.park.edu/center-for-peace-journalism/peace-journalist.html, date accessed: 17 November 2014.

Lynch, J. and Galtung, J. (2010) *Reporting Conflict: New Directions in Peace Journalism*. St Lucia: University of Queensland Press.

Lynch, J. and McGoldrick, A. (2005a) *Peace Journalism*. Stroud: Hawthorn Press.

Lynch, J. and McGoldrick, A. (2005b) 'War and Peace Journalism in the Holy Land', *Social Alternatives*, 24 (1): 11–15.

McGoldrick, A. and Lynch, J. (2014) 'Audience Responses to Peace Journalism', *Journalism Studies*. Published online 18 December doi: 10.1080/1461670X.2014.992621.

McLaughlin, G. (2002) *The War Correspondent*. London: Pluto Press.

Mills, C.W. (2000) *The Sociological Imagination*. Kindle Edition: Oxford University Press.

Noakes, J.A. and Gwinn Wilkins, K. (2002) 'Shifting Frames of the Palestinian Movement in US News', *Media Culture & Society*, 24 (5): 649–71.

Philo, G. (2007) 'Can Discourse Analysis Successfully Explain the Content of Media and Journalistic Practice?', *Journalism Studies*, 8 (2): 175–96.

Philo, G. and Berry, M. (2011) *More Bad News from Israel*. London: Pluto Press.

Philo, G. and Happer, C. (2013) *Communicating Climate Change and Energy Security. New Methods in Understanding Audiences*. New York: Routledge.

Ravid. B., Landau, D., Benn, A. and Rosner, S. (2007) 'Olmert to Haaretz: Two-State Solution or Israel Done For', *Haaretz*. 29 November, http://www.haaretz.com/news/olmert-to-haaretz-two-state-solution-or-israel-is-done-for-1.234201, date accessed: 27 March 2015.

Rinnawi, K. (2007) 'De-legitimization of Media Mechanisms: Israeli Press Coverage of the Al-Aqsa Intifada', *International Communication Gazette*, 69 (2): 149–78.
Ruigrok, N., Van Atteveldt, W. and Takens, J. (2009) 'Shifting Frames in a Deadlocked Conflict?', *De Nederlandse Nieuwsmonitor*, www.nieuwsmonitor.net/d/11/ShiftingFrames.pdf, date accessed: 29 March 2013.
Schudson, M. (2001) 'The Objectivity Norm in American Journalism', *Journalism*, 2 (2): 149–70.
Starkey, G. (2007) *Balance and Bias in Journalism. Representation, Regulation and Democracy*. Basingstoke: Palgrave Macmillan.
Strenger, C. (2014) 'Psychological Obstacles to Peace in Israel', *Haaretz* 4 July, http://www.haaretz.com/mobile/1.601122?v=6D64FA00ED968D96A657C76E7A773EA1, date accessed: 17 November 2014.
Wolfsfeld, G. (2004) *Media and the Path to Peace*. Cambridge: Cambridge University Press.
Wright, E.O. (2010) *Envisioning Real Utopias*. London and New York: Verso.
Zelizer, B. (2004a) 'When Facts, Truth, and Reality are God-Terms: On Journalism's Uneasy Place in Cultural Studies', *Communication and Critical/Cultural Studies*, 1 (1): 100–19.
Zelizer, B. (2004b) *Taking Journalism Seriously*. Thousand Oaks, CA, London and New Delhi: Sage.
Zelizer, B., Park, D. and Gudelunas, D. (2002) 'How Bias Shapes the News: Challenging *The New York Times*' Status as a Newspaper of Record on the Middle East', *Journalism: Theory, Practice, and Criticism*, 3 (3): 283–307.

11
Sociology and Journalism: The Search for a Historical Imagination

Kevin Williams

Sociology has been accused of 'abandoning' the study of communication. Scholars such as Jefferson Pooley and Elihu Katz argue that despite occupying a prominent place in the development of the study of communication, American sociology today pays little attention to communication, the media and journalism. The growth of communication research has been accompanied by a migration from the discipline of many with a background or an interest in media sociology. Those remaining have either stopped doing communication research or are increasingly unfamiliar with the literature of media and communication studies. The gap that has developed between communication and sociology in the US is in part attributed to media research drifting into the territory of journalism schools. This location has posed a problem for the legitimacy of mass communication research as it is a subject area with 'its roots in, and an on-going commitment to, vocational training' (Pooley and Katz 2008:777). The perceived lack of 'status' of journalism schools has cemented a rupture which has left sociology in the US studying every aspect of popular modern culture except the media.

The perception of abandonment is not shared in the European context in any formal sense. There are no journal debates reflecting on the relationship between sociology and communication. Pooley and Katz speculate that the lack of discussion of a break between sociology and communication in Britain is at least in part a consequence of the way in which mass communication research was anchored in or close to sociology departments. They state that 'many leading British media researchers identify as, and are housed within, departments of sociology' (Pooley and Katz 2008:778). They do not make any reference to the relationship outside the Anglo-American world. This is not surprising as the periodic reviews of the state of the field have largely ignored the

European tradition of mass communication research. Outside Europe the situation is worse, as the regular calls for the 'internationalising' or 'de-Westernising' of media studies indicate (Curran and Park 2000; Thussu 2009). Daya Thussu (2009:16) notes that the study of mass communication, like the social sciences and humanities generally, has been affected by an 'epistemological essentialism, rooted as it is within an Anglo-American intellectual tradition'. The globalisation of communication and education is to some extent increasing awareness of this limitation and there is more engagement with other cultures and knowledge systems, but the field of mass communication research has been and still is overwhelming an Anglo-American endeavour.

Pooley and Katz's notion of abandonment has to be contextualised by the growing interest sociology is showing in the impact of new media and information technology on social relations. The explosion of social media has made it difficult for the discipline to continue to ignore communication. Some have referred to the 'reluctant sociologist' to describe the discipline's engagement with the social consequences of the digital world (Farrell and Petersen 2010). However, the recent tectonic shift in information technology has touched most major areas of sociological enquiry, particularly identity, youth and gender. In the process there has been reconciliation between mass and inter-personal communication, which traditionally has divided the study of communication. There is talk of the emergence of 'digital sociology' (Lupton 2014). Much of the speculation about the impact of new media on the institutions and interactions of modern life – as well as the more general consideration of the relationship between sociology and communication – has lacked an historical context and input.

This short chapter considers the ways in which the 'historical deficit' has influenced the study and understanding of one specific area of the field – journalism. Journalism is today an expanding area of mass communication studies, but it has been neglected. The study of journalism has institutionally been segregated from media and communication studies in many countries – whether because of the vocational pull of journalism education or lack of 'status' according to journalism research. But neglect also reflects the taken-for-granted view many have of journalism. We know what it is; it has an immutable quality. As a result there has been little incentive to explore forms of journalism and limited effort to examine its history. Journalism history, like media history in general, is 'uncared for, marginalised and visited only occasionally' (Bailey 2009:xxi). The lack of history means that we are unaware of how journalistic practices and textual forms have changed to imbue the concept with different meanings. It is not just the absence of journalism history that is a problem; the history that has emerged can be criticised for presenting a particular view of the profession. Rooted in national frameworks, it fails to capture the interactions across borders that have shaped journalism's development.

Calls for history

There have been in recent years numerous interventions from scholars to explain why the study of mass communication has been reluctant to be involved with history. Calls are made for a greater engagement with the past. One of the most significant was that of James Curran (2002), who presented a range of different approaches that could be adopted to the study of mass communication history. His six narratives in search of media historians generated considerable debate and provided the discussion of media history with a set of theoretical foundations. While these narratives have application to a variety of societies, Curran's conceptualisation of media history is anchored in a 'national' history, that of the British Isles. Like media historians everywhere, his knowledge and understanding of the media's past is rooted in his own national consciousness. This has until recently been reinforced by the process of media research which is embedded in national archives and records. It is only with digitalisation that access to broader and more international databases has become available. Curran has emphasised the importance of comparative media research in a number of contexts and supports the need for more comparative media history. Comparative research challenges the national tradition of media history that dominates the field. There is nevertheless the matter of how comparative research is conducted. It is not enough to compare and contrast national media systems; it is essential to focus on cross-national interactions and the interface of the national and transnational, to 'de-territorialise' comparative media history (see Hepp and Couldry 2009).

The absence of history is not only experienced through the lack of consideration of the past of the media. It is also felt in another way – the failure of mass communication studies to engage with its own history. The limited mapping of the historical development of media and communication research is often attributed to the insecurity that pervades the field (Golding 2005). The consequence of this limitation is that it has enabled the telling of particular stories about the discipline, and this has influenced the way in which the media and communication are studied, researched and ultimately understood today. Key theories, theorists and significant turning points are taken for granted. That they are anchored in specific circumstances in distinctive periods and in particular societies is often overlooked. This is perhaps more applicable to certain aspects of the communication process. Audience research, for example, often generalises from the particular experience of one society, and that society is the United States. Orson Welles's Mercury Theatre radio presentation in 1938 is often deployed to describe the power of the media and the hypodermic approach to understanding the influence of the media (see Winston, Chapter 12, this volume). There is less consideration of the peculiar circumstances of American society in the late 1930s, the particular make-up of the American radio audience and the intellectual understanding of the emerging mass media in the US at this time.[1] Whether we can generalise from this episode at all is questionable. But the widespread use of Welles's example in the teaching of media and communication studies in a number of societies illustrates a lack of commitment to historiography.

There is a reluctance to explore the way in which political and cultural factors gave rise to and shaped the development of mass communication research. Timothy Glander (2000) notes that the history of mass communication and media studies has until recently refrained from asking difficult questions about the origins of the field. Sifting through the documentary remains of the formative years of the field, he identifies how interpretations, values and practices have been influenced by the politics and culture of the Cold War. There is, he argues, little awareness of how much the study of mass communication, particularly in the US, has uncritically inherited from this period. Dispersed throughout these early years are the seeds of alternative approaches such as associated with 'propaganda analysis', which historical analysis could reclaim to provide the field with a different set of foundations.

Journalism history

Journalism studies as an area of systematic academic investigation has only emerged relatively recently. Its attitude towards history resembles that of the field of mass communication in general. History is of 'limited interest' for journalism studies; it is 'a sort of detachable sub-field' and 'it is unusual that the theories of journalism studies historicize their objects' (Nerone 2013:18). The neglect of history has major implications for what is studied and how it is studied. The history of journalism that is undertaken 'predominantly' focuses on 'events and developments in a nation state framework' (Broersma 2010:10). National accounts prevail and few attempts are made to compare national narratives, let alone produce international histories of an activity that from its earliest days was a transnational phenomenon. The historiography of the field of journalism studies has similarly been neglected. The newness of the term 'journalism studies' belies the fact that it is a 'relatively new name for a fairly old field' (Nerone 2013:17) which we can trace back at least to early sociological interest in news and journalism at the end of the nineteenth century. The story told about evolution of journalism studies follows a particular pattern. Anchored in a national framework, it is characterised by an emphasis on the genre of news, disagreement between skills and scholarship, disciplinary and methodological confusion, and an Anglo-American focus.

The impetus for more journalism history comes from the challenge presented by the considerable quantitative and qualitative change taking place in contemporary communication technology. The communications 'revolution' or 'crisis', depending on whom you read, threatens the 'end of journalism'. The study of mass communication is going through fundamental change – particularly if you read the proponents of Media Studies 2.0. Understanding past debates and approaches enables us to put the present changes to the profession and the discipline into some context. Old media were once new. How scholarship explains the advent of the cinema, newsreels, radio and television on the practices and processes of journalism has something to teach us about present debates concerning the arrival of the internet and social media. Going further back there is a resonance between the early pamphlets, journals and embryonic newspapers of eighteenth-century print culture and the culture of today's social media which emphasises the importance of historical knowledge. History enables us to interrogate far more effectively some of the basic concepts deployed to analyse the media and journalism today, such as the 'public sphere' or 'moral panics' or 'hegemony'. Perhaps most significantly in light of the debate about sociology and communication history, it forces scholars to investigate journalism in a social context. Social relations shape journalism and vice versa; the nature of the relationship is a matter of conjecture but the incorporation of history into the study of journalism ensures that more attention is paid to social factors. It will also help us with the most elusive evaluation, the impact of journalism on the course of society. New technology is facilitating the scholarly scrutiny of past media content, which provides insight into the output of journalism. There are many problems and issues to 'doing' historical content analysis, but it does provide the opportunity to examine the past performance of journalism which hitherto has not been possible. The rest of this chapter explores the kind of journalism history that is beginning to emerge and critically evaluates some of the assumptions that underpin it. The starting point is the prediction of journalism's imminent death.

Crisis in the state of Journalism

Contemporary debates about the present and future state of journalism centre on the 'death' of the profession (Deuze 2006). The demise of journalism is seen to have been precipitated by the arrival of new media technologies which have undermined traditional practice (see Bromley 1997). Mark Deuze is emphatic that in our era of liquid news 'any definition of journalism as a profession working truthfully, operating as a watchdog for the good of society as a whole and enabling citizens to be self-governing is not only naive, but also one-dimensional' (2005:458). A picture is painted of a new era in which boundaries between different types of information providers such as bloggers, tweeters and journalists are becoming increasingly blurred, calling into question the value of the 'journalistic function' to society. Convergence is the term used to describe how technology and journalism are transforming into one entity, centred on digital web platforms with user-generated content, story curation and aggregation and niche information services. Depending on whom you read, this entity offers the potential for or is actually creating a profound shift in our understanding of what constitutes journalism, the role of journalism and who is a journalist (see Franklin 2012).

The discussion of the impact of new media technology on journalism is couched in technophilia and an obsession with gadgetry. This has led some advocates of new media within the industry and the academy to accentuate or exaggerate the 'crisis' in journalism. It is also a discussion that is by and large anchored in developments in the Western world, in particular the US. Outside North America and Western Europe not only are newspapers thriving but journalism is expanding. Any generalisation about the contemporary state of journalism is confronted by the robust health of journalism in many parts of the world, which challenges the notion of 'crisis' that figures so prominently on the curriculum or research agenda in the West. More significantly, the discussion about the present and future state of the profession eschews an historical understanding of what is often airily dismissed as 'legacy' journalism. On the appearance of the new, the old apparently reveals its distinctive shape and form. All the contradictions and complexities melt away to be replaced by the certainties of a profession that emphasises 'accuracy, independence and impartiality' (Riordan 2014) and is embedded in established rituals of practice and performance.

Historical analysis reveals that what is being replaced or eroded or challenged, depending how far along the road to change you have walked, old or traditional journalism is more diverse and complex than many acknowledge. Journalism as a profession, form and set of practices and performances is continually evolving and the boundary between the journalist and non-journalist has been the subject of negotiation since the days of the embryonic newspapers of the seventeenth century. That most perceptive of journalism historians, Mark Hampton (1999; 2004; 2005), has examined nineteenth- and early twentieth-century contests over who counted as a journalist. Documenting the evolution of journalism reveals the extent to which the profession has continually struggled to establish itself in relation to other forms of information provision and analysis. The roots of today's 'crisis' have to be seen in a longer historical context in which journalism has changed and adapted in the face of social, cultural, economic and political developments and the challenge of alternative information providers. This is manifest in the struggle between partisanship and independence which characterises journalism history.

It is generally accepted that there was a shift from an 'ideologically charged, reflective journalism' to a 'more neutral, fact-based practice' which is termed the 'news paradigm' in the latter part of the nineteenth century (Hoyer and Pottker 2005). There is a 'grand narrative' of the evolution of journalism which describes innovations pioneered in North America and Britain and their diffusion into media systems in Europe and more recently to other parts of the world. This diffusion is seen in different ways: for some it is an example of cultural imperialism or 'Americanisation' while others see it as part of the process of modernisation by which universal standards of journalistic practice are evolving across the world. In the scholarly literature the shift is usually differentiated as a move from 'old' to 'new' journalism as the style and form as well as the way in which news was gathered changed fundamentally. This interpretation is primarily associated with Jean Chalaby (1998), who attributes the shift to the commercialisation of the newspaper industry. Before this, Chalaby asserts, everything was publicity. Such an interpretation is challenged by historians such as Mitchell Stephens (1988), who take a longer view of journalism. Commitments by early newspapers to reproduce faithful and accurate accounts of what is happening in the world are cited to indicate the efforts of pre-commercialisation editors to produce independent judgement and non-partisan reports. Of course the gap between the pronouncements of editors about their practices and what they actually do in practice has to be taken into account – but this applies to any period of newspaper history.

The important point is that partisanship and independence have existed alongside each other throughout the history of journalism. The evolution of the profession can be seen as cyclical, which not only highlights the regularity of boundary contestations but also accounts for how at certain times partisanship or independence is in the ascendancy. Harbers and den Harder (2010) believe the traditional narrative is 'an overly rigid straitjacket'. Diversity of style, form and practice is something that characterises journalism history, and the journalism of opinion remains part of the story of journalism in the twentieth and twenty-first centuries. Partisanship has never gone away; in fact, in many media systems, partisanship is the primary mode of operation for journalists. There is evidence to indicate that partisan journalism is re-establishing itself in the Anglo-American world, with the growth of talk shows, the blogosphere and Twitter. Fox News is an example of the extent to which partisan reporting has re-emerged in the mainstream news media.

Much of the debate around journalism history revolves around contrary definitions of journalism. How we define journalism has implications for the way in which we understand the profession and its history. Scholarly understanding of what journalism is tends to anchored in the context of news. Influential compendiums such as *The Handbook of Journalism Studies* and *The Routledge Companion to News and Journalism* make a link between journalism and news (Allan 2010; Wahl-Jorgensen and Hanitzsch 2009). Other aspects of journalism such as editorial or leader writing or feature articles and opinion pieces are often described in relation to news: editorials comment on the news of the day while feature reporting provides the background or context to the news. That the vast number of people who describe what they do as 'journalism' have nothing to do with the reporting of news is often overlooked. Textbooks acknowledge that journalists work in a variety of ways to acquire and disseminate information, but they usually define journalists as men and women who present information as news. The debate about the 'future of journalism' is overwhelmingly driven by consideration of the fate of news, and it is fair to say that most evaluations of the quality and performance of journalism are anchored in the study of the news genre.

Equating journalism with news makes it easier to accept Chalaby's interpretation of the profession as an invention of the mid- to late nineteenth century. A broader understanding lends more credibility to Stephens' emphasis on the longevity of journalism. Stephens (1988) argues that all societies, past or present, have a 'thirst for news', tracing a similar fascination with news in the Greek agora and the Roman Forum, where spoken news was enhanced by the posting of daily handwritten news sheets. Stephens' conception of news is more fluid. He sees it as synonymous with information, gossip and rumour whereas Chalaby is more comfortable restricting news to matters of current affairs and politics. This is in accord with Chalaby's lack of sympathy with the political press that characterised French society in the nineteenth century. His dismissal of everything prior to the arrival of the commercial press, or the Anglo-American news revolution, as publicity is a rejection of the journalism of opinion practised in France following the 1789 Revolution. For Chalaby – and the grand narrative – the adoption of American practices, styles and forms is the pinnacle of the profession's development (see Broersma 2010). The result is that other journalistic styles and forms not centred on the 'news paradigm' are downplayed or ignored.

Some scholars see the grand narrative as something of a simplification. The 'new' did not replace the 'old'. Rather, as with all things new, there was cultural resistance; a process of adaptation marked the introduction of new techniques such as the interview and the inverted pyramid (Broersma 2007). Empirical studies of the content of newspapers raise doubts about the shift – or at least extend the time frame within which it happened. Frank Harbers and Bas den Harder (2010), as part of the excellent historical work generated by the Groningen Centre for Journalism Studies, show from their content analysis of the British and Dutch press in the twentieth century that 'new journalistic routines and forms associated with the "news paradigm" were still far from established in 1925 and still greatly developed even between 1965 and 2005' (Harbers and den Harder 2010:29). The continuation of a journalism of opinion is reflected today in newsrooms in many parts of Europe, where the division of labour between reporting and editorialising that has characterised Anglo-American news culture for much of the twentieth century is not replicated. The notion of 'redaction' indicates that many European journalists are more likely to perform the whole range of functions, news-gathering and reporting, writing editorials and commentary as well as technical production, which are carried out by several individuals in Britain and the US (Esser 1998:379; Kepplinger and Kocher 1990:292).[2] Redaction does not clearly discriminate between news *and* opinion that has been taken for granted in modern journalism. In this context it could be argued that new media technology is moving Anglo-American journalism towards the practice of redaction as work demarcations break down inside newsrooms.

The grand narrative of journalism history neglects journalistic diversity between and within countries. Paying more attention to the variety of journalistic cultures and discourses is not only about acknowledging partisan reporting. History can be used to identify the different kinds of journalism that have emerged. Journalism in terms of its occupational culture and legitimacy is always being reshaped, and it is associated with other things than news such as advice, analysis and advocacy. Take the examples of music, arts and travel journalists: they do not inform audiences about events or products they evaluate, appraise and review. There is an expectation that journalism should provide 'judgements of taste' (see Fürsich 2012). Travel journalism, for example, evokes the norms and expectations of the profession such as objectivity and accuracy, but it also encourages personal reflection, commentary and a literary form. Often the outlet of publication determines the type of travel journalism that is produced – a newspaper makes different demands from a travel magazine or journal. But it is also the case that certain forms of journalism demand judgements of taste or the imparting of advice; they are often dismissed as a 'soft' variety of journalism not worthy of study (see Hanusch and Fürsich 2014). That these forms have not figured prominently in journalism history has helped to mask the diversity of journalism forms and practices.

Pre-eminence of politics

The failure of scholarship until recently to embrace different forms and types of journalism relates to the overwhelming emphasis placed on the relationship between news, journalism and democracy. Most scholars focus on journalism that relates to politics because it 'makes the strongest claim to public importance' (Schudson 2003:15). The extent to which news as a form of political journalism is significant in shaping people's view of the world is increasingly a matter for discussion. As scholars slowly overcome their reluctance to study the 'softer' types of journalism, they discover that other forms of journalism play an important role in shaping people's perceptions and understanding of society. Folker Hanusch and Elfriede Fürsich (2014:9) draw attention to how travel journalism functions like international news to provide both information and cultural frames about others. They justify the importance of studying travel journalism by 'the exponential growth' of media content devoted to travel and tourism (Hanusch and Fürsich 2014:5). Writing about travel for public consumption has a long history which can be traced back to the eighteenth century (for examples see Steward 2005). This aspect of journalism history – like others – has been lost in the welter of research generated on the role of journalism in the development of a free press and defence of democracy.

The emphasis on the press and journalism as the midwife of democracy has led scholars to ignore or downplay other aspects of the profession. Forty years ago James Carey described the focus on the relationship between journalism and democracy as 'something of an embarrassment' (Carey 1997:86) He argued that journalism history was 'oppressively chronological' and 'needlessly pre-occupied with the biographies of editors and publishers' (Carey 1997:87). This preoccupation was the outcome of the 'Whig interpretation of history', which preferences the notion of progress. Underpinned by the concept of the 'fourth estate' journalism history has documented the progress of the free press and its contribution to political and civil rights. This was what the great works of nineteenth-century journalism history stressed (for example, Andrews 1847; Fox Bourne 1887) but Carey saw its legacy lingering on, freezing out consideration of reporting practices and writing styles and formats. As he put it, the 'central story in journalism has been largely banished from our remembrance of things past' (Carey 1997:90). Scholars are now beginning to pay more attention to the changing occupational culture of journalism and the organisational, technological, social-economic and political contexts in which journalists work. Such research enables us to examine how transformations in 'media work' have influenced the process of representation; but the pull of traditional journalism history remains strong.

Journalism history today may be less influenced by the Whig interpretation, but it is possible to argue that Habermas (1989) and his concept of the public sphere produce the same effect – the preferencing of journalism and politics. The public sphere can be seen as a 'tragic version of Whig press history' (Schudson 2008:249). As a piece of historical analysis, Habermas's work is far from robust; it draws on secondhand sources and is based on particular types of 'newspapers' and the writers who produced them. The emphasis he places on the *Tatler* and the *Spectator* as representative of newspapers and periodicals in Britain in the early eighteenth century is misleading, as is the portrayal of the coffee houses as peaceful centres of rational discourse (see Cowan 2004). Habermas constructs the idea of journalism as a rational activity geared to produce the exchange of ideas about politics and society.[3] This is problematic as a depiction of those involved in the press and print culture in the early eighteenth century. Recent studies indicate many news publications were more commercial and better organised than Habermas assumes, and they devoted as much space to entertainment and sensation as to ideas, information and issues (see Clarke 2004; King 1987; Rogers 1992; Snell 2007). The emergence of Grub Street in the late seventeenth century established some sort of system for the generation of stories. Described as writers who hired out their service, the Grub Street hack was paid by line. Their approach to the collection of news was 'audacious and unscrupulous' (Chibnall 1980:189). Stories of misdemeanours, gossip and scandal, crime and social unrest were processed. The main purpose of the Grub Street hacks – as opposed to periodical writers and pamphleteers – was not to facilitate the exchange of ideas or provide a platform for public deliberation but to increase sales, reflect readers' fears and confirm their prejudices. Habermas downplays the diversity of those involved in the early period of journalism, ignoring the different kinds of periodical journalism practised.

Journalism across cultures

Habermas's work has the virtue of considering the extent to which the political journalism that was first developed in Britain was replicated in other parts of Europe. Most journalism history rarely engages with the international dimension. There are a few works that compare national histories (see Hallin and Mancini 2004), but journalism histories 'predominantly study events and developments in a nation state framework without structurally considering international developments and cross-border influences' (Broersma 2010:10). Or to put it more bluntly, journalism history is 'dangerously and unflaggingly parochial' (Stephens 2000). The result is that the variety of interactions and the countless notions that 'drift' across national borders are 'underplayed or ignored' and 'crucial connections and lineages' are obscured and 'telling comparisons' missed (Stephens 2000). In an era in which globalisation has stimulated transnational study in most disciplines, the confinement of journalism history to national frameworks seems anachronistic and perverse.

A transnational history of journalism would stress its cosmopolitan nature from the days of the embryonic newspapers of the early seventeenth century. The corantos of the 1620s were international in content and produced through the interaction of information gatherers in different cities of Europe and sometimes beyond. Many corantos epitomise the global-local nexus that pervades modern media discourse. Disseminated locally, usually in major cities or ports in Europe, they often contained nothing but international stories or rather a hodgepodge of unedited translations of material from continental publications. The development of new techniques of news reporting in the US from the 1830s onwards, seen as crucial to the advancement of Anglo-American journalism, was strongly influenced by Europeans – migrants and visitors – and their understanding of European reading publics. Take Joseph Pulitzer, or 'Joey the German' as he was nicknamed – even though he was Hungarian. His journalistic experience was honed working on a newspaper serving the German-speaking community in St Louis, and it was through his attempt to address the migrant German-speaking community that he developed some of the presentational and technical skills central to the new journalism in the United States. The nineteenth century was an age of migration, and looking at national histories of journalism of the period it is striking how many journalists travelled and how much they wrote about their travels. The creative interaction is manifest in Europeans going to America and Americans coming to Europe, so that it is possible to identify the 'new American journalism had various European routes' (Hoyer 2007:37).

The dissemination of styles, forms and practice in the nineteenth century was intimately tied up with the expansion of Empire. The imperial powers extended their influence through the extension of information and communication networks as much as military force and political diplomacy. Historians have documented the technological and political advance of these systems, such as cable and the telegraph. Less attention has been paid to the software and the diffusion of journalism, with the exception of the various studies of the international news agencies. However, wherever representatives of the European empires went they established newspapers and news publications. The assumption is that these publications were simply the outlet for imperial values and views, and they represented the transfer of Western ways of doing things. Transnational histories indicate that matters were more complicated and complex. The process by which Western values were incorporated or adapted or assimilated into colonial societies was a matter of give and take. Power was unequal in these transactions, but the imposition of values, methods and practices was atypical. Recent scholarship on empire has focused on the reciprocal relationship between colonisers and the colonised (for example, Bhabha 1995). The interaction is portrayed as a heterogeneous and varied process of unequal negotiation between colonial powers and local peoples, with the press seen as a primary site of contestation (see Codell 2003). Colonial reporting should not be simply seen as a form of metropolitan propaganda as it incorporated 'the traces of the political forces at work in both domestic and overseas locations' (Naranch 2007). Journalism history needs to treat journalism in a way which is inclusive of difference, both within societies and between them.

Finding a field

Focusing on journalism history in transnational terms provides a guide for a re-evaluation of the history of journalism studies. Traditional descriptions of the evolution of journalism studies emphasise national developments as part of telling the story of a field that emerged in the United States from the 1930s onwards but with its prehistory firmly rooted in German social theorists of the late nineteenth century (see Wahl-Jorgensen and Hanitzsch 2009:4–9). Reference is usually made to Max Weber's failure to heed his own call in 1910 to produce a comprehensive survey of journalists. The call is seen as recognition of the importance of the social role of journalism and the press. However, it is not until the 1970s and 1980s that sociology is seen as exerting a 'stronger influence' on journalism research (Wahl-Jorgensen and Hanitzsch 2009:6). Revisionist historiography of journalism studies can take issue with key 'turning points' and key personnel in the emergence of journalism studies. The absence of leading German researchers such as Kurt Baschwitz, one of the founders of the journal the *Gazette* (see Wieten 2005) who did not go to the US prior to the Second World War, is an example. But it is the evolution of the relationship between sociology and journalism that is perhaps more interesting.

There has been a long and close relationship between sociology and journalism which is often neglected. The history of this relationship highlights the considerable influence, both negative and positive, that each has had on the other. Herbert Spencer's *The Study of Sociology* was partly published in response to the simplification of social issues presented in the press (Golding 2005). The connections between some of the founding fathers of sociology and the profession of journalism are often highlighted. Robert Park, a leading light of the Chicago School, was a city reporter, and this background helped to 'shape his sociological habitus and his belief in the academic value of "nosing around"' (Anderson 2015:6). Less attention is paid to what journalism and sociology have learned from one another. Today there are calls for sociology to be more accessible and jargon free and for journalists to use sociological analysis in their work (Sternheimer 2008). Such calls neglect the close relationship at the start of the twentieth century. Anderson (2015:3) has traced how in the US 'journalism once included a plethora of material and methods that today would be considered "sociological" and how early sociologists refer to the importance of learning from journalistic production and method'. Many building the discipline made use of both journalistic and sociological methods, particularly in connection with the activity of the Social Survey Movement. However, as sociology established itself, the boundary we acknowledge today between sociology and journalism was erected. This boundary is not and never has been impermeable; Anderson describes the relationship as 'a line with zigs and zags, moments of embrace and moments of revulsion' (2015:3). It also differs between countries. Nobody abandoned journalism – or for that matter communication studies; it is simply that the relationship has waxed and waned. At critical moments they have reconnected; one such moment is the arrival of the digital world. Transnational histories of journalism demand a sociological input to make sense of the interactions within and between societies and their consequences for the meaning of journalism. Hence there is a need to acknowledge the importance and longevity of sociology to the study of journalism.

Notes

1. For a discussion of the reception of the broadcast in the US context, see Pooley and Socolow (2013).
2. In many parts of Europe one term – *redakteur* in Germany, *redactar* in Spain, *redacteur* in France – is used to describe all those working in the newsroom.
3. Many would stress that journalism was not recognised as a particular form of work or activity at this time. Certainly the term journalism was not regularly used to describe what news writers and information providers did. However, many of the means by which information was processed, disseminated and presented by journalists today would have been familiar to those in the press and periodical world of the early eighteenth century.

References

Allan, S. (2010) *The Routledge Companion to News and Journalism*. London: Routledge.

Anderson, C.W. (2015). 'Drawing Boundary Lines between Journalism and Sociology, 1895–1999', in M. Carlson and S.C. Lewis (eds.) *Boundaries of Journalism: Professionalism, Practices, and Participation*. New York: Routledge, pp. 201–17.

Andrews, A. (1998 [1847]) *The History of British Journalism*. London: Routledge/Thoemmes Press.

Bailey, M. (2009) *Narrating Media History*. London: Routledge.
Bhabha, H. (1995) *Location of Culture*. London: Routledge.
Broersma, M. (2010) 'Transnational Journalism History', *m&z*, 4: 10–15.
Broersma, M. (ed.) (2007) *Form and Style in Journalism: European Newspapers and the representation of News 1880–2005*. Leuven-Paris-Dudley, MA: Peeters.
Bromley, M. (1997) 'The End of Journalism? Changes in Workplace Practices in the Press and Broadcasting in the 1990s', in M. Bromley and T. O'Malley (eds.) *A Journalism Reader*. London: Routledge, pp. 330–50.
Carey, J. (1997) 'The Problems of Journalism History', in E.S. Munson and C. Warren (eds.) *James Carey: A Reader*. Minneapolis: University of Minnesota Press, pp. 86–95.
Chalaby, J. (1998) *The Invention of Journalism*. Basingstoke: Macmillan.
Chibnall, S. (1980) *Law-and-order News: An Analysis of Crime Reporting in the British Press*. London: Tavistock.
Clarke, B. (2004) *From Grub Street to Fleet Street: An Illustrated History of British Newspaper to 1899*. Aldershot: Ashgate.
Codell, J. (ed.) (2003) *Imperial Co-histories: National Identities and the British Colonial Press*. Madison, WI: Fairleigh Dickinson Press.
Cowan, B. (2004) 'Mr Spectator and the Coffeehouse Public Sphere', *Eighteenth-Century Studies*, 37 (3): 345–66.
Curran, J. (2002) 'Media and the Making of British Society c1700–2000', *Media History*, 8 (2): 135–54.
Curran, J. and Park, M. (2000) *De-westernising Media Studies*. London: Routledge.
Deuze, M. (2005) 'What Is Journalism? Professional Identity and Ideology of Journalists Reconsidered', *Journalism*, 6 (4): 442–64.
Deuze, M. (2006) 'Global Journalism Education: A Conceptual Approach' *Journalism Studies*, 7 (1): 19–34.
Esser, F. (1998) 'Editorial Structures and Work Principles in British and German Newspapers', *European Journal of Communication*, 13 (3): 375–405.
Farrell, D. and Petersen, J.C. (2010) 'The Growth of Internet Research Methods and the Reluctant Sociologist', *Sociological Inquiry*, 80 (1): 114–25.
Fox Bourne, H. (1887/1998) *English Newspapers*. London: Routledge/Thoemmes Press.
Franklin, B. (2012) 'The Future of Journalism', *Journalism Studies*, 13 (5–6): 663–81.
Fürsich, E. (2012) 'Lifestyle Journalism as Popular Journalism', *Journalism Practice*, 6 (1): 12–25.
Glander, T. (2000) *Origins of Mass Communications Research During the American Cold War*. Mahwah, NJ: Lawrence Erlbaum Associates.
Golding, P. (2005) 'Looking Back and Looking Forward: The Risks and Prospects of a Not-So-Young Field', *Gazette: The International Journal for Communication Studies*, 67 (6): 53–42.
Habermas, J. (1989) *The Structural Transformation of the State: An Inquiry into a Category of Bourgeois Society*. London: Polity Press.
Hallin, D. and Mancini, H. (2004) *Comparing Media Systems: Three Models of Media and Politics*. Cambridge: Cambridge University Press.
Hampton, M. (1999) 'Journalism and the "Professional Ideal" in Britain: the Institute of Journalists', 1884–1907', *Historical Research*, 72 (178): 183–201.

Hampton, M. (2004) *Visions of the Press in Britain, 1850–1950*. Chicago: University of Illinois Press.

Hampton, M. (2005) 'Defining Journalism in Late Nineteenth Century Britain', *Critical Studies in Media Communication*, 22 (2): 138–55.

Hanusch, T. and Fürsich, E. (2014) *Travel Journalism: Exploring Production, Impact and Culture*. Basingstoke: Palgrave Macmillan.

Harbers, F. and den Harder, B. (2010) 'On the Spot: New Ways of Reporting in British and Dutch Newspaper Journalism 1925–2005', *m/z*, 4: 29–38.

Hepp, S. and Couldry, N. (2009) 'What Should Comparative Media Research be Comparing? Towards a Transcultural Approach to Media Cultures' in D. Thussu (ed.) *Internationalizing Media Studies*. London: Routledge, pp. 32–47.

Hoyer, S. (2007) 'Rumours of Modernity' in M. Broersma (ed.) *Form and Style in Journalism: European Newspapers and the Representation of News 1880–2005*. Leuven, Paris and Dudley, MA: Peeters, pp. 27–46.

Hoyer, S. and Pottker, H. (eds.) (2005) *Diffusion of the News Paradigm 1850–2000*. Goteborg: Nordicom.

Kepplinger, H.M. and Kocher, R. (1990) 'Professionalism in the Media World?', *European Journal of Communication*, 5 (2): 285–311.

King, P. (1987) 'Newspaper Reporting, Prosecution Practice and Perceptions of Urban Crime: The Colchester Crime Wave of 1765', *Continuity and Change*, 2 (3): 423–54.

Lupton, D. (2014) *Digital Sociology*. London: Routledge.

Naranch, B. (2007) 'Covering the Colonies: Overseas Journalism and the German Empire Building, 1884–1890'. Paper presented to International Interdisciplinary Conference on German Colonialism and Post Colonialism San Francisco State University, 6–7 September.

Nerone, J. (2013) 'Why Journalism History Matters to Journalism Studies', *American Journalism*, 30 (1): 15–28.

Pooley, J. and Katz, E. (2008) 'Further Notes on Why American Sociology Abandoned Mass Communication Research', *Journal of Communication*, 58 (4): 767–86.

Pooley, J. and Socolow, M.J. (2013) 'War of the Words: The Invasion from Mars and Its Legacy for Mass Communication Scholarship' in J. Hayes, K. Battles, and W. Hilton-Morrow (eds.) *War of the Worlds to Social Media: Mediated Communication in Times of Crisis*. New York: Peter Lang, pp. 35–56.

Riordan, K. (2014) *Accuracy, Independence, and Impartiality: How Legacy Media and Digital Natives Approach Standards in the Digital Age*. Oxford: Reuters Institute, Oxford University.

Rogers, N. (1992) 'Confronting the Crime Wave: The Debate over Social Reform and Regulation, 1749–53', in L. Davison, T. Hitchcock, T. Keirn, and R. Shoemaker (eds.) *Stilling the Grumbling Hive: The Response to Social and Economic Problems in England, 1689–1750*. Stroud: Alan Sutton, pp. 77–95.

Schudson, M. (2003) *The Sociology of News*, New York: WW Norton.

Schudson, M. (2008) 'Public Spheres, Imagined Communities and the Underdeveloped Historical Understanding of Journalism', in B. Zelizer (ed.) *Explorations in Communication and History*. London: Routledge, pp. 181–9.

Snell, E. (2007) 'Discourses of Criminality in the Eighteenth Century Press: The Presentation of Crime in The Kentish Post, 1717–1768', *Continuity and Change*, 22 (1): 13–47.

Stephens, M. (1988) *A History of News*. New York: Viking.
Stephens, M. (2000) 'Call for an International History of Journalism', *American Journalism*, 17 (2): 97–100.
Sternheimer, K, (2008) 'What's the Difference between Sociology and Journalism?', *Everyday Sociology Blog*, 29 September, http://nortonbooks.typepad.com/everydaysociology/2008/09/whats-the-diffe.html, date accessed: 4 May 2015.
Steward, J. (2005) ' "How and Where to Go": The role of Travel Journalism in Britain and the Evolution of Foreign Tourism 1840–1914', in J.K. Walton (ed.) *Histories of Tourism: Representation, Identity and Conflict*. London: Channelview, pp. 39–54.
Thussu, D. (2009) *Internationalizing Media Studies*. London: Routledge.
Wahl-Jorgensen, K. and Hanitzsch, T. (2009) *The Handbook of Journalism Studies*. London: Routledge.
Wieten, J. (2005) 'Kurt Baschwitz and the Founding Of Gazette', *Gazette* 12/2005; 67 (6): 523–530.

12
The Martian Invasion and the Sociological Imagination

Brian Winston

The Martians invaded Earth at 20:00 hours, Halloween's eve, 30 October, 1938. They landed in a field on the Wilmuth farm, Grover's Mill, New Jersey (40°19′00″N 74°36′34″W) and a large number of people were killed. Thousands more, across the United States, listening to live radio news-reports, panicked.

I am not here concerned with the fact that this event at Grover's Mill did not happen; that it was, in fact, a fiction – that week's *Mercury Theater of the Air* presentation on CBS directed by, and starring, Orson Welles. Fiction in the guise of news is unremarkable, after all: it is even to be found buried in the news itself. 'Truth', it should not be forgotten, is for the press as much a branding device as it is an earnest of quality. We can see this in its archive from, say, the French *canard* – news-book – with its true (*véritable*) report of a dragon seen in the skies above Paris in 1567 through the astronomer Sir John Herschel's observation via a giant telescope of creatures on the moon reported by Benjamin Day's *New York Daily Sun* in 1835 to all the fabrications, embellishments and entrapments of yesterday's papers (Fellow 2013:88; Janković 2000:195). The Herschel story appeared in the *New York Sun* on 6 May 1835 as a sensational spoiler to disrupt the launch of its first one cent rival, the *New York Herald*; but that paper's publisher, James Gordon Bennett Sr, would become – and more successfully so than Day – a purveyor of such stunts. He was, after all, the man who (reportedly) said: 'Many a good newspaper story has been ruined by over verification.' Of few major news stories is this truer than of the received myth of the impact of the Welles broadcast.

The salient point is not, then, that there were no deaths in Grover's Mill at the hand of Martians that night, nor that the 'reports' of them were actually coming from a studio in Manhattan rather than New Jersey. It is, simply, that 'thousands' in the rest of America did not, in fact, 'panic' on hearing these. Of course, claiming that they had demonstrated radio's effectiveness, and this certainly displeased neither the broadcasters nor their advertising paymasters. Orson Welles, at 23, was also prepared to believe, in line with his emerging *enfant terrible* public persona, that he had caused mayhem. But I wish to examine the consequences for another group of Americans who gained advantage from credulity – the sociologists. Arguably, the impact on them was, and is, the programme's most profound and enduring legacy. As Lowery and Defleur put it in a standard work on media research:

> What occurred that October night was one of the most remarkable media events of all time. If nothing else was proved that night, it was demonstrated to many people that radio could have a powerful impact on its audience.
>
> (Lowery and Defleur 1995:45)

Simply, though, it proved no such thing because the panic no more happened – at least in the sense suggested by the received account – than did the Martian invasion itself. Yet, as a determinant of the sociological imagination, *The War of the Worlds* supposed impact, uninterrogated and – of course – inter alia, remains foundational for media effects research into the present.

Be that – for the moment – as it may: first consider that the broadcast incontrovertibly did provide the papers with an excuse to attack the radio. Although many US radio stations were owned by newspaper publishers, there had been considerable friction between the media. Eventually, in 1933, a species of 'peace treaty', the Biltmore Agreement, was signed to allow radio access to the news wires for limited newscasts. However, one of its provisions also permitted unrestricted coverage of exceptional events; and this was the 1930s – the Lindbergh kidnapping, the *Hindenburg* airship disaster, the invasions of Manchuria and Ethiopia, the Spanish Civil War, Hitler and so on (McChesney 1993:171). By 1938, radio was so effectively exploiting the loophole that print journalists were increasingly eager to undermine its legitimacy as a news source; hence the 'splashes' screaming 'panic' across the country on the morning after the Welles broadcast. It is the newspaper industry that was really spooked by *The War of the Worlds* (or claimed to be so), and it sensationalised the programme's supposed impact as a basis for a censorship demand. Editorially, the press collectively called on the

Federal Communications Commission (FCC) to impose some standard of social responsibility on those to whom it had granted broadcasting licences. It is in the making of this case that the seeds of the 'panic' can be found.

The New York Daily News ran three pictures on its cover under the banner 'FAKE RADIO WAR STIRS TERROR THROUGH U.S.': a Martian space ship (a direct descendant of the Parisian dragon, no doubt – the image is uncaptioned), Orson Welles (shot from below with horror lighting) and a woman, her arm broken (we are told) as a result of a fall only tenuously related to the broadcast. Her caption is: ' "War" Victim'. Even among the less yellow sections of the American press sensationalism ruled: 'Radio Listeners, Taking War Drama as Fact' is a typical headline, this taken from *The New York Times*. The 'standfirst' reads: 'Many Flee Homes in Panic to Escape "Gas Raid from Mars" – Phone Calls Swamp Police at Broadcast of Welles Fantasy...' and the report begins: 'A wave of mass hysteria seized thousands of radio listeners throughout the nation....' Nevertheless, no actual hysteric who had supposedly fled their home was interviewed and, after the 'jump' to page four, few informants were named and those that were stated they were panicked not by the broadcast but by others telling them about it. The only actually disturbed listener *The Times* interviewed was a Mr Louis Walker of 1322 Clay Avenue, in the Bronx, who claimed to have switched into the broadcast, nearly having a heart attack, he said. The story, then, is of unnamed masses jamming switchboards, besieging police stations, running into the street with wet clothes on their faces to avoid the Martian 'gas'. In short, there is no triangulated evidence to support mass hysteria.

Moreover, the broadcast itself is deeply unconvincing. Rushed on air – because of the company's live theatrical commitments – and lacking the auditory depth and sophistication of much radio production at this time, the programme – replete with station air-checks and so on – is clearly inauthentic. Of course, there are those amongst us who grapple with the concept of fiction but millions, then as now, do not. There is but one moment in the show which might convince and, indeed, this is when Mr Walker reported joining the audience: 17 minutes 27 seconds into the drama. He then heard the supposed eye-witness reporter (played by Frank Readick) describing the first fatal Martian attack in a fair duplication of Herb Morrison's famous – and then recent – emotional eye-witness recorded account of the fatal crash of the airship *Hindenburg*, which had really happened the previous year, 7 May 1937.

'Remote' (or in UK parlance 'outside') broadcasting had been pioneered by the Canadian Broadcast Corporation's live reports from the location of a mining disaster in Nova Scotia in April 1936, and programme interruptions for news bulletins had featured from February 1938, reporting on the threat of a European war as Hitler demanded control of the Sudetenland from Czechoslovakia. The Welles production simulated, albeit inauthentically, such actual and newly introduced live or recorded location reporting techniques. To get the moment at 17 minutes 27 seconds, Welles had the cast listen to the Morrison recording, and Readick apparently did so repeatedly:

> MORRISON: It burst into flames! It burst into flames, and it's falling, it's crashing! Watch it, watch it!... It's burning and bursting into flames... Oh, the humanity....

and reproduced it – in Howard Koch's script based on H. G. Wells's novel – thus:

> 'REPORTER' (READICK): There's a jet of flame springing from the mirror, and it leaps right at the advancing men. It strikes them head on! Good Lord, they're turning into flame!
> (SCREAMS AND UNEARTHLY SHRIEKS)
> ... it's spreading everywhere. It's coming this way. About twenty yards to my right
> (CRASH OF MICROPHONE... THEN DEAD SILENCE)[1]

But one would have had to rush out of the house (with the wet towel) 30 seconds later, because by 17 minutes 57 seconds, the 'announcer', having apologised for losing contact with the 'reporter', then reads an asinine 'late bulletin' about one 'Professor Endlekoffer' who says all is well on Mars. Mr Walker can be forgiven for believing, at least momentarily, in the broadcast's 'remote' report but not in this 'bulletin'. There is even less excuse – although much reason – for Hadley Cantril's credulity about the broadcast's aftermath.

The FCC quickly indicated that there was no basis for regulatory action, and there the matter might have rested had it not been for Cantril. He had been President Roosevelt's private pollster and, in 1938, was chair of the Department of Psychology at Princeton. He had also instigated and obtained funding from the Rockefeller Foundation for a Princeton Radio Research Project (PRRP) (Korzi 2000:56; Pooley and Socolow 2013a:1922–3). It is his response to the newspapers' coverage that was to provide media sociology with an important paradigm for the investigation of audience effects: study of supposedly direct consequences of exceptional media events as assessed by surveys of public response, extrapolated into assumptions about general social impacts.

By 1938, continued funding for the PRRP had become uncertain and *The War of the Worlds* brouhaha suggested an investigation which would secure its future. Cantril approached Frank Stanton of CBS, a key figure in radio's burgeoning interest in audience measurement, for emergency extra funding for a 'firehouse' project on the broadcast's impact. Stanton, who had been instrumental in helping Cantril secure the initial Rockefeller grant, came up with the money.

The power and influence of the media constituted a largely uninterrogated given. Had not Goebbels explained in 1933, to general assent, 'it would not have been possible for us [Nazis] to take power or to use it in the ways we have without the radio' (Goebbels 1933)? And did not 'it pays to advertise' have the status of a proverb? The investigation of the efficacy of publicity campaigns, from the early 1920s on, had become an established commercial activity of itself. One research tool to hand for assessing public response was the opinion poll, which Cantril as a social psychologist was adept at using. It had gained status as a result of its accuracy in predicting election results and it was, of course, more generally a useful technique in the service of an essential broadcasting need. To maintain its viability as an advertising medium, American radio had to measure its audience to match the audited bureaux of press circulation. American advertising agencies demanded, at a minimum, 'proof' of the scope of listenership, and broader survey questions were soon also asked – for example, on the acceptability of female announcers (Hilmes 1997:142–3). The *War of the Worlds* incident, therefore, seemed ripe for study. What Cantril brought to the media research table with his investigation of the 'panic' was an expansion of the survey technique via the introduction of in-depth interviews to embrace the psychological, his discipline. Of course, in-depth interviews too had a long history (for example, Mayhew et al. 1851–62), but they had not been previously used so directly in an investigation into media effects.

The first thing to note about the report that emerged from the PRRP, published as *The Invasion from Mars: A Study in the Psychology of Panic* (1940), is that, despite his background, Cantril, in this instance, largely chose to ignore the survey data (Cantril et al. 1940 [1982]). He barely cites, and totally ignores the implication of, the most fundamental data available to him outside his own research – the ratings. Full national figures were unavailable, but of the 5000 households phoned by the C.E. Hooper ratings service during transmission only 2 per cent indicated that the radio was tuned to CBS at the time of the call. Cantril, ignoring this, does mention an unpublished CBS survey conducted by Stanton in the week following the broadcast (but then Stanton had paid Cantril for the work, after all); although he avoids drawing the obvious conclusion from it. Of CBS's 920 respondents, careful selected demographically and interviewed face to face (not by telephone), only 12–1.3 per cent – admitted to hearing the broadcast from the outset. Cantril ignores this number, explicating instead other of Stanton's findings, for example about subjects' 'critical ability' to discern a fiction (Cantril et al. 1940[1982]:77; Pooley and Socolow 2013a:1931).[2]

There were 34 million US households in 1938 so 2 per cent yields a maximum figure – assuming all had sets and all were on – of some 600,000 homes. This show cannot be remotely considered a hit. In fact, *The Mercury Theater of the Air* was a 'sustaining' (that is, unsponsored) production of the network itself, offered, in the name of quality, as a sacrifice against rival programming which dominated the time slot – in this case a popular variety show on NBC. (It is even suggested that Wells arranged for the first 'live report' from 'Grover's Mill' to coincide with an NBC commercial break in order to catch programme switchers, such as Louis Walker.) Stanton, despite his financial support, was to say later, with more than a grain of truth, that nobody was listening (Dunham 1997:33–4). The clearest positive result of the broadcast was that, thus helped by the newspapers, Welles acquired a sponsor – Campbell's Soup. No wonder that CBS was happy to cooperate with Cantril. Cantril, to justify his 'panic', began by glossing the possibility that the audience was comparatively limited. On the contrary, he calculated it, in defiance of the ratings and on the (erroneous) grounds these were all established through telephone survey, as six million. Each home would need to have 5.5 listeners given the Hooper result for this to be remotely the case. Moreover, Cantril estimated, for no very obvious reason, that a million of these listeners panicked (Cantril et al. 1940 [1982]:47).

Nor did Cantril claim – à la Mayhew – any sort of representational validity for his sample. The CBS money was not enough to allow for interviewing beyond Orange, New Jersey. Within a week of the broadcast some 30 people had been questioned, and subsequently some 135 in-depth interviews in total were taken. Subjects were found 'by personal enquiry and initiative of the interviewers'. Initiative was needed because contacting names mentioned in the papers yielded only six people willing to cooperate, a fact Cantril attributes to the shame of the duped. Thus: 'Over 100 [of the 135] were selected because they were known [to the investigators] to have been upset by the broadcast' (Cantril et al. 1940 [1982]:xiii). To interview at random might have revealed – or come closer to revealing – how limited the programme's impact actually was. Given the funding context, prophylactics against such an outcome – inflating the audience size, pre-selecting interviewees – are unsurprising. Cantril further ensured that he was providing proof positive of causality on an extensive and serious scale by conflating, in the results, various levels of subjects' response; for example, melding 'frightened', 'disturbed' or 'excited' by the programme with being 'panicked' (Pooley and Socolow 2013b).

He also found correlation between educational level among his 'intuitively' selected respondents and their susceptibility to media-induced panic – their 'critical ability' (Orr 2006:59). Michael Denning notes that this reflects a certain underlying 'deep contempt for working class culture' embedded in the study (Denning 1998:558). The questions of Cantril's survey might seem disingenuous:

Do you think there is some form of life on Mars comparable to ours?

- very possible
- slightly possible
- not at all
- no opinions

but current scholarship indicates that, on the eve of war – with Europe already in flames as the results were being prepared for publication – more was at stake than a mere investigation into audience reception of an entertainment (Pooley and Socolow 2013b; 2013c). The issue of morale maintenance and manipulation of opinion – seen as being most pressing among the lower orders – loomed large. A vision of all-powerful media – the received orthodoxy of 'hypodermic needle' or 'magic bullet' model of its direct effects on both thought and action – was a given of *bien pensant* opinion. Hitler, surely, demonstrated it.

Any assessment of media impact, however, needs to distinguish between attitude/opinion formation (which can be seen as self-attested, discovered by questioning and so on) and media-provoked action (which can be externally verified). Robert Merton draws a distinction between propaganda as 'one-way' repetitive communication (for example, Hitler's repetitions of 'big lies' to compel belief) and persuasive messages as 'two way', producing action as a consequence of 'reciprocal interplay' – that which today might be termed 'interactivity' (Merton et al. 1946:33–40). Jacques Elul, on the other hand, discerns a division in propaganda – neutrally defined overall as persuasive messages – as having either direct and indirect (which he terms 'sociological') outcomes (Elul 1964:15). Attitude formation (Mertonian propaganda) is indirect, provoked action (Mertonian persuasion) direct. The Cantril study, with its easily critiqued procedures and therefore tendentious conclusions, blurs this distinction. The 'panic' noted in the study was all internally attested, while the externally verifiable consequences (on telephone switchboards, police stations and so on) remained untriangulated.

In Pooley and Socolow's account, Cantril emerges as a somewhat egocentric opportunist, sidelining colleagues essential to the project (Hazel Gudet and Herta Hertzog) and seriously falling out with Paul Lazarsfeld (Hertzog's husband), the director of PRRP, whom he had appointed in 1937 (Pooley and Socolow 2013a:1923–4). Lazarsfeld, although committed to the study and in general given to collaborative work, felt Cantril ignored his prerogatives as the PRRP's director. He soon removed himself from Princeton to establish and lead Columbia University's Office of Radio Research (later the Bureau of Applied Social Research). There he co-opted Robert Merton who had joined the Columbia sociology faculty at the same time. Merton, 'who would become perhaps the most influential American sociologist of the 20th century', had little taste for 'applied' research. Nevertheless, he was persuaded by Lazarsfeld to become an associate director of the Bureau (Simonson 2006:271). Merton was a trained sociologist, unlike the psychologist Cantril (and unlike Lazarsfeld whose doctorate was in mathematics), and he was, initially, sceptical about the efficacy of the investigative tools available (such as interviewing) as a serious technique to determine media impact. But another major 'media event' in 1943, the first since the Welles broadcast, presented an opportunity to refine such approaches, and he acceded to Lazarsfeld's request that he replicate *The Invasion from Mars* study.

From 8 a.m., 21 September 1943 through to 2 a.m. the following morning, Kate Smith, an enormously popular – somewhat 'homely' and certainly patriotic – singer, had made 65 short appeals on CBS, about every 15 minutes for the 18 hours, specifically selling War Bonds. Each interstitial concluded with the repeated 'Will you buy a bond?' (Merton et al. 1946:36). Between stints at the microphone, calls were taken from listeners making pledges and explaining why they were doing so, the substance of which Smith then incorporated in her subsequent scripted appeals to the audience. This use of the telephone allowed for 'the simulacrum of personal contact', interactivity contributing to the 'two-way' persuasiveness involved (Merton et al. 1946:69). It reinforced Smith's 'you and I' rhetoric. Unlike the *War of the Worlds* 'panic', the direct impact of her effort required no newspaper exaggerations and fabrications. It could be unambiguously measured in the tallied amount of pledges to buy bonds made by telephone or in writing. Eventually, this totalled some $39 million. At $18.75 a bond, Smith received pledges 'selling' over two million of them (Horten 2003:194). The 'marathon' was another exceptional 'media event', seemingly demonstrating what Merton was to call 'the tyranny of radio'. (Scannell 2007:65–6; Simonson 2004).

The contrast to Cantril's procedures was pronounced and a wide array of integrated methods of inquiry were deployed. A thorough content analysis of recurrent themes (for example 'patriotism') in Smith's interstitial 'continuities' (aka scripts) was undertaken and used to contextualise the responses found in a poll of 978 of a 'carefully selected cross section of the population of Greater New York', diverse as to class, ethnicity, education and religion. A hundred extended focused interviews, in a mode developed by Hertzog (one of Cantril's sidelined colleagues), were also conducted (Merton et al. 1946:16; Simonson 2006:280). Of these, 75 respondents had pledged to buy and 25 had not.

Smith had ignored the most obvious selling point: the ten-year bonds bought for $18.75 would be redeemable for $25. Smith had made sacrifice for the war effort central in her appeals, and Merton noted that in 50 per cent of his respondents this rather than investment was given as the primary reason for making the pledge. Other reasons given for buying bonds were specific variations on sacrifice – collective effort, family members in the forces and so on. But also present was an element of competition. This was the third drive on CBS in which Smith had been involved. Radio appeals were not unusual, and radio had been specifically utilised in previous official war-bond drives – together with a complete panoply of communication modes from posters and press advertising to movie shorts, from celebrity appearances to (even) classroom exhortations. What distinguished CBS's 1943 effort was the format – the repeated interstitial appeals. Dance marathons, 'endurance entertainment', had been a ubiquitous American quasi-sporting fad arising in 1923 from general competitions to establish 'world records' (Martin 1994).[3] The marathon format explains a reported concern amongst Merton's respondents for Smith's endurance. This encouraged persistent listening. The ludic element was further echoed by Smith's repeated exhortations that previous totals be exceeded.

Merton and his colleagues also paid much attention to Smith's persona. Her signature song was Irving Berlin's 'God Bless America'. So popular had she made it that an abortive campaign began for it to replace 'The Star Spangled Banner' as the national anthem. She had sung it for George VI and Queen Elizabeth at the White House during a state visit. As well as a prime-time entertainment hour on CBS, she also had a weekly 'agony aunt' 15-minute programme in which she responded to listeners' letters. With an audience of ten million, this was the most popular daytime broadcast in America (Scannell 2007:64). Finally, 'prominent was her physical appearance in the responses' (Merton et al. 1946:146–7). A Southerner, she was a matronly figure with an exceptionally warm microphone voice.

Despite the care with which this context was documented and the reality of the $39 million raised, nevertheless the claim of direct causality needs explication. More than the 'tyranny of radio' was involved. The broadcast was entirely licet and exhortationary – it was a fund-raiser and it raised funds. People pledging (unlike those supposedly running into the street with towels on the heads) were not being persuaded into deviant behaviour. However, and much less much unmentioned, the 'sacrifice' involved in buying a bond was cushioned by the promised 33 per cent return on the investment in 1953. Sacrifice and patriotism aside, the ludic element was also seductive. The broadcaster's celebrity persona was perfectly matched to the task. As the marathon was broadcast by CBS, members of the audience were being bombarded with messages to buy bonds at every turn. The country was in the midst of the Third War Bond Loan Drive, which had began on 9 September 1943. It ended three weeks later having handsomely exceeded the ambitious goal of raising $15 billion, by some 60 per cent: $25.1 billion. Smith's $39 million represents 1.5 per cent of this.

Officials of the Office of War Information (OWI), which had overall charge of the drives, felt that the Smith exercise was beginning to suggest a personal public relations effort. Despite continued popularity, she was not invited to repeat it for the following three annual drives.

Peter Simonson (2006) mounts an elegant case for the recuperation of *Mass Persuasion* (Merton et al. 1946), drawing attention to the sophistication of Merton's thinking around notions of 'pseudo-*Gemeinschaft*' and 'public image', but it is significant that his defence of the work significantly does not embrace the central, and essential, claim of causality. Paddy Scannell suggests that revisiting Lazarsfeld and Merton corrects the widely received notion, widely received by the 1970s, that the empirical tradition of effects research (whose foundational moments can be seen in these analyses of the Welles and Smith broadcasts) was 'mindless'. Lazarsfeld and Merton's thinking clearly prefigured a modern agenda of concern with the media as 'soft disciplinary agents of the economic and social status quo' (Scannell 2007:72). What remains true, though, is the fact that, despite it being commonly retailed to the contrary, these 'key incidents of [media] effects' do not actually 'strengthen' an understanding of media impact, much less prove it (Philo 1990:3).

The model of all-powerful media was inevitably to be refined as the weight of research failed effectively to demonstrate it effectively. Lazarsfeld's evolution of a 'Two-step Flow' from media to mass opinion marks the first stage of this process. Re-enforcement rather than initiation came to be held as a likelier and more common media effect. The difficulty of demonstrating causality eventually reached the dead end of the 'null effect' hypothesis and the development of a 'uses and gratifications' model before being swept away by the theorising of postmodernism. But, throughout, the grail of demonstrating direct effect remains – and if it eluded the knights of pure sociology then the champions of social psychology were ever ready to seek it.

The *locus classicus* of the cognate lab-based (or lab-like) research tradition is Albert Bandura's 'Bobo Doll' experiment of 1958. Never mind that it has nothing to do with mass communication per se, it is the *fons et origo* of social psychology research as applied to the media. Such are the accretions on this endlessly cited study that I abstract a summary from the original paper:

> *Subjects*
>
> The subjects were 36 boys and 36 girls enrolled in the Stanford University Nursery' School. They ranged in age from 37 to 69 months, with a mean age of 52 months...
>
> *Experimental Design*
>
> ...Half the experimental subjects were exposed to aggressive models and half were exposed to models that were subdued and nonaggressive in their behavior...
>
> After having settled the subject in his corner, the experimenter escorted the model to the opposite corner of the room which contained a small table and chair, a tinker toy set, a mallet, and a 5-foot inflated Bobo doll...
>
> With subjects in the *nonaggressive condition*, the model assembled the tinker toys in a quiet subdued manner totally ignoring the Bobo doll...

In contrast, with subjects in the *aggressive condition*, the model began by assembling the tinker toys but after approximately a minute had elapsed, the model turned to the Bobo doll and spent the remainder of the period aggressing toward it.

Experimental Conditions

...At the end of ten minutes, the experimenter entered the room, informed the subject that he would now go to another game room, and bid the model goodbye.

Test for Delayed Imitation

The experimental room contained a variety of toys. The aggressive toys included a 3-foot Bobo doll...

Complete Imitation of Models' Behavior

Subjects in the aggression condition reproduced a good deal of physical and verbal aggressive behavior resembling that of the models... subjects in the nonaggressive and control groups... exhibited virtually no imitative aggression...

(Bandura et al. 1961: 575–82)

Conclusion: young children watching violent behaviour imitate it.

Certainly, young 'faculty brats' at Stanford in the late 1950s did so when exposed to unknown adults suddenly introduced into their environment, a nursery where familiar adult teachers presumably normally played with them. Instead the stranger began playing violently on his or her own with a toy designed to be hit. Bandura, 'the most cited of living psychologists', was a pioneer of such experimentation and is ranked by his peers as the fourth most influential twentieth-century figure in the field after Skinner, Piaget and Freud (Haggbloom et al. 2002).

Leave aside as an irony that this 'experiment', the founding 'proof' upon which never-abating concerns about the impact of violent media turn, would today be prohibited as an unethically exposing exposure of children to corruption and/or distress. Ignoring that, even if we accept the viability of extrapolation from laboratory to the real world, what are we told? That children learn by imitation of actually witnessed behaviour; that a toy designed to be hit gets hit? As with Merton's demonstration that a charitable media appeal evokes charitable responses, does not the obviousness render any broad conclusions for media impact unsafe?

For example, ask children exposed to film of aggression on the doll, as did Kniverton and Stevenson in 1970, if they were familiar with the toy, and one discovers that those that were, were five times less likely to bop it than those for whom it was a novelty (Kniverton and Stevenson 1970). Such prior experience and knowledge are factors which monocausal explanations exclude. They 'contaminate' ('confound', the statisticians would say) the claim of causation. Media sociology textbooks nevertheless retail accounts of the Bobo Doll experiment, insisting that it shows that violent behaviour arises as a consequence of children watching 'a character on film behaving in an aggressive manner' (Gunter and McAleer 1997:107).

'Aggression' commonly appears to be tested by demonstrating that a research subject has a heightened proclivity to administer (virtual) electric shocks or blasts of white noise on others. Experiments 'showing', for example, increases of such 'aggression' as a consequence of playing violent video games were being reported on a monthly basis by 2006 (Anderson et al. 2010). Undiverted by any doubts as to the relevance of these projects to actual circumstances, social psychology nevertheless assures us that 'only experiments can hope to provide persuasive evidence of causality' (Griffiths 1997:206). And not just about violence.

Melvyn Defleur, for example, in another classic 1950s study, was concerned with the question of message diffusion. He used a light aircraft to drop leaflets over a number of villages in Washington State, and followed up by tracing who picked them up and who passed them on. He found that: 'as transmitters of the leaflet via *pass-on diffusion*, children were more active in more segments of the population than were adults' (Defleur and Larsen 1958:176). It is, one can safely claim, incontrovertible that leaflets dropped unexpectedly from the sky (at least in rural Washington State) will be picked up and passed on largely by children. As a guide to the causes of actual behaviour, though, the evidence is as useful as that of a *Candid Camera* stunt. The entire tradition speaks more to the creativity of social psychology than to the realities of media impact. But, as with Cantril's study, one can note the seriousness of Defleur's context. The leaflet stated that in case of enemy attack, planes might deliver instructions in this form. He and his colleagues were involved in testing how communication with the masses might be maintained in the event that other mass media systems were knocked out in a nuclear war. (Not for nothing did Defleur name this Project Revere in honour of Paul, his ride and his warning of imminent arrival of an enemy – then the British). And so it goes.

For example, George Gerbner's (1998) 'Cultivation Theory' revisits Cantril's correlation between increased media impact and lower educational attainment and economic standing. He suggested that such socially disadvantaged long-term heavy users of television were likely to be more fearful of violence than are light users (more educated and of a higher class). Given the mayhem suffusing media this seems self-evident. But 'Cultivation Theory' isolates media, and so no more avoids the 'contamination' problem (as in the presence of factors other than the media) than does any other positivist research design. Heavy media users, for example, are more likely to be living in more deprived areas where the experience of real violence is likely to be greater (Wober and Gunter 1998). The correlation could as much reflect a rationally grounded response to experience as it does media impact.

It is the detail of these researches that rendered the legacies of *The War of the Worlds* as well as the Bobo Doll experiment mindless, at least in those quarters not given to replicating them. As Sonia Livingstone concludes, 'Despite the volume of research, the debate about media effects... remains unresolved' (Livingstone 1996:306). Nevertheless, correlations are not without considerable significance and it would be improper, as David Miller and Greg Philo correctly insist, to conclude that the manifest failings of positivism prove the 'null effect' thesis (Miller and Philo 1999:21). 'We can accept that what people understand and believe is not simply a result of what we are told by the media'. 'Contamination' does not totally 'confound' all results, and it cannot be the case that we can write off 'the effect of media simply because a small number of stimuli are not seen to have much effect on developed systems of belief' (Philo 1990:6–7).

Impact can occur. Perhaps this is most carefully demonstrated in connection with health communication campaigns. Information – new (for example, the 'five-a-day' campaign on the value of eating fruits and vegetables) and old (on the value of exercise) – can be transmitted via media, and subsequent reception studies have repeatedly noted small to moderate effects on understanding (Leavy et al. 2011; Noar 2006). Moreover, ways can be found to overcome the considerable difficulties of producing sound – or at least less contaminated – evidence from surveys.

Philo's invitation to research subjects to write, as journalists, thus revealing significant correlation to the contours of media coverage in their understanding of any given topic, would be a good example of this (Philo 1990:12). Coupled with an examination of the subjects' acknowledged media sources, this technique allows for a more specific isolation of media effect. The 'journalism' can be mapped against the sources to reveal repeated errors. However, except in very specific and limited circumstances where the mendacity of a media story is known, examples of which Philo provides, this cannot be easily extended to demonstrate causality as regards opinion formation more generally. For one thing, as Charles Peirce insists, one needs 'previous acquaintance with what the sign denotes' to make any sense of it' (Peirce 1966:179). This inevitably must include more than the immediate media coverage; so therein contamination must still lie. The subjects' reading of the media source texts, as Philo carefully outlines, is conditioned by prior knowledge and factors such as class-formation. Moreover, the unpacking of opinion (in contrast to the identification of the specifics of fraudulent reporting) requires a judgement of bias in the specific original texts on the part of the researchers; a contentious matter itself and one subject to (potential?) bias. Nevertheless, the process goes further towards providing evidence of direct effect than has been previously possible.

The developed sophistication here in play is something of the exception that proves the rule that effects research, otherwise, too often lacks the rigour of good investigative journalism, never mind meeting the standards of proof lawyers demand of any evidence. And what is concerning about that is that the majority of such work, however 'unsafe' its findings, is too commonly used to justify the social control of the media. Cantril showed the way to the usefulness of academic research for the communications industries and authorities. Today a 'regulator' such as Ofcom is quick to support Cantil's sociological decedents' search for evidence of effect, albeit with no sounder outcomes. Ofcom has a statutory 'role in protecting TV viewers' which it does via the imposition of a production code. This, though, is arguably an improper, barely disguised, censorship system, and little else can justify it in a liberal democracy other than the supposed impact of the media on popular understanding.

Thus, when a quantitative survey in 2013 revealed that the code's prohibition of violence before 9 p.m. to 'protect' children is nugatory, with 80 per cent of parents being unconcerned, Ofcom sought qualitative data of audience opinion for justification (Anon (Jigsaw) 2014:1). It secured the services of Jigsaw Research: 'We believe that research works best when it is colourful and imaginative – when it is a springboard for creativity and opportunity. We call this Thinking in Colour' (Jigsaw Research 2014). Jigsaw then distributed 127 'viewing journals', held 14 'discussion groups' of six to eight subjects to comment on a total of 15 violent clips taken from soap operas, and conduct 14 in-depth interviews (Anon (Jigsaw) 2014:8–9, 13–7, 47) And from this they find, for instance:

> Cumulative Overall Impact:
>
> ...A number of different factors, taken together, can have a cumulative impact on the viewer. These factors might include music or 'an atmosphere of unease' which can add to the viewers discomfort by creating a sense of threat or menace.
>
> (Anon (Jigsaw) 2014:5)

So 'factors' (for example music) *can* cause 'discomfort' evidenced by a 'sense' of threat or menace: just as Cantril found in 1938. The 9 p.m. 'watershed' remains.

And Bandura's legacy?

First we must jump from the lab (or other controlled environments) to the 'real' world, a leap which many might not want to make. Were experiments less reliant on violent toys, mock torture, leaflets falling like manna from heaven and so on, believing their results would still require more faith than logic. Demonstrating media-induced behaviour modification is fundamentally less 'safe' than are the conclusions drawn from audience research. Correlation and causation are the Scylla and Charybdis between which conclusions drown (see Cumberbatch and Howitt 1989). And outside the lab, this is still the case. Little behaviour modification – as opposed to attitude formation – has been observed. For example: 'In terms of health promotion, a large portion of health campaigns have not led to substantial health behaviour change among members of the US population' (Anderson et al. 2010:1). Despite effectively raising awareness, people ate no more fruit and vegetables (Foerster and Hudes 1994).

Nevertheless causation does occur – although it might be supposed where it does, that this is primarily evidence of social deviancy in the receivers. The most – perhaps only – clear body of repeated media causation is with suicide. So well attested is copy-catting as a consequence of media consumption, imitation is known as the 'Werther Effect'.[4] For instance: following the opening of the Vienna subway in 1978 and its emergence as a site for suicides, a suicide prevention group successfully campaigned for media restraint. In 1987, 'splashes' with suicide notes and images of the dead ceased to appear until suicide was no longer reported at all. The suicide rate was slashed by 84.2 per cent (Etzersdorfer and Sonneck 1998). This arguably goes beyond correlation but, note, it needed neither sociology's attitude surveys nor social psychology's media impact experimentation to be proved.

Demonstrating direct causation at this level of evidential certainty has to be what is in question in any polity which has adopted the principle of free expression. This right's only legitimate constraint can be that it 'do no harm' (Winston 2012:260). It is not, then, media-induced emotions, opinions or beliefs but media-induced action (such as violence) where effect needs to be demonstrated. People can believe or not believe that the Martians invaded as they will, and for whatever reason; it is their actions based on this belief – for example besieging police stations, imitating suicide – that afford reasons for the control of expression. And suicide aside, however pervasive assumptions to the contrary, effects research does not yield the evidence needed to justify such control. It is not that we know less than the tradition claims to; this all matters because authorities claim to 'protect' the public on the basis of the effects literature. This demands that these claims are treated with extreme suspicion.

Rather like news of the panic caused by invasions from Mars.

Notes

1. Welles's first major appearance on radio had been as an 'announcer' in an experimental drama by Archibald McLeish broadcast on CBS in 1937. Michael Denning suggests his climactic speech in this production, the arrival through smoke and glare of a gigantic 'conqueror' figure, is also here echoed (Denning 1998:382–3).
2. The 'critical ability' factor in evaluating the authenticity of realistic fictional texts accords with Umberto Eco's concept of the 'inferential walk' (Eco 1979[1994]:33). More generally, it is also reflected in Charles Peirce's triadic 'percepts' to test the validity of any referent (Peirce 1966:179).
3. The last was in 1952.
4. Goethe's novel, *The Sorrow of Young Werther* (1774), about a man who kills himself for love, was (anecdotally) said to have caused imitative suicides.

Bibliography

Anderson, C.A., Shibuya, A., Ihori, N., Swing, E.L., Bushman, B.J., Sakamoto, A., Rothstein, H.R., & Saleem, M. (2010) 'Violent Video Game Effects on Aggression, Empathy, and Prosocial Behavior in Eastern and Western Countries: A Meta-Analytic Review', *Psychological Bulletin*, 136 (2): 151–73.

Anon (1938) 'Radio Listeners, Taking War Drama as Fact', *New York Times*, 31 October.

Anon (Jigsaw) (2014) *Audience Attitude Towards Violent Content on Television*. OFCOM/Jigsaw, http://stakeholders.ofcom.org.uk/binaries/research/tv-research/violence/Violence_on_TV_Report.pdf, date accessed: 22 November 2014.

Bandura, A., Ross, D. and Ross, S.A. (1961) 'Transmission of Aggression through Imitation of Aggressive Models', *Journal of Abnormal and Social Psychology*, 63 (3): 575–82.

Cantril, H., with (uncredited) Gaudet, H. and Hertzog, H. (1940[1982]) *The Invasion from Mars: A Study in the Psychology of Panic*. Princeton, NJ: Princeton University Press.

Cumberbatch, G. and Howitt, D. (1989) *A Measure of Uncertainty: The Effects of the Mass Media*. London: John Lilley.

Defleur, M. and Larsen, O. (1958) *The Flow of Information: An Experiment in Mass Communication*. New York: Harper.

Denning, M. (1998) *The Cultural Front: The Laboring of American Culture in the Twentieth Century*. London: Verso.

Dunham, C. (1997) *Fighting for the First Amendment: Stanton of CBS vs. Congress and the Nixon White House*. Westport, CT: Praeger.

Eco, U. (1979 [1994]) *The Role of the Reader: Explorations in the Semiotics of Texts*. Bloomington: Indiana University Press.

Eco, U. (1994) *Six Walks in the Fictional Woods*. Cambridge, MA: Harvard University Press.

Ellul, J. (1964) *The Technological Society*. New York: Vintage.

Elul, J. (1965) *Propaganda: The Formation of Men's Attitudes*. New York: Vintage Books.

Etzersdorfer, E. and Sonneck, G. (1998) 'Preventing Suicide by Influencing Mass Media Reporting: the Viennese Experience 1980–1986', *Archives of Suicide Research*, 4 (1): 67–74.

Fellow, A. (2013) *American Media History*. Boston, MA: Wadsworth.

Foerster, S.B. and Hudes, M. (1994) *California Dietary Practices Survey*. Sacramento, CA: Californian Department of Health Services and California Public Health Foundation.

Gerbner, G. (1998) 'Cultivation Analysis: An overview', *Mass Communication and Society*, 1 (3/4): 175–94.

Goebbels, J. (1933) *The Radio as the Eight Great Power*, http://research.calvin.edu/german-propaganda-archive/goeb56.htm, date accessed: 16 November 2014.

Grant, A. and Meadows, J. (2006) *Communication Technology Update*. Oxford: Focal.

Griffiths, M. (1999) 'Violent Video Games and Aggression: A Review of the Literature', *Aggression and Violent Behavior*, 4 (2): 203–12.

Gunter, B. and McAleer, J. (1997) *Children and Television*. London: Routledge.

Haggbloom, S., Warnick, R., Warnick, J.E., Jones, V.K., Yarbrough, G.L., Russell, T.M., Borecky, C.M., McGahhey, R., Powell III, J.L., Beavers, J. and Monte, E. (2002) 'The 100 Most Eminent Psychologists of the 20th Century', *Review of General Psychology*, 6 (2): 139–52.

Hilmes, M. (1997) *Radio Voices: American Broadcasting 1922–1952*. Minneapolis: University of Minnesota Press.

Horten, G. (2003) *Radio Goes to War: The Cultural Politics of Propaganda During World War II*. Berkeley: University of California Press.

Janković, V. (2000) *Reading the Skies: A Cultural History of English Weather, 1650–1820*. Manchester: Manchester University Press.

Jigsaw Research (2014) http://www.jigsaw-research.co.uk, date accessed: 22 November 2014.

Kniverton, B. and Stevenson, G. (1970) 'The Effect of Pre-experience on Imitation of an Aggressive Film Model', *British Journal of Social & Clinical Psychology*, 9 (1): 31–6.

Korzi, M. (2000) 'Lapsed Memory: The Roots of American Public Opinion Research', *Polity*, 33 (1): 49–74.

Leavy, J.E., Bull, F.C., Rosenberg, M. and Bauman, A. (2011) 'Physical Activity Mass Media Campaigns and their Evaluation: A Systematic Review of the Literature 2003–2010', *Health Education Research*, 26 (6): 1060–85.

Livingstone, S. (1996) 'On the Continuing Problems of Media Effects Research' in J. Curran and M. Gurevitch (eds.) *Mass Media and Society*. 2nd Ed. London: Edward Arnold, pp. 305–24.

Lowery, S.A. and DeFleur, M.L. (1995) *Milestones in Mass Communication Research: Media Effects*. 3rd Ed. White Plains, NY: Longman.

Mark Griffiths, M. (1997) 'Video Games and Aggression' *The Psychologist*, September: 397–401.

Martin, C. (1994) *Dance Marathons: Performing American Culture of the 1920s and 1930s*. Jackson: University Press of Mississippi.

Mayhew, H., Tuckniss, W. and Beard, R. (1851–1862) *London Labour and the London Poor: A Cyclopaedia of the Condition and Earnings of those that will Work, those that cannot Work, and those that will not Work*. 4 Vols. London: George Woodfall and Son/Griffin, Bohn, and Company.

McChesney, R.W. (1993) *Telecommunications, Mass Media, and Democracy*. New York: Oxford University Press.

Merton, R., Fiske, M., Curtis, A. (1946) *Mass Persuasion*. Westport, CT: Greenwood.

Miller, D. and Philo, G. (1999) 'The Effective Media', in G. Philo (Ed.) *Message Received*. Harlow: Addison Wesley, pp. 21–32.

Noar, S. (2006) 'A 10-Year Retrospective of Research in Health Mass Media Campaigns: Where Do We Go From Here?', *Journal of Health Communications*, 11 (1): 21–42.

Orr, J. (2006) *Panic Diaries: A Genealogy of Panic Disorder*. Durham, NC: Duke University Press.

Peirce, C.S. (1966) *Collected Papers of Charles S. Peirce*. Cambridge, MA: Harvard University Press.

Philo, G. (1990) *Seeing & Believing: The Influence of Television*. London: Routledge.

Pooley, J. and Socolow, M. (2013a) 'Checking Up on The Invasion from Mars: Hadley Cantril, Paul Lazarsfeld, and the Making of a Misremembered Classic', *International Journal of Communication*, 7: 1920–48.

Pooley, J. and Socolow, M. (2013b) 'The Myth of the *War of the Worlds* Panic', *Slate*. http://www.slate.com/articles/arts/history/2013/10/orson_welles_war_of_the_worlds_panic_myth_the_infamous_radio_broadcast_did.html, date accessed: 15 November 2013.

Pooley, J. and Socolow, M.J. (2013c) 'War of the Words: The Invasion from Mars and Its Legacy for Mass Communication Scholarship', in J. Hayes, K. Battles, and W. Hilton-Morrow (eds.) *War of the Worlds to Social Media: Mediated Communication in Times of Crisis*. New York: Peter Lang, pp. 35–56.

Scannell, P. (2007) *Media and Communication*. London: Sage.

Simonson, P. (2004) 'Introduction', in R. Merton, M. Fiske, and A. Curtis (1946) *Mass Persuasion*. Westport, CT: Greenwood, pp. XI–XLIX.

Simonson, P. (2006) 'Celebrity, Public Image and American Political Life: Rereading Robert Merton's Mass Persuasion', *Political Communication*, 23 (3): 272–84.
Winston, B. (2012) *The Right to Offend*. London: Bloomsbury.
Wober, M. and Gunter, B. (1998) *Television and Social Control*. New York: St Martins.
Wright, K., Sparks, L. and O'Hair, H. (2013) *Health Communication in the 21st Century*. Malden, MA: Wiley-Blackwell.

Conclusion: Stretching the Sociological Imagination in the Neo-Liberal Academy

Matt Dawson, Bridget Fowler, David Miller and Andrew Smith

In this concluding chapter we return to the sociological imagination and consider the practical effects of changes in the role and status of sociology and how the discipline has been affected by the political economy of higher education. We look in turn at the marketisation of the academy, and at the threat these changes pose to job security and status. We turn next to the consequences of research assessment processes on the autonomy of academics, and on their ability to determine their own work patterns and topics. This is followed by a brief discussion of the challenges faced by those committed to teaching social theory in such conditions. Finally, we discuss the politics of the so-called 'impact agenda', suggesting that the space for the production of natural and scientific knowledge has also been damaged by the rise of policy-related institutions (think tanks) in civil society.

Markets, universities and the new mode of funding

The contributions to this book have been arranged around the concept of a sociological imagination and have debated how it might be further enhanced. But at present in the UK, following the earlier US example, universities are being fundamentally restructured around a new mode of funding. This has profound repercussions for sociology. Thus the likely removal of the current cap on student fees in England will herald a new dimension of marketisation. As David Willetts (then minister for universities and science) remarked, the 'most powerful driver of reform [*sic*] is to let new providers [private universities] into the system' (cited in Collini 2013:6). Even if partial public funding remains 'the withdrawal of state funding from undergraduate degree programmes in arts, humanities and social sciences represents the privatisation of English higher education' (Campaign for the Public University n.d.).

Such objectives are championed in the Browne Report (2010). Browne adroitly deploys the progressive vocabulary of the Greens – *Securing a Sustainable Future for Higher Education* (our emphasis) – for his neo-liberal goals. His report dresses up in 'dynamic' (2010:49) clothes a policy curiously denuded of evidence-based backing, which can only have regressive consequences. In this model everything is deemed right about postgraduate funding – a Panglossian vision of inequities in practical access to Masters' degrees not shared by educational researchers. Making a conspicuous break with the 1963 Robbins Report, Browne's main goal is unabashedly to restructure universities in line with 'what employers need'. Unsurprisingly, the subsequent changes to English universities outlined in the Coalition White Paper of summer 2011 implemented virtually all of Browne's recommendations.

The consequence has been that most English students now gain loans to pay fees and are under heightened pressure to undertake vocationally useful degrees. This trend is expected to affect the popularity of arts and social sciences over the long term, especially the likelihood of students from 'untraditional university origins' opting for sociology. In turn, a decline in student numbers has immediate material consequences. Such universities desperately seek to recruit students under the threat that their academic staff will otherwise become compulsorily redundant. This, of course, is in a context where redundancy precludes academics from competing for funded research and therefore threatens life-long damage to careers. Moreover, the potential for heads of subject to choose to 'let go' those doing unpopular research subtly threatens academic freedom, in a manner unprecedented since the Second World War.

The growing extension of the market in universities has been examined most closely in the US under the heading of academic capitalism (see, for example, Slaughter and Rhoades 2004). They note that it has been accompanied by four main features: knowledge production as profitable business; the mass marketing of courses and teaching materials beyond the student body; the exponential growth of an academic precariat; the decline in servicing the needs of local communities. Thus, first, there has been a much greater prioritisation of research over teaching, together with the commodification of research 'outputs'. As an example, prior to 1980 about 250 patents per annum went to American universities, mostly in the STEM subjects (science, technology, engineering and medicine); in 1998, this had increased to 3151 (Slaughter and Rhoades 2004:312). In turn, investment in American universities is strongest not just where there is the highest public funding in the form of research grants, but where the business interest is greatest. Strikingly – at least to those in the UK's social sciences – corporations have even begun to shape university research agenda, including the intricate processes of reviewing grant proposals (Slaughter and Rhoades 2004:311).

Second, organisation for much greater instrumental rationality has meant that teaching at the level of individual universities becomes more subject to commodification.[1] Of course, this occurs partly through higher fees: thus, for example, Piketty (2014:485) reports that Harvard parents now have a joint income of $450,000, 'which corresponds to the income of the top two per cent of the US income hierarchy'. But it also occurs through other forms of marketisation, including sales of the relevant academics' lectures, as well as textbooks, which benefit the universities where they work.

Third, the mark of the new academic capitalism is a permanent dual-labour market for academic staff. A primary market caters for research 'stars' – highly paid professors in well-founded and prestigious laboratories or institutes – whilst the secondary academic market buys the labour of part-time, casualised workers and postgraduates. This swollen academic 'contingent labour-force', now often forced to work without offices, is one sector of the wider 'precariat'. Part-time teaching in America has doubled in the last 20 years (Slaughter and Rhoades 2004:320).

Finally, there has been a decline of interest in the older public university in supplying the teaching needs of local communities, especially of ethnic minorities, since '[a]s colleges and universities shift towards revenue generation through academic capitalism, they invest less in historic, democratic missions of providing increased access and upward social mobility to less advantaged populations of students' (Slaughter and Rhoades 2004:308). Paradoxically, this changed mode of academic production in the US has not in fact led to a reduction of public subsidy but rather to its transfer from one section to another. In general, the neoliberal university is correlated with increased inequalities – with especial benefits for large companies, the wealthy (not least vice-chancellors and principals) and the professional upper middle class.

Research has also drawn attention to the growth of higher management in universities, the parallel establishment of the top-down 'right to manage' as in other branches of the public sector (Warner 2015; on the right to manage, see Beynon, Chapter 4, this volume) along with the dramatic decline or threats of decline in the collegial powers of academic senates (McGettigan 2013).

Yet there have also been important forms of academic resistance to these changes that are shaping a new professional ethic. The consequences of making universities so driven by league table monetary rewards and economic employability have been drawn out in two biting polemics by Stefan Collini (2012 and 2013), by Marina Warner on the 'cruel optimism' possessed at first by academics (2014; 2015) and by a Voltairean satire on the 'winner take all' mentality of the new university marketisation by Martins (2004). These diverse forms of opposition have culminated in a new collective manifesto – that of the Campaign for a Public University, cited above, in which John Holmwood has had a vital role (see his foreword to this volume).

Collini (2012:164) has drawn out with great lucidity the underlying premises of 'HiEdBizUK plc' (2012:21). He has pointed out how much progress in commercial research and development is invisibly indebted to the much more open-ended research in universities. He has stressed the inappropriate use of business market analogies in university competitive models:

> There may be *rivalry* between different national groups of scholars, as between individuals, but not [in] any meaningful sense *competition*. British archeologists are enriched, not impoverished if any of their colleagues from another country unearths a key bit of the jigsaw of an ancient civilization.
>
> (Collini 2012:164)

Like Martins, he has radically challenged the narrowed focus of governments and some employers on universities as engines of economic growth and social mobility. Arguing forcefully that individuals' upward ascent via the university ladder should only supplement and not substitute for the redistribution of material wealth, he draws attention to universities' neglected wider functions. An interest in the possession of ideas, 'whether in history and literature, or physics and biology' (Collini 2012:88), is, he holds, common in the general public, if not for themselves, then as an aspiration for the education of their children. We can only note in passing that this is also a claim backed by the research of Jonathan Rose (2002).

Perhaps paradoxically, we, as sociologists, can be indebted to Collini for addressing the current governmental disdain for anything other than the generation of new theories or positivist accumulation of facts. For as he points out, this neglects the value of philosophical modes of enquiry into clarity of expression, historical and literary understanding and the interpretation of thought more broadly; hence, ultimately, explaining. Such concerns with the phenomenology of actors' lives extend surely beyond the humanities, which he wants to valorise, to much crucial interpretative work in sociological enquiry.

Power, as Lukes has trenchantly reminded us, is not just about who wins given the conflicting parties' standing, nor even about who sets our agendas or finances the parties. Rather, it is also about a third dimension, often omitted:

> [I]s not the supreme and most insidious exercise of power to prevent people... from having grievances not least by shaping their perceptions, cognitions and preferences in such a way that they accept their role in the existing order of things either because they can see or imagine no alternative to it, or because they see it as natural and unchangeable?
>
> (Lukes 2005:28)

We need to apply this three-dimensional model to the field of university education, especially to the new mode of funding and its implications for deepening inequalities. It requires a modicum of sociological imagination but more crucially *the craft* of those trained in the discipline to show how such structures are organised in the interests of power. Of course, if sociology is cut – along with certain arts subjects such as philosophy – such a recognition of the nature of power, interests and the mobilisation of bias is less likely.

The Research Excellence Framework (REF): A matter of time

The rise of neo-liberal management in British universities discussed above and the thoroughgoing imposition of auditing practices on academic life pose very evident and very significant challenges to our sociological imaginations. To a considerable extent such changes are exemplified in the periodic and increasingly elaborate research assessment exercises which have become a part of British higher education since 1986. The REF and its predecessor the RAE (Research Assessment Exercise), as is well recognised, have the effect of giving a new priority to instrumental or strategic thinking in academic life. In that respect they might well appear to constitute an absolutely characteristic example of what Weber meant by the shift from 'value' to 'means-end' rationality. Presented and justified as mere mechanisms, as means of measuring the 'originality, significance, rigour' (and now 'impact') of research, they come to be treated as goals in their own right, so that by a (widely resisted) inversion, research and scholarship are reframed as means of competition in what Holmwood and McKay (2015) have called the 'fight for cash and glory'. Such an interpretation, of course, may well be insufficiently cynical. It seems highly likely that this instrumentalism is itself instrumental. University managers clearly prize these research assessment processes, at least in part, because the ability to orientate towards them *as if they were* goals makes them all the more effective as the means of bringing a series of new practices of scrutiny and discipline to bear on individual academics and on departments. They are, in that respect, means masquerading as ends masquerading as means.

In a powerful chapter at the end of *Pascalian Meditations*, Bourdieu points out the extent to which forms of social power depend upon an ability to organise and arrange time, and are expressed in particular relationships to time, particular kinds of temporal experience (2000:Chapter 6). His argument owes a debt, perhaps, to Marx's own famous emphasis on the politics of time, and his situating of the contest over the length of the working day at the heart of his account of labour under capitalism. One way of bringing our sociological imaginations to bear on the REF and related processes is to think about them as involving just this: a social struggle over time. This is the case, firstly, because the REF is part of a wider development, along with the imposition of Key Performance Indicators and Annual Performance Reviews, by which the autonomy of the academic field is eroded through an attack on its established temporality. The REF contributes to this insofar as it gives real force and presence in our working lives to the characteristically neo-liberal idea that the success or failure – the value – of intellectual labour can be gauged in a fixed, quantitative way rather than in an open-ended, long-term and discursive way, and because it ties reputational or material advantages, or disadvantages, to the outcome of a formalised process based on that assumption. Bourdieu reminds us, of course, that social 'games', including the 'games' of scholarship and research, are not 'fair games' (Bourdieu 2000:215). One of the inheritances of a socially privileged background is an ability to anticipate the forthcoming states of the field in which a person is involved, with all of the positional advantages which follow from that. In that respect, we cannot naively read as 'pure' or disinterested the long-term outcomes of the discursive processes by which academic judgements conventionally accord value or worth to particular works. Nevertheless, such judgements have an importantly provisional quality, in the sense that they remain open to processes of long-term contestation and revision within the academic field. It is that historicity and that provisionality which is effectively short-circuited by the 'time' of the REF, which makes individual evaluative judgements, even where these are arrived at through processes of peer-review, definitive and beyond contest. Whilst it may be objected that this overstates the effect of the REF, given that the 'scoring' for individual papers and books is not made public, the process clearly relies upon and instantiates a different form of temporality in academic life, tending to make us less invested in the long-term and discursive process of scholarly evaluation, and, in that respect, eroding our sense of investment – our sense of 'being invested' – in the future of the field. We need only think, for example, of the idea that a particular act of scholarship, research or theoretical synthesis has the capacity to be 'lasting' or to make a 'lasting' contribution. This conventional commendation vouchsafes the long-term qualitative evaluation of significance and quality to future discussion in the field, and by the same token constitutes a statement of practical faith in that field's own lastingness. Such a judgement is literally unthinkable in terms of the temporality of the REF, with its one-off (and instantly disposable) attributions of value.

By the same token, these processes affect directly the experience of academics at the level of daily practice. Bourdieu (2000:206) describes the 'scholastic' attitude as being defined by a 'particularly free relationship to what is normally called time... a suspending of urgency, the pressure of "things to do", of business and busyness' so that such an attitude is characterised above all by a 'relationship of externality' as regards time and everyday practices: 'that of a subject facing an object'. Outside a relatively small number of privileged situations, it is hard to imagine many contemporary British academics recognising themselves or their working lives in these words. The attack on the 'time' of the academic field, on the temporality by which value is judged in that context and the historical openness to which such judgements are subject, has, as a corollary in the conditions of academic production, the imposition of new kinds of urgency, new pressures to 'do things', new 'busyness' (and, yes, of course, an attempt to construe academic life as indeed a form of 'business'). In this immediate sense, the rise of an audit culture appears to entail an old-fashioned struggle over 'productivity', over the length of the academic working day, of the intensity of the work undertaken in that time and over the level of 'output' produced. Here too, however, we should recognise an instrumental instrumentalism at play. As far as research is concerned (as opposed to teaching or other activities which may directly 'generate revenue' for universities), it is not really levels of 'productivity' as such which are at stake here but the imposition of the very idea that research and scholarship are activities which are amenable to a measurement in terms of productivity at all. That is to say, an assumption whose first premise is that academic work results in 'products' about which the most pertinent question is not 'how lasting' will this be, but 'how many' (how many items added to the online repository; how many citations accumulated on Google Scholar)? It is in this sense that the challenge to the long-run temporality of the academic field, on the one hand, and the challenge to the everyday conditions of academic labour, on the other, can be said to be two sides of the same coin.

Perhaps our response to this situation needs to be correspondingly double-sided. On the one hand, however much we need to continue to be critical about the inequalities which structure and are reproduced by the academic field, it remains important that we defend the autonomy of that field and the space it provides for forms of inquiry and reflection whose outcomes are not simply determined by the interests of corporations, institutions or powerful individuals. One thinks here of Bourdieu's own qualified defence of the artistic field at the end of *The Rules of Art* (1996:postscript), a defence offered not because he was oblivious to the unequal nature of competition in that field, but because the relative autonomy of that competition, vis-à-vis forces in the wider field of power, kept open a precious space for critical intervention and response to those very forces. The academic field, surely, warrants the same qualified defence for broadly the same reasons. On the other hand, if the changing working experience of academics undermines the conditions that allow us to adopt a 'scholastic attitude', then it may perform an unwitting service for our sociological imaginations. The nub of sociological craftsmanship for Mills, after all, was a breaking down of the separation between life and work, between wider social experience and the ways in which we go about making sense of such experience sociologically (for example, Mills 2008:46–7). If we can no longer find ourselves comfortably occupying an intellectual space that allows us a sense of 'externality' as regards time, this may be a loss of privilege from which we can learn. This is not to suggest that we should not contest the attempts to direct and control our day-to-day working practices. But in contesting these changes we necessarily find ourselves involved in struggles homologous to those in which many others are simultaneously involved in the context of neo-liberalism. Thus, if nothing else, this sense of changing time must remind us whose side we should be on.

Teaching theory and the sociological imagination

This book has indicated John Eldridge's interest in, and contributions to, the field of social theory. These have not been limited to research but include the teaching of social theory he performed for many years on the postgraduate Current Issues in Social Theory and undergraduate Classical Sociological Theory courses at Glasgow. Such activity is in keeping with Mills's conception of the sociological imagination which required, and advocated, theoretical insight. Mills's goal of converting private troubles into public issues necessitates at some point the abstract and generalised thinking produced in theory. The importance of this was part of the reason why Mills was so famously critical of the 'Byzantine oddity of associated and disassociated Concepts, the mannerism of verbiage' found in what he dismissed as 'grand theory'. Instead Mills encouraged the 'simplicity of the clear statement' in sociological communication (Mills 1959:224). Therefore, not only was theory important to sociological understanding but this should also be an accessible process, intended to communicate its theoretical insight to as wide an audience as possible. How possible is such a vision today?

It is easy to find grounds for pessimism here. For example, it has been claimed that the changes in Research Council funding priorities, towards 'applied' research with clear 'impact pathways', makes the funding of theoretical research more scarce. Furthermore, the increased pressures of the REF and its short-term focus discussed above encourages the publication of multiple papers over a short period, discouraging theoretical development (Holmwood 2010). Others have expressed fears concerning sociology's current 'presentism' and the way it encourages 'intellectual entrepreneurs' who are characterised by a tendency to make dubious theoretical claims of 'newness' (Inglis 2014). These entrepreneurs are, in turn, cut off from questions of methodology and untroubled by the absence of empirical evidence (Gane 2011). This has left some to claim that sociology suffers fundamental flaws in its attempt to critique neo-liberalism as a theoretical project (Johnson 2014). Meanwhile, debates concerning sociology's over-reliance on the problematic 'classics' (Marshall and Witz 2004), or, conversely, its ignorance of the intellectually valuable and underappreciated classics (Turner 2006) rumble on.

The above contributions all have valuable points to make. However, they tend to overlook how theory is taught. In the second half of the twentieth century there was a shift from teaching theory as a collection of schools towards teaching *theorists*. Whereas the former encouraged a linear narrative concerning the development of sociological theorising, the latter creates a field which:

> appears to the present-day newcomer in a completely different light: a vast expanse with a lot of criss-crossing tracts, paths and gorges trodden in all directions by clearly distinguishable figures of more and less distinguished personalities, each busy in blazing a new trail rather than keeping to one already blazed.
> (Bauman et al. 2014:56)

Most students will now encounter a course of *social theorists*, perhaps mostly dead white men, each with their own concepts, perspectives and contributions. Such an approach also encourages a further shift towards the idea of 'theory with a capital T' where individual theorists and their unique insights are valorised, with their thought 'enshrined in "texts" to be endlessly pored over like chicken entrails' (Stanley and Wise 1990:24).

Confronted with such a way of teaching theory – a core course in which you have to master complex texts – students perhaps understandably turn away and adopt a 'grin and bear it' approach before they can turn to the more interesting courses; or, even more worryingly, fear that they are 'not smart enough' to master these complex texts. Given what we know about the sociology of education, it seems likely those from working-class backgrounds may be more likely to adopt such a perspective. Therefore, this is likely to reproduce the supposed exclusivity of the theoretical field.

The above should not be taken as an all-out condemnation of having a compulsory course on social theorists. What it does require is an awareness of how theory is taught across the curriculum. When encountered as 'theories of', whether that is theories of class on a class course; theories of deviance on a deviance course and so on, such theories are readily discussed and appreciated by students. The same could be true of a theory course. A social theory ultimately operates a 'way of seeing' (Plummer 2010:29) in which the hidden rules of social life, its conflicts and consensuses, suddenly become clear to us. Therefore, theorists can be taught as grappling with the issues of the social world as it is and thus demonstrate 'its relevance to experience and humans' struggles with their own life problems' (Bauman et al. 2014:105).

We doubt there are many sociologists who disagree with this; the question is, how can it be achieved in the teaching conditions of a neoliberal context? The answer is that social theory teaching must begin not with the field of social theory but with the world as it is. The controversies of social theorists, the context in which they wrote, their relation to other writers and so on are all important for students to know. However, they are best engaged with once the value of the theory to explain, and perhaps critique, neo-liberal society is established. Some theory texts are difficult reads and contain the 'Byzantine' verbiage of which Mills was so critical. But if teaching employs 'the simplicity of the clear statement' advocated by Mills, it not only demonstrates the value of social theory, but also its 'accessibility' as a way of seeing for all students. By doing so, social theory teaching can help realise the connection of private troubles and public issues so central to the sociological imagination.

Disembedding the production of knowledge

Over his career, John Eldridge (1981) was a keen observer of the evolution of the discipline of sociology and how it interacted with political life. In the half-century or so the discipline has expanded, diversified and embraced a variety of intellectual approaches to understanding society. It has also come under a number of attacks. These have been predicated in part by the view that sociology was having too great an impact on society as opposed to one that was too slight.

Perhaps the most significant attack in Britain was a report written by the Nottingham University sociologist Julius Gould and published in 1977 by the Institute for the Study of Conflict, a right-wing propaganda group linked to British intelligence and backed by the Central Intelligence Agency (CIA) and large corporations like Shell and BP (Powerbase 2015). *The Attack on Higher Education: Marxist and Radical Penetration* claimed that:

> groups and individuals in the fields of education and culture have shown by their theory and, more importantly, by their practice that they reject key notions long associated with the idea of an open, plural society: notions such as freedom of expression and association
> (*The Times* 1977a)

The report was described by one of its targets, the sociologist Robert Young, as 'the closest British academic life got to a McCarthy-ite witch-hunt of radicals' (Young 2005), and although *The Times* published extracts of the report, it also criticised Gould for the 'alarmist tone which goes beyond his evidence' (*The Times*, 1977b).

Another key instance occurred in the early 1980s, when the Conservative government, in the person of Education Secretary Keith Joseph, took action against social science in general and sociology in particular by renaming the Social Science Research Councils the Economic and Social Research Council (Posner 2002). Both of these examples suggest a desire to manage the impact that sociology and social science might have, specifically to lessen it or change its character.

These two examples provide a counterpoint to the current 'impact agenda' where academics in general are encouraged to influence society. In a way the attacks on the discipline highlight one of the submerged elements of the impact agenda.

Impact is assumed to be a good thing, to be always positive. But of course – in principle – we can think of negative impacts on society. As soon as we try to list them we have to recognise that the whole question of positive or negative impact is at least potentially contestable. Increasing inequality in society or, for that matter, increasing racism would not unanimously be seen as positive impacts. In many areas the question of which way society should develop is profoundly contested. The fact that there can be negative 'impacts' raises the whole question of the actual experience of impact, and by implication how policy on higher education might affect how disciplines operate. In common with the open attacks on sociology in the 1970s and 1980s there is a political dimension to this. The impact agenda is a new part of the REF, the intention of which (like the RAE) is to distribute research funds selectively. The 'basic idea', notes Tarak Barkawi (2013), 'is to rank all the departments in any one discipline and channel funding to the "best" departments, while cutting funding to the rest', thus intensifying hierarchies within university departments, and indeed between universities (Callinicos 2006).

Successive rounds of the RAE/REF from 1986 onwards have taken place in the context of declining public funding. The gaps are filled by student fees (in England and Wales) and by an increasing need to gain funding from external funding agencies. Corporations are the main source of such income. This has had a very significant 'impact' on the ability of academics to carry out basic research, and shapes by extension the kinds of impacts that they can have on policy and society more broadly.

Encroachment of private interests further upon production of knowledge

The 1980s onwards saw significant encroachment of the private sector on the territory of the university, with the attendant tendency to undermine autonomous intellectual production. This pattern has been evident in those countries at the forefront of neo-liberal transformation, especially the UK (Miller and Philo 2002; Monbiot 2000), the US (Krimsky 2003; Soley 1995) and latterly Canada (Brownlee 2015).

It is also widely noted that knowledge production, especially the production of (natural) scientific knowledge is vulnerable to compromise particularly when the scientific process interfaces with vested interests, predominantly from the corporate sector. (Krimsky 2003) The examples of the health effects of tobacco and the resistance to the scientific consensus on climate change are well known (McGarity and Wagner 2008; Michaels 2008; Oreskes and Conway 2010), but similar processes are evident in relation to the chemicals, food, alcohol and other industries (Markowitz and Rosner 2002; Miller and Harkins 2010).

Disembedding of knowledge production

Accompanying the increasing penetration of academic by corporate interests, there has been a wider reconfiguration of the relationship between the public (higher education) and private production of knowledge. Thus the neo-liberalisation of the university sector has been accompanied by a sort of 'disembedding' of intellectual production more generally. In *The Great Transformation,* Polanyi (1944:57) discussed disembedding in relation to the rise of capitalism, which 'means no less than the running of society as an adjunct to the market. Instead of economy being embedded in social relations, social relations are embedded in the economic system'. Arguably this is similar to the process described by the anthropologist of policy, Janine Wedel (2010), as the creation of a 'shadow elite', which is distant from the formal mechanisms of political accountability in liberal democracy. The notion of disembedding implies that 'shadow elites' remove or insulate themselves from previously existing forms of democratic accountability, effectively displacing or undermining previous regimes (Bollier 2009). In the current case we might think in particular about changes in the production of 'research' and 'policy advice' in the past four decades. To take the most obvious example, that of the rise of the think tank, we can see how this might work. The political scientist Diane Stone (2007) suggests there are 'three myths' about think tanks: that they 'bridge research and policy', 'serve the public interest' and 'build knowledge'. None of these, she says, is true. As Medvetz (2012: 82) argues in his study of think tanks:

> [Think tanks] must go to elaborate lengths to create and maintain the perception that they are independent from the state and the

market, especially in light of their profound dependence on the same institutions for their material support, relevance, and personnel.

(Medvetz 2012:82)

'Nearly all think tanks', he notes, 'rely heavily on short term donations and must therefore orient their work to the market for funding' (Medvetz 2012:144). We can also point to the role of think tanks as partisan ideologues and/or lobbyists. Wedel characterises think tanks as vehicles 'to launder ideologically charged influence into difficult-to-trace advocacy' (2014:181). Protestations of neutrality and detachment dismissed, we turn to the historical role played by the think tank. Medvetz (2012:225) is clear that their growth over the last 40 years 'has played a pivotal role in undermining the relevance of autonomously produced social scientific knowledge', which has 'effectively limited the range of options available to more autonomous intellectuals, or those less willing to tailor their work to the demands of moneyed sponsors and politicians'.

Indeed there is evidence that there are some key actors in the think tank revolution who see the creation of think tanks as a means to strategically undermine the way in which higher education works. In 2009, after the death of Irving Kristol (dubbed the 'godfather of neoconservatism'), British journalist Melanie Phillips praised him for being 'the first public intellectual to understand and articulate a defence of western civilisation against the onslaught mounted by the moral and cultural relativism of the nihilistic left'. She recalled that when she met Kristol he asked her:

Why hasn't anyone done there what we did [in the US], set up publications and think-tanks and talk radio to break the power of the Left in the universities? I just can't understand why everyone is just sitting there and letting it happen! What's wrong with them all?

(cited in Miller et al. 2011:416)

The more think tanks, lobby consultancies and policy planning groups dominate the landscape of intellectual production, the less relevance will sociology have. A clear implication for the stretching of the sociological imagination is to turn sustained sociological attention on to these denizens of the knowledge production industry, as well as maintaining a focus on the impact of neo-liberal governance on the ability of the universities to produce independent science and social science.

Note

1. In the US, new universities emerge as profitable enterprises tapping into the precariat's need for constant requalification, not least via postal Masters courses. Many offer what Collini, quoting McGettigan, (2013:3) nicely calls 'subprime degrees', for which, even with huge drop-out rates, the institution may still be profitable:

   > the University of Phoenix... at its peak in 2010... was said to have some 600,000 students and annual revenue in excess of $4 billion expenditure (in October 2012 it announced plans to close 115 campuses owing to a drastic drop in its profits). The senate investigation showed that 60 per cent of students dropped out within two years [... yet] 89 per cent of revenue comes from Federal student loans.
   >
   > (Collini 2013:5)

   Collini notes that in the UK private capital is now entering higher education – the money paid to private colleges (both charities and profit-making) had trebled in 2011–12, now reaching £100m (Collini 2013:4–5).

References

Barkawi, T (2013) 'The Neoliberal Assault on Academia', *Al Jazeera English*, 25 April. http://www.aljazeera.com/indepth/opinion/2013/04/20134238284530760.html, date accessed: 6 May 2015.

Bollier, D. (2009) 'Why Karl Polanyi Still Matters', *On the Commons*, 24 February. http://www.onthecommons.org/why-karl-polanyi-still-matters, date accessed: 6 May 2015.

Brownlee, J. (2015) *Academia Inc. How Corporatization Is Transforming Canadian Universities*. Winnipeg: Fernwood Publishing.

Bauman, Z., Jacobsen, M. and Tester, K. (2014) *What Use is Sociology?*. Cambridge: Polity Press.

Bourdieu, P. (1996) *Rules of Art: Genesis and Structure of the Literary Field*. Cambridge: Polity Press.

Bourdieu, P. (2000) *Pascalian Meditations*. Cambridge: Polity Press.

Browne, J. (2010) *Securing a Sustainable Future for Higher Education*. Independent Review of Higher Education Funding and Student Finances, https://www.gov.uk/government/uploads/system/uploads/attachment_data/file/422565/bis-10-1208-securing-sustainable-higher-education-browne-report.pdf, date accessed: 28 April 2015.

Callinicos, A. (2006) *Universities in a Neoliberal World*. London: Bookmarks.

Campaign for the Public University (n.d.) 'Manifesto', *Campaign for the Public University*, http://publicuniversity.org.uk/manifesto/, date accessed: 6 May 2015.

Collini, S. (2012) *What are Universities For?* London: Penguin.

Collini, S. (2013) 'Sold Out', *London Review of Books*, 24 October, 3–12.

Eldridge, J. (1981) *Recent British Sociology*. Basingstoke: Macmillan.

Gane, N. (2011) 'Measure, Value and the Current Crises of Sociology', *Sociological Review*, 59 (s2): 151–73.

Holmwood, J. (2010) 'Sociology's Misfortune: Disciplines, Interdisciplinarity and the Impact of Audit Culture', *British Journal of Sociology*, 61 (4): 639–58.

Holmwood, J. and McKay, S. (2015) 'As REF 2014 Goes By: a Fight for Cash and Glory...(with Apologies to Casablanca)', *The Sociological Review Blog*. http://www.thesociologicalreview.com/information/news/as-ref-2014-goes-by-a-fight-for-cash-and-glory-with-apologies-to-casablanca.html, date accessed: 2 April 2015.

Inglis, D. (2014) 'What is Worth Defending in Sociology Today? Presentism, Historical Vision and the Uses of Sociology', *Cultural Sociology*, 8 (1): 99–118.

Johnson, P. (2014) 'Sociology and the Critique of Neoliberalism: Reflections on Peter Wagner and Axel Honneth', *European Journal of Social Theory*, 17 (4): 516–33.

Krimsky, S. (2003) *Science in the Private Interest*. New York: Rowman and Littlefield.

Lukes, S. (2005) *Power: A Radical View*. 2nd ed., Hampshire: Palgrave Macmillan.

Markowitz, G. and Rosner, D. (2002) *Deceit and Denial: The Deadly Politics of Industrial Pollution*. Berkeley: University of California Press.

Marshall, B. and Witz, A. (eds.) (2004) *Engendering the Social: Feminist Encounters with Sociological Theory*. Milton Keynes: Open University Press.

Martins, H. (2004) 'The Marketisation of Universities and some Contradictions of Academic Capitalism', *Metacritica*, 4: http://revistas.ulusofona.pt/index.php/metacritica/article/view/2747/2099, date accessed: 3 May 2015.

McGarity, T. and Wagner W. (2008) *Bending Science: How Special Interests Corrupt Public Health Research*. Cambridge, MA: Harvard University Press.

McGettigan, A. (2013) *The Great University Gamble: Money, Markets and the Future of Higher Education*. London: Pluto.

Medvetz, T. (2012) *Think Tanks in America*. Chicago, IL: University of Chicago Press.

Michaels, D. (2008) *Doubt is Their Product*. Oxford: Oxford University Press.

Miller, D. and Harkins, C. (2010) 'Corporate Strategy, Corporate Capture: Food and Alcohol Industry Lobbying and Public Health', *Critical Social Policy*, 30 (4): 1–26.

Miller, D. and Philo, G. (2002) 'Silencing Dissent in Academia: The Commercialisation of Science', *The Psychologist*, 15 (5): 244–6.

Miller, D., Mills, T. and Harkins, S. (2011) 'Teaching about Terrorism in the United Kingdom: How it is Done and What Problems it Causes', *Critical Studies on Terrorism*, 4 (3): 405–20.

Mills, C.W. (1959) *The Sociological Imagination*. Oxford: Oxford University Press.

Mills, C.W. (2008) *The Politics of Truth*. Oxford: Oxford University Press.

Monbiot, G. (2000) *Captive State: The Corporate Takeover of Britain*. London: Macmillan.

Oreskes, N. and Conway, E.M. (2010) *Merchants of Doubt: How a Handful of Scientists Obscured the Truth on Issues from Tobacco Smoke to Global Warming*. New York: Bloomsbury.

Piketty, T. (2014) *Capital in the Twenty-First Century*. Cambridge, MA: The Belknap Press.

Plummer, K. (2010) *Sociology: The Basics*. London: Routledge.

Polanyi, K. (1944) *The Great Transformation*. New York: Farrar and Rinehart.

Posner, M. (2002) 'Social Sciences under Attack in the UK (1981–1983)', *La revue pour l'histoire du CNRS*, 7: http://histoire-cnrs.revues.org/547, date accessed: 6 May 2015.

Powerbase (2015) 'Institute for the Study of Conflict', http://www.powerbase.info/index.php/Institute_for_the_Study_of_Conflict, date accessed: 27 April 2015.
Rose, J. (2002) *The Intellectual Life of the British Working Classes*. New Haven, CT: Yale.
Slaughter, S. and Rhoades, G. (2004) *Academic Capitalism and the New Economy: Markets, State and Higher Education*. Baltimore, MD and London: Johns Hopkins University Press.
Soley, L. (1995) *Leasing the Ivory Tower: The Corporate Takeover of Academia*. Boston, MA: South End Press.
Stanley, L. and Wise, S. (1990) 'Method, Methodology and Epistemology in Feminist Research Processes', in L. Stanley (ed.) *Feminist Praxis: Research, Theory and Epistemology in Feminist Sociology*. London: Routledge, pp. 20–60.
Stone, D. (2007) 'Recycling Bins, Garbage Cans or Think Tanks? Three Myths Regarding Policy Analysis Institutes', *Public Administration*, 85 (2): 259–78.
The Times (1977a) 'Gould Report Calls for Rebuttal of Attacks on Education in Britain by Extreme Radicals', *The Times*, 21 September 1977: 4.
The Times (1977b) 'The Enemies of Liberty', *The Times*, 21 September 1977: 15.
Turner, B. (2006) 'Classical Sociology and Cosmopolitanism: A Critical Defence of the Social', *British Journal of Sociology*, 57 (1): 133–51.
Warner, M. (2014) 'Diary', *London Review of Books*, 36 (17): 42–3.
Warner, M. (2015) 'Learning My Lesson: On the Disfiguring of Higher Education', *London Review of Books*, 37 (6): 8–14.
Wedel, J. (2010) *Shadow Elite: How the World's New Power Brokers Undermine Democracy, Government, and the Free Market*. New York: Basic Books.
Wedel, J. (2014) *Unaccountable: How Elite Power Brokers Corrupt our Finances, Freedom and Security*. New York: Pegasus Books.
Young, R.M. (2005) 'Introduction' to 'Mystifications in the Scientific Foundations of Sociology', *Science or Society?: Bulletin of the Cambridge Society for Social Responsibility in Science*, 2 (June 1971): 9–11. Available from: http://human-nature.com/rmyoung/papers/paper88.html

Appendix: Bibliography of the Writings of John Eric Thomas Eldridge (b. 1936)

Prepared by Alison Eldridge

1959
Race Relations in Leicester University, unpublished thesis, Leicester University Library Collection.

1960
'Overseas Students at Leicester University: Some Problems of Adjustment and Communication', *Race*, 27 October.

1961
The Selection and Training of Supervisors in the Black Country. (with Jones, C.F.) Stafford: Staffordshire College of Commerce.

1963
'Shrinkage in Industry', *New Society*, 16: 17 January.

1965
'Plant Bargaining in Steel: North East Coast Case Studies', *Sociological Review*, 13 (2): 131–48.

1966
'Redundancy Conflict in an Isolated Steel Community', *Journal of Management Studies*, 3 (3): 285–304.

1968
Industrial Disputes: Essays in the Sociology of Industrial Relations. London: Routledge and Kegan Paul.

1969
'The British Blue Collar Worker', *International Journal of Comparative Sociology*, 10 (1–2): 80–94.

1970
Max Weber: The Interpretation of Social Reality. London: Michael Joseph.

1971
'Sociology and Industrial Life', Inaugural lecture, Bradford University, published in *Mens en Maatschappij, Driemaandelijks tijdschrift voore sociale wetenschappen*, 46e (4).
Sociology and Industrial Life. London: Michael Joseph.
'Weber's Approach to the Sociological Study of Industrial Workers', in A. Sahay, A (Ed.) *Max Weber and Modern Sociology*. London: Routledge Kegan Paul, pp. 97–111.

1972
'On the Social System: Selected Writings by L J Henderson', Book Review, *Sociology*, 6 (2): 298.

1973
Sociology and Industrial Life. Nelson University Paperbacks: The Making of Sociology Series, London: Nelson (originally published in 1971).
'Industrial Conflict: Some Problems of Theory and Method', in J. Child (Ed.) *Man and Organisation*. London: George Allen and Unwin Ltd, pp. 158–84.
'Sociological Imagination and Industrial Life', in M. Warner (Ed.) *The Sociology of the Workplace*. London: George Allen and Unwin Ltd, pp. 274–86.
'Wages and Accidents: An Exploratory Paper' (with Kaye, B.M.) in A. Tewings (Ed.) *Onderenening en Vakbeweging*. Rotterdam: Universitaire den Rotterdam.

1974
A Sociology of Organisations. (with Crombie, A.D.) London: Allen and Unwin 1974 (reprinted in 2013).
'Pilots and Management: Industrial relations in UK Airlines: Cousins, J. (1972)', Book Review, *Sociology*, 8 (2): 336.
'Sociological Analysis: Sahay, A. (1972)', Book Review, *Sociology*, 8 (2): 352–3.

1975
'Panaceas and Pragmatism in Industrial Relations', Third Lerner Memorial Lecture, given to the Manchester Industrial Relations Society at the University of Manchester, 1974. Published in *Industrial Relations Journal*, 6 (1): 4–13.

1976
Bad News. Glasgow University Media Group. London: Routledge Kegan Paul. (reprinted in 2009 as part of Routledge Revivals series).
'Sociological Knowledge: Notes in the Margin', *Epworth Review*, (3): 1.

1980
More Bad News. Glasgow University Media Group. London: Routledge Kegan Paul. (reprinted in 2009 as part of Routledge Revivals series).
Industrial Democracy. (with MacInnes, J. and Cressey, P.) Glasgow University Centre for Democracy and Participation Research Paper.

1981
'Space for Sociology', Presidential Address delivered to the Annual Conference of the BSA, Lancaster University, April 1980, *Sociology*, 15 (1): 94–103.
'Participation Prospects: Some Scottish Evidence' (with MacInnes, J. and Cressey, P.), *Dept of Employment Gazette*, 89 (3).
'Industrial Democracy and Participation: A Scottish Survey' (with MacInnes, J. Cressey, P. and Norris, G.) *UK Dept of Employment Research Paper*, no 28, London: HMSO.
'Images of Sociology', *Working Papers in Sociology*. Glasgow: Glasgow University (Extended Version of Lecture Given at the Annual Conference of the BSA, April 1981).

1982
Industrial Democracy and the Division of Labour. Discussion Paper 5, Centre for Research in Industrial Democracy and Participation. Glasgow: University of Glasgow.

1983
C. Wright Mills. London: Tavistock Publications and Ellis Horwood.
Industrial Relations and the New Right. Open Lectures in Industrial Relations. Nottingham Trent: Polytechnic.
'Organizational Democracy and Political Processes', in C. Crouch and F. Heller (eds.) *International Yearbook of Organizational Democracy, Vol. I*. Oxford: Wiley.

1984
'Through a Glass Darkly: Reflections on Television', *Churchman*, 98 (2), 117–25.
'Garfinkel and Ethnomethodology; Heritage, J (1984)', Book Review, *Times Educational Supplement*.

1985
War and Peace News. Glasgow University Media Group. Milton Keynes: Open University Press.
Just Managing: Authority and Democracy in Industry. (with MacInnes, J. and Cressey, P.) Buckingham: Open University Press.

1986
'War, Peace and Power', in H. Davis (Ed.) *Ethics and Defence: Power and Responsibility in the Nuclear Age*. Oxford: Blackwell Publishers, pp. 188–206.
'Public Opinion and the Media', in H. Davis (Ed.) *Ethics and Defence: Power and Responsibility in the Nuclear Age*. Oxford, Blackwell Publishers, pp. 208–26.
'Essays on the History of British Sociological Research; Bulmer, M (Ed) (1985)', Book Review; *Sociological Review*, 34 (3): 657–9.

1987
'Mass Media, Public Opinion and Democracy', Presidential Address (Sociology Section) British Association for the Advancement of Science, Belfast.

1988
'Content Analysis in Perspective: The Approach of the Glasgow University Media Group', International Association for Mass Communication Research, 16th Conference, Barcelona.
'Feasible Futures: Reflections on Industrial Society', Cameron Wallace Lecture published by Scottish Churches Industrial Mission.

1990
Industrial Sociology and Economic Crisis. (with MacInnes, J. and Cressey, P.) Harvester: Wheatsheaf.
'Sociology in Britain: A Going Concern', in C.G.A. Bryant and H. Becker (eds.) *What Has Sociology Achieved?* London: Macmillan, pp. 157–78.

1991
Taking Out Moscow. Collaborative SRT Project, Edinburgh: St Andrew's Press.

1993
Getting The Message: News, Truth and Power. Glasgow University Media Group (eds.) London: Routledge.
'News, Truth and Power', in Glasgow University Media Group (eds.) *Getting The Message: News, Truth and Power*. London: Routledge, pp. 3–33.
'Whose Illusion? Whose Reality?', in Glasgow University Media Group (eds.) *Getting The Message: News, Truth and Power*. London: Routledge, pp. 331–50.
News Content, Language and Visuals. Glasgow University Media Group (eds.) London: Routledge.

'Introduction: That Was the World That Was', in *News Content, Language and Visuals*. Glasgow University Media Group (eds.) London: Routledge, pp. 1–26.
'Ill News Comes Often on the Back of Worse', in *News Content, Language and Visuals*. Glasgow University Media Group (eds.) London: Routledge, pp. 27–38.

1994
Raymond Williams: Making Connections. (with Eldridge, L.) London: Routledge.
'Work and Authority: Some Weberian Perspectives', in L. Ray and M. Reed (eds.) *Organising Modernity: New Weberian Perspectives on Work, Organisation and Society*. London, Routledge, pp. 81–97.

1996
'How Many Cheers For Community?', *The Scottish Journal of Community Work and Development*, 1: 33–9.
'Towards an Imperfect Future: A Discussion Article', *Epworth Review*, 23 (3).
'A Very Special Case: The BBC from John Reith to John Birt', *Cultural Policy*, 2 (2): 269–80.
'Rhetoric and Marxism, Aune, J.A. (1994)', Book Review, *American Journal of Sociology*, 101 (5): 1461–2.

1997
The Mass Media and Power in Modern Britain. (with Kitzinger, J. and Williams, K.) Oxford: Oxford University Press.
'A Russian Rollercoaster', Review Article, *Work, Employment and Society*, 11 (2): 365–7.

1998
'A Benchmark in Industrial Sociology: W G Baldamus on *'Efficiency and Effort'* (1961)', *Historical Studies in Industrial Relations*, 6: 133–61
'Explaining Food Scares in the Media' (with Miller, D. MacIntyre, S. and Reilly, J.), in A. Murcott (Ed.) *The Nation's Diet*, August, Longman, pp. 228–49.

1999
'Culture at Work', in P. Glavanis and H. Beynon (eds.) *Patterns of Social Inequality: Essays for Richard Brown*. Essex: Longman Publishing, pp. 97–108.
'Risk Society: Now you See it, Now you Don't', in G. Philo (Ed.) *Message Received*. Essex: Longman Publishing, pp. 106–27.
'Thinking about Risk: A Review Essay' (with Hill, A.), *Risk and Society*, 1 (3): 343–50.
'Frankenstein's Footsteps: Science, Genetics and Popular Culture: Turney, J. (1998)', Book Review, *Science and Christian Belief*, 11 (1): 95–6.

2000
For Sociology. (edited with J. MacInnes, C. Warhurst, S. Scott and A. Witz) London: Routledge-Cavendish.
'Sociology and the Third Way' in J. Eldridge et al. (eds.) *For Sociology*. London: Routledge-Cavendish, pp. 131–44.
'Ill News Comes Often on the Back of Worse', in E. Buscombe (Ed.) *British Television: A Reader*. Oxford, Oxford University Press, pp. 235–47 (originally published in 1995).

2001
'On the Cusp of the Cultural', in R. Burgess and A. Murcott (eds.) *Developments in Sociology*. Prentice Hall: Pearson Education, pp. 79–98.
'Science and Technology: The Growth of Knowledge in an Uncertain World', Breaking New Ground, The First Scottish Ecumenical Assembly.
'Towards A Democratic Science; Scientific Narration and Civic Communication: Brown, R.H. (1999)', Book Review, *Science and Christian Belief*, 13 (2): 178–80.

2002
'Gouldner, Alvin W. (1920–80)', in M. Warner (Ed.) *International Encyclopaedia of Business and Management*. London: Thomson Learning, pp. 250–4.
'Durkheim, Emile (1858–1917)', in M. Warner (Ed.) *International Encyclopaedia of Business and Management*. London: Thomson Learning, pp. 1493–96.

2003
'Post Modernism and Industrial Relations', in P. Ackers and A. Wilkinson (eds.) *Understanding Work and Employment, Industrial Relations in Transition*. Oxford: Oxford University Press, pp. 325–36. (Extension 'Whatever Happened to Post Modernism?' given at British Industrial Relations Association annual conference, Manchester).
'Risk and Relativity: BSE and the British Media' (with Reilly, J), in N. Pidgeon, R. Kasperson and P. Slovic (eds.) *The Social Amplification of Risk*. Cambridge: Cambridge University Press, pp. 138–55.
'C Wright Mills' *White Collar* Revisited', *Historical Studies in Industrial Relations*, 16: 141–67.
'Norbert Elias et la Théorie de la Civilisation: Bonny, Y., de Quevoz, J.M. and Neveu, E. (eds.) (2003)', Book Review, *Sociology*, 38 (5): 1065–6.

2005
'What Effect does the Treatment of Violence on TV have on People's Conduct? A Controversy Reconsidered', in S. Hurley and N. Chater (eds.) *Perspectives on Imitation*, Vol. 2, Cambridge, MA: MIT Press, pp. 243–56.
'The British Sociological Association: A Sociological History: Platt, J. (2003)', Book Review, *British Journal of Sociology*, 56 (2): 319–20.

2006
'The Work of the Glasgow University Media Group: An Insider's Story', in D. Berry and J. Theobald (eds.) *Radical Mass Media Criticism: A Cultural Genealogy*, Black Rose Books, pp. 109–24.
'In Praise of The Guardian', *Fifth Estate* [online], March.

2007
'A Tract for the Times: Joan Woodward's *Management and Technology* (1958)', *Historical Studies in Industrial Relations*, 23/24: 181–207.
'Merton and Lazarfeld's Studies in Radio and Film Propaganda; An Exposition and Commentary'; Propaganda, Spin and Lobbying in a Global Age conference, Strathclyde University, Glasgow September 7.
'Beyond 2000: Remembering Raymond Williams', *Fifth Estate* [online], April.

2009
'Industrial Sociology in the UK: Reminiscences and Reflections', *Sociology*, 43 (5): 829–45.

'John Riches – An Appreciation', in P. Middleton, A. Paddison and K. Wenell (eds.) *Paul, Grace and Freedom*. London, T & T Clark, pp. xiii–vii.
'The Political Economy of Work: Spencer, D (2009)', Book Review, *Historical Studies in Industrial Relations*, 27–28: 253–5.
'Cricket, Lovely Cricket: A Summer Digression', *Fifth Estate* [online], August.

2010
'Baldamus's Adventures in Cross Classification', in M. Erickson and C. Turner (eds.) *The Sociology of Wilhelm Baldamus: Paradox and Inference*. Farnham: Ashgate, pp. 19–34 (extension of conference paper given at BSA Annual conference, 2008).
'Working Models of Religious Engagement with Emerging Technology' (with Donald Bruce), Church of Scotland SRT Project and the Conference of European Churches, Faith and Science: fissures in post-secular societies, University of Nottingham May.

2011
'Work and Authority in Industry: The Research Strategy of Reinhard Bendix', *Historical Studies in Industrial Relations*, 31/32: 155–79.
'Half-Remembrance of Things Past: Critics and Cuts of Old', *Sociological Research Online*, 16 (3): http://www.socresonline.org.uk/16/3/20.html.
'Dancing with Ghosts: Why the Sociological Classics Still Matter', paper delivered at the Regional Conference of Post Graduate Students, Glasgow University.

2013
'Stuart Hall', in D. Coole et al. (Ed.) *Encyclopaedia for Political Thought*. Oxford: Blackwell Publishers.

2014
'Between Science and the Humanities: Sociology as a Third Culture', in J. Scott and J. Holmwood (Eds.) *The Palgrave Handbook of Sociology in Britain*. Hampshire: Palgrave Macmillan, pp. 338–59.
Tom Burns and the Practice of Sociology. Edinburgh University Working Papers in Sociology.
'Stimulating the Sociological Imagination: Stretching Exercises', paper given at 'Stretching the Sociological Imagination': conference in honour of John Eldridge, Glasgow University, September (extended version published in this volume).

Forthcoming
'Dorothy Wedderburn', *The Oxford Dictionary of National Biography*. Oxford: Oxford University Press.
'The Neoliberal Labyrinth', Extended Review, *Historical Studies in Industrial Relations*.

Index

Abbot, A., 104
academic battles/conflicts, 125–6
academic capitalism, 248
academic field, 128–9, 135, 251–2
academic precariat, 247–9
academic research, 247–9, 255–9
Académie Francaise, 102
academy, 109, 126
Addams, Jane, 102, 110
aesthetic sensibility, 126
aggression, 237–8
alienation, 9, 46, 47, 108, 110
Americanisation of journalism, 214
Anderson, Benedict, 149
Anderson Perry, 128
Annual Performance Reviews, 251
anomie, 9, 37
Anscombe, Elizabeth, 134
antagonistic cooperation, 11
apartheid, 111, 128, 133
Archer, Margaret, 110
Army Information Teams, 175
Aron, Raymond, 5, 131
Arthur Guinness Company of, Dublin, 29
Aryanpour, Amir, 132
Ashmore, Jonathan, 130
attitude formation, 232
Attridge, Derek, 131
audience belief/behaviour, xi, xii
Auschwitz, 132
Autogestion, 102
autonomy
 academic, 120–37, 253–9
 of the imagination, 102

Baird, Vera, 78
balance, 60, 104, 133, 163, 190, 192, 194–6, 199–201
Baldamus, Wilhelm 'Gi', 27, 43, 47–9, 55, 57
Baldwin, Thomas, 131

Bamberger, Bill and Davidson, Cathy, 28
Bandura, A., 236–7, 241
Bannister, Roger, 38
Barber, E., 17
Barthes, Roland, 126, 131
Baschwitz, Kurt, 221
Batchelor, George, 135
Baudrillard, J., 109
Bauman, Z., 7–8, 108–9, 116
BBC, xiv, 16, 159
Bechhofer, Frank, 83
Beharrell, P., x
belief transformation, xxi, 202
belief, xiv, xv, xxi, 19, 52, 73, 152, 156–7, 165, 192–3, 197, 201–3, 221, 239, 242
Benjamin, Walter, 149
Bennett, James Gordon Sr, 226
Berger, Peter, 9, 110, 112
Biltmore Agreement, 227
'Black' activities/operations, 174, 176, 179
Bloody Sunday Inquiry, 171, 175–6
Bobo Doll, 236–9
bogus self–employment, 85, 88
Boltanski, L., 105, 128
Bondi, Herman, 130
Bourdieu, P., xx, 120, 122–135, 137–8, 251–3
Brassed Off, 66
Bretscher, Mark, 130
British Coalfields, 65–82
British Sociological Association, xi, xix–xx, 142, 155
Brittan, Leon, 76
Browne Review/Report, x, 247
Bullock, Alan, 128
Burawoy, M, 49, 54–5, 104, 149, 155
Bureau of Applied Social Research (BASR), 168, 233
bureaucracy, 5, 83, 158

Bureau of Social Science Research, 169
Burns, Tom, 83, 136, 150
Butler, J., 142

Cabinet Ministerial Group on Coal (CMGC), 68, 72, 74, 76, 78
Campaign for Coal, 69, 80
Canadian Broadcast Corporation, 228
canon (academic), 120, 146–7
Cantril, Hadley, 168, 229–34, 238, 240–1
Capitalism, 5, 32–3, 56–7, 69, 83, 103, 111, 131, 145, 247–8, 251, 258
Causation, 238, 241–3
CBS, 226–8, 233–5, 242
Celynen South colliery, 65
Chiapello, E., 128
Church, 126, 135
Churchill, W., 132
CIA, 168–9
Cicourel, A., 12
Circuit of Communications (production, content, reception and circulation), xi
civilization, 145–7, 259
classification of academic spaces, 125–6
Clydebridge steelworks, 83
Cobain, Iain, 169–71, 181
Coercion, 58, 168–9, 182, 185
Cohen, Percy, 133
Cohen, Stanley, 133
Collective action, 83, 95
collective bargaining, 53, 59
collective memory, 120, 122–3
collective power, 39
collective representations, 122
collective unconscious, 123
Collini, Stefan, 249
communication(s), xiv, xxi, 120, 164, 166–8, 176, 182, 228, 240
Communist Manifesto, The, 9
community, xviii, 34, 68, 71, 79, 103, 105, 147
comparative media history, 210
conditions of work, 88–9, 90
Conduct After Capture, 181
Conflict of the Faculties, The, 125

conflict, xv, xix, xxi, 1, 11, 14, 16, 39, 52–3, 58, 78, 83–4, 95, 107, 121, 126, 131–2, 138, 142, 189, 190–9, 200–5
Connell, R., 112, 144
conservative surgery, 103
constructivism, 54
content analysis, xiv, 120, 159, 212, 216
control, 91
cooperative corporation of intellectuals, 130
cooperatives, 127, 128
Cooper, Frederik, 106
Copper Green, 184
corantos, 219–20
corporatism, 53
Counter–propaganda, 173, 176
Craib, Ian, 136
Cressey, P., 49, 61
Crick, F., 18, 130
crisis, xix, 2, 55, 61–2, 83–4, 90, 96, 122, 141, 144, 212–14
critique, 102–6
  artistic, 105
  social, 105
cross–classification, 2–4, 5, 20, 43–5, 47–9, 50, 52–7, 59, 61–3
Crouch, C., 49, 52–3, 55
Crozier, Michel, 135
cultural capital, 124–5, 155
cultural imperialism, 112, 214, 221
culture, xviii, 5–6, 12–13, 26–8, 40–1, 50, 88, 112, 122, 129, 138, 141, 143–4, 146–7, 149–50
Cynheidre colliery, 65–6

Daily Mail, The, 170
Daily Telegraph, The, 122, 134
Darwin, Charles, 4
Defence Intelligence and Security Centre, 180
Defence and Overseas Policy (Official) Committee (Ancillary Measures), 175
Defence School of Intelligence, 180
Defence SERE Training Organisation, 181
Defleur, Melvyn, 238

deindustrialization, xxi, 27, 32, 40–1
democratization of cognition/nature, 152
in-depth interviews, 191, 230–1
Derrida, J., 131
Diageo Archive, 28, 30–1, 33–8, 41, 52
Digital sociology, 209
discourse analysis, 191
distinction, 120
division of labour, 33, 36–9, 40, 154
DNA, 18, 130
dominant class, 124, 127
dominant memory, 122–3
Donohue, J., 18
Downes, David, 133
Dramaturgy, 10, 142
Du Bois, W.E.B., 102, 108, 111
Durkheim, Emile, 9, 14, 37, 39, 101–2, 106–8, 115–16, 122–3, 143, 153–4
Dworkin, Angela, 102, 108

Ecole des Hautes Etudes en Sciences Sociales, 129
Ecole Normale d'Administration, 135
Ecole Normale Supérieure, 129
Economic reality, 91
Economist, The, 131
economy, 68–9
Eco, Umberto, 18, 23, 242
education, 257–8
educational affinities, 129
Edwards, P., 52, 55–6, 62
Eighth Military Information Support Group (Airborne), 181
Eldridge, John, x, xiii, xiv, xvii, xx, xxi, 1, 25, 26, 39, 41, 43, 45, 47–9, 55, 61–2, 83, 96, 101–2, 111, 115, 116, 120–2, 131, 137, 138, 141, 150, 158, 159, 164–5, 254, 256
Elias, Norbert, xix, 11
empirical evidence, 145, 150, 152, 157, 159, 163, 182, 254
empirical sociology, 141
Employment Appeal Tribunal, 87–8
Employment Status Indicator, 90
Employment Tribunal, 90–1
endurance, 73, 81
engager, 85–6, 89, 90–1, 93–4

English Literature, 142, 146, 148, 151, 158
enlightenment, 152
Epstein, Bill, 133
ethnographic approach, 26, 54–5, 198, 203–4
ethnographic media studies, 203–4
European Working Conditions Survey (EWCS), 88
Ewbank, Inga-Stina, 134
explicit managerial ideology, 58
explicit power (authority plus coercion), 58–9
external explanations, 54

Falklands conflict, 16
Falsely Self-Employed (FSE), 85–9, 90–6
falsification, 89, 90–3
Fauconnet, Paul, 115
Federal Communications Commission, 228–9
Fiddles, 50–2, 57, 59
field, 25, 123–4, 129, 130–2, 134–5, 137–8, 251–5
field of education, 250
field struggles, 134
Firquats, 175
Fleming, A., 16–17
flexibility, 84–5
  employment, 84–9, 90
flow, 13, 202, 236
focused interviews, 234
Fontane, Theodor, 134
Foreign Office, 172
Fourth Military Information Support Group, 181
Franklin, R., 18
Freud, S., 17–18, 237

Galton, Francis, 154
Galtung, J., 199
game (metaphor), 11, 12, 182
Gazette, 221
Geddes, P., 101–2, 104, 108, 112
Gellner, E., 142
Gemeinschaft, 25, 146, 148, 235
George, Alexander, L., 169
German Historical Institute, The, 131

Ghodse, Hamid, 132
Giddens, A., 101, 107, 109, 110–12, 143–4
gift exchanges, 120, 129, 137
Glander, T., 166
Glasgow Media Group, x, xi, xv, xviii, xix, xxi, xxii, 16, 20, 164, 190–2, 202–3
globalisation, 6, 83–4, 209, 219
Global political struggles, 132–4
Goffman, E., 10, 121, 142
Gold, Thomas, 130
Gouldner, A., 121, 155, 158
grammar school, 127
Grandes Écoles, 127
Grangemouth oil refinery, 83
Greenham Common, 163
grid, 50–2
group, 50–2
Grub Street, 219
Guardian, The, 121–2, 131–2, 133–6, 143, 149
Gudet, Hazel and Hertzog, Herta, 233
Guinness (Brewery, Park Royal), 25, 27–9, 30–3, 37–8, 38
Guinness, E., 30, 34
Guinness Time, 29, 33–5, 37

Haaretz, 194
Habermas, J., 218–19
habitus, 123, 125–6, 221
Halbwachs, M., 120, 122–3
Halford, Susan, 27
Hancock, H., 12, 80
Harle, J., 12
Havel, V., 128
hegemonic masculinity, 145
hegemony, 144, 212
Her Majesty's Revenue and Customs (HMRC), 85–6, 88–9, 90–2, 96
Herschel, J (Sir), 226
Hersh, Seymour, 184
Hill, Christopher, 122, 130
historical sociology, 208–9, 210–13
history of journalism, 208–13
Hobbes, T., 128
Hobhouse, L.T., 101, 107, 109, 111
Hobsbawm, Eric, 126
Hoffman, R., 17

Holmwood, J., x, 120, 249, 251
House of Commons, 169–70
Hoyle, Fred, 128
Human nature, 113, 152–3
Husbands, Christopher, 133

ideal types, 5–6, 51, 57
ideal type transiency, 6
identity, 142–4, 159
impact agenda, x, xii, 246, 257
imperial journalism, 220
implicit managerial ideology, 58–9
implicit power, 58–9
improvisation, 12–16
Independent, The, 121–2, 128–9, 131, 133–6
independent journalism, 215
independent schools, 127
individual, 9–10, 37–9, 46, 51, 105
individual emancipation, 105
individualised worker, 52, 94
industrial change, 32
industrial citizenship, 36, 38, 41
industrial restructuring, 32
industrial sociology, (25–100), xiv, xix, 26, 83, 95, 100
inequality, 113, 122, 137, 145, 257
information policy, 172–4, 219, 220
Information Policy Unit, 174
Information Research Department (IRD), 172–3, 176
information technology, 157, 209
insecurity, 94
Institute for Propaganda Analysis, 168
integration, 92, 95
intellectual craftsmanship, 2, 4, 43, 253
intelligentsia, 124–5
internal explanations, 54
International Wages for Housework, 107
intersectoral dialogue, 198, 204
Invalides, 121
IRA, 172
Iranian Revolution, 128, 132
Israel-Palestine conflict, xxi, 189, 190–5, 200, 202
Ivy League, 127

James, Selma, 102, 107
Jarrett, K., 13
job security, 246
job status, 246
job typology, 57, 58
Joint Services Intelligence Organisation, 181
Joint Warfare Establishment, 173
Jolles, Charlotte, 134
journalism, xiv, xxi, xxii, 33, 189, 191, 193, 195–9, 200–2, 204–5, 208–9, 210, 211–22, 239, 240, 250–3
journalists, xiv, 27, 129, 172, 192, 194, 196, 200–5, 213–18, 220–2, 227, 239
juxtaposition, 4, 6, 20

Kant, I., 120, 125
Karski, Jan, 132
Key Performance Indicators, 251
kinetic activity, 182–4
knowledge, 143, 147

Labour Force Survey (LFS), 88
labour market, 28, 142, 145, 248
Labour Party, 72, 107
Labour Process Theory, 39
language, 150–1
Laslett, Peter, 130
Lasswell, H., 165–7
Lazarsfeld, Paul, 165–8, 233, 235–6
leadership, 5
Leavis, F. R., 146–9, 155–7
Lee, Elizabeth Briant, 168
Lefebvre, Henri, 102, 105, 107, 111
Le Monde, 122
Levitas, Ruth, 101, 112, 114, 115–16
Lewis, Edward, 130
liberalism, 53
libertarian socialism, 111
Lipshitz, Howard, 130
literary criticism, 142–8, 149, 151
Luyendijk, Loris, 195

MacGregor, I, 68–9, 73
MacInnes, John, 49, 61, 141
macro-micro, 4–5, 11

macroscopic, 3–4
Magic Bullet Model, 232
management, 34, 38, 52, 56, 58, 59, 60–1, 68, 72, 73, 75, 79
managerialism, 120
Mannheim, Karl, 101, 104–5, 108, 120, 124–5
manual labour, 26
Marcuse, Herbert, 102, 105, 106, 111
marketization, 96, 120, 137, 246, 248–9
Mars, G., 49, 50–2, 55
Martins, Herminio, 133
Marx, Karl, 4, 9, 102, 111, 124, 135, 143, 148, 153, 155, 251
masculine domination, 128
masculinity, 144–5
Mastership of Balliol, 122
May Day Manifesto, 67
McClung Lee, Alfred, 167–8
Mead, Herbert, 102, 108
'Means-end' rationality, 250
means of production, 9, 164
mechanistic organizational structures, 58
media content, xiv, 192, 212, 216, 218
media coverage, xiv, 27, 164, 191, 193–4, 239, 240
media effects, xix, 196, 200–1, 222, 229, 230, 232, 236
media history, xxii, 209, 269
Media Monitoring Unit, 163
media studies, 25, 121, 163–4, 189, 191–9, 202–4, 209, 211–12
media, xi, xii, xv, xix, 25, 27, 75, 87, 120, 121, 141, 150, 161, 163–4, 166, 177, 191–9, 200–5
Mehldau, B., 13
mental health beliefs, xv
Merton, R., 16–19, 165, 232, 234–7
metaphors and similes, 7–8, 11, 14, 142
methodology (sociological), xi, xiv, xx, 4, 14–15, 158, 190–1, 222, 234, 254
method (scientific), 154–7
migrant labour, 6, 7
Military Intelligence Brigade, 180
Miller, Chrissie, 134

Mills, C. Wright, xi, xix, 1–4, 20, 40–1, 43–9, 50–1, 55, 57, 121, 131, 132, 142, 189, 190, 192–3, 197, 199, 253–4, 256
miners' strike, 65, 68, 77, 80
miners' wives, 65, 80
Ministry of Defence, 170, 175, 179, 180, 182
models of political economy, 53
molecular, 3, 4, 18, 130
Mommsen, Wolfgang, 131
Mooney, Hugh, 171–6
morality, moral regulation, 9, 39, 149, 154
moral order, 9, 149
moral values, 148–9, 152
Moynihan, Daniel, 112
mutuality of obligation, 91

Nantgarw colliery, 66
narrative, 32, 36, 52, 142–3, 146, 191, 194–5, 197–9, 201, 203–4, 210, 212, 214, 216–17
National Coal Board, 67
National Executive Committee (NEC), 71
National Insurance, 86
National Union of Mineworkers, 67–9
Nazism, 111, 128, 132
NBC, 231
neo-corporatism, 53
neo-liberalism, 27, 53, 113, 128, 136, 253–4
neutrality, 195–6, 259
Newbridge, 65
New Labour, 79, 80, 113–14
new media, 209–10
News Paradigm, 214
news, xiii, xiv, xv, xix, xxii, 16, 74–5, 141, 143, 191, 199, 200, 212, 216, 219, 226–7, 229
New York Daily News, The, 228
New York (Daily) Sun, The, 226, 228
New York Herald, The, 226
New York Times, The, 131, 228
1984, 151
nomad capitalism, 69
non-alienation, 47

Normalisation of New Forms of Employment, 88, 93–5
Nostalgia, xxi, 40
Null Effect Hypothesis, 236

obituaries, 120–32, 134–7
objectivity, 163, 192, 195, 200, 217
obligation, 50, 91, 96, 113, 130, 161
occupation, 26, 32, 44, 50–2, 85–6, 92, 102, 127, 137, 194–5
Office of War Information (OWI), 235
O'Hagan, Andrew, 74
Olmert, Ehud, 194
one-state solution, 194–5
ONS, 85
ontological security, 147, 152, 154
order (social), 7, 10, 69, 76, 144–5, 147–8, 157
Organic solidarity, 38, 52, 62
Orgreave Coking Plant, 66, 76–8
Orson Welles' *Mercury Theatre*, 211, 226
Orwell, George, 150–1
Owen, David, 172
Oxbridge, 127, 131, 137

Palazzo di Propaganda Fide, 165
panic, 227–8, 230–4, 242
Panthéon, 121
Park, Robert, 221
partisanship, 214–15
paternalism, 36, 37, 42
'Patrick Geddes Heritage Trail', 104
Peace Journalism, xxi, 198–9, 200, 202, 205
performativity, 142
perspectivism, 122
philosophical inquiry, 249
Picard, Raymond, 126, 131
pictorial workspace, 50, 54, 57, 60, 62
pluralised identities, 105
political authority, 5
Political Warfare Executive, 178
Pontifical Academy of Social Sciences, 110
Pooley, Jefferson and Katz, Elihu, 208
Pope Gregory XV, 164
Port Stanley, 163
postmodernism, 109, 236

Index 275

poststructuralism, 109
power, xiv, 39, 44–7, 57–9, 60–1, 66, 73, 84, 90, 103, 106, 120–1, 125–6, 130, 132, 142, 144–5, 185, 194, 250–1, 253
praxis, 111–12
precarity, 79, 95, 247–8, 270
pre-modern knowledge, 147
Pride, 66
Princeton Radio Research Project (PRRP), 229, 233
private interests, 257
privatization, 69, 246
propaganda, 163–9, 171–3, 176–9, 184–5, 232–3
propaganda analysis, 167–9
provoked action, 233
Psychological Operations Group, 181
psychological operations ('Psyops'), 163, 169, 170–3, 176–8, 181, 185
psychological warfare, 168, 170–1, 178, 185
Psychological Warfare Unit, 170–1
public, 141, 149
Public Order Act, 76
Public Records Office, 171
Public Relations, 163, 235
Pulitzer, Joseph, 220

Qualter, Terence, 165
Quetelet, A., 154

Radical individualism, 122
Rahman, Tariq, 136
rational democracy, 102
rationalism, 125, 148, 155
rationality, 5, 106, 136, 248
reactionary elitism, 145
realism, 49
realist rationalism, 125
redaction, 216–17
redundant, 49, 68–9, 74, 247
Rees, Merlyn, 75
reflexivity, 125, 142–3, 147, 189, 190
relationist understanding/thinking, 124
relativism, 143, 147, 151, 154–5, 158, 259
representation(s), 122, 195, 199, 200

Republican Party, 107, 110
Rerum Novarum, 110
Research Assessment Exercise, x, 250
Research Excellence Framework (REF), xii, 250–2, 257
resistance to interrogation, 170–1
Rew, Alan, 133
Rex, John, 133
Ridley, Nicholas, 72
Riot Police, 77–8
Robbins Report, xi, 157, 247
Rockefeller Foundation, 166–7
Roosevelt, F., 132, 229
Roper, Michael, 136
Rose, Gillian, 134
Rowbotham, Sheila, 102

Sacra Congregatio de Propaganda Fide, 164
Said, Edward, 126, 130, 136
Sargisson, L., 109
SAS, 164, 175
Saunders, Peter, 110
Save Easington Area Mines (SEAM), 70
Scargill, Arthur, xiv, 68, 71, 73, 76
science, 152–3, 155–7
'Science as a Vocation', 155–7
scientific writing, 18
Scott, Sir Giles Gilbert, 30–1
self-employment, 83–9, 90, 92–6
Self-realisation, 143
self and society, 10, 143
serendipity, 16–18, 19, 20
serious playfulness, 49, 56
Service Delivery Partners, 87
A Seventh Man, 6, 9
shadow elite, 258
Siddall, N., 73
Simmel, Georg, 11
Skinner, Quentin, 130
Smith, Kate, 233–4
Snow, C.P., 146
social class, 5, 52, 72, 83, 122, 124–5, 127, 132, 138, 142, 154, 159, 234, 255
social cohesion, 19, 105
social credit, 103
social democracy, 109, 110
social integration, 8, 95

socialism, 67, 103, 110, 111
social media, 209
social memory, 120
social movements, 14–15, 83–4, 109
social reconstruction, 9, 101, 112–14
social solidarity, 14–15, 71–2, 95
social structure, 1, 14, 46, 48–9
social transformation, 190, 197, 199, 200
society as a metaphor, 7–12, 14, 20
society, xviii, xix, 2, 5, 7–9, 10–12, 14–15, 20, 74, 78, 79, 94–5, 104, 106, 112, 113, 144, 257
sociological alternatives, 101–2, 104–9, 111, 189
sociological craftsmanship, 253
sociological imagination, xi, xix, 1–2, 4, 6, 8, 16, 20, 25, 41, 45–6, 96, 102, 110, 114, 122, 142, 154, 157, 189, 190, 191, 193, 197, 199, 259
Sociological Society, 114–15
sociology, xiv, xviii, 1, 7, 9, 11, 15–16, 27, 39–40, 101–5, 107–8, 110, 112, 114–16, 133, 141–2, 144, 147, 149, 153, 159, 256–7, 259
  of knowledge, 47, 124
  of media, 163–262
  normative, 102, 105, 107, 115, 199, 202
  of obituaries, 120–6
  public, 104, 141, 149
  punk, 104
  of work, 25–100
solidarity/ies, 14, 15, 71, 129, 130
Spectator, The, 218
Spencer, Herbert, 221
sport, 32
stage (metaphor), 9–10
Stalinism, 128
state, 109, 142, 145, 158, 163, 258
status, 5, 44
Statutory Maternity Pay, 86
Statutory Sick Pay, 86
STEM, 247
Stepping Stones, 75
Stewart, Colonel Bob, 179
Stoate, R., 78
strategic communication, 177

Strenger, Carlo, 203
structure and agency, 11–12, 17, 26, 144, 154
structures of feeling, 25, 27, 40, 121
structures of power, 45–6, 142
Studholme, Maggie, 107
subjective conditions, 46
subordinate memory, 123
suicide, 154, 241
Symbolic Interactionism, 121

Tatham, Steve, 177, 179, 181
Tatler, The, 218
Tax Law Review Committee of the Institute for Fiscal Studies, 85
Taylor, Laurie, 133
Taylor, Philip, 166
teaching, 246–8, 254
Tebbitt, Norman, 163
Thatcher, Margaret, x, 16, 68, 72, 74–5, 121, 135
Think Tanks, 258–9
'Third Way', 92, 101–4, 107–8, 111
Thompson, E.P., 4, 78, 135
Times, The, 121, 132, 135, 256
torture, 169, 170, 181, 182, 184, 241
Touraine, A., 14–15, 83–4, 95
Trades Union Congress (TUC), 85
trade unions, xi, 15, 52, 69, 70–2, 74, 75, 79–81, 83, 95
transformative sociology/media studies, 249, 250–3, 258
Transnational Journalism, 189, 197–8, 199–200, 202, 204
Travel Journalism, 217–18
Tugwell, Colonel Maurice, 172
Turner, C., 49–50, 54, 128
'two-states' solution, 194
two-step flow model, 236
typologies, 44–5, 52

unadjusted worker, 46–7
un-alienated worker, 46–7
uses and gratifications model, 236
Utopia, 5, 101, 109, 112–16
Utopianism, 109–14, 116

value-free science, 146–7, 152, 155–6

Wade, William, 130
Wales Institute of Social & Economic Research, Data & Methods (WISERD), xviii, 86, 96
Walker, Peter, 73
Wallace, Colin, 172–4
Walton, Paul, x
Warner, Anne, 130
Warner, Lloyd, 65, 79
Warner, Maria, 249
War of the Worlds, 230, 234, 239
Watson, J., 18
Weber, Max, xix, 5–6, 17, 107, 111, 135, 143, 147–8, 153, 155–7, 221, 250
Welfare Capitalism, 33
Welfare State, 95, 109–11
Wells, H.G., 114, 229, 231
White, Martin, 114
Wilkins, M., 18

Willetts, David, 246
Williams, Bernard, 130, 136
Williams, David, 130
Williams, Raymond, xix, 8, 12, 27, 40, 67, 76, 79, 121, 146, 164
Wittgenstein, L., 142
Wollheim, Richard, 130, 135–6
Woodward, J., 27, 143
Woodward, Joan and Bendix, Reinhard, 27
Work, 25–7, 34–5, 40, 51–2, 84–5, 88–9
Working class, 19, 26, 124–5, 128, 137
Working class culture, 232
Workplace Employment Relations Study (WERS), 88
World War II, 178
Worsley, Peter, 132

Zinn, Howard, 135

Printed and bound by CPI Group (UK) Ltd, Croydon, CR0 4YY